Staging
Britain's Past

ARDEN STUDIES IN EARLY MODERN DRAMA

Series editors:
Lisa Hopkins, Sheffield Hallam University, UK
Douglas Bruster, University of Texas at Austin, USA

Published titles

Early Modern Theatre and the Figure of Disability
by Genevieve Love
ISBN: 978-1-350-01720-7

Imagining Cleopatra
by Yasmin Arshad
ISBN: 978-1-350-05896-5

Staging Britain's Past

Pre-Roman Britain in Early Modern Drama

Kim Gilchrist

THE ARDEN SHAKESPEARE

LONDON • NEW YORK • OXFORD • NEW DELHI • SYDNEY

THE ARDEN SHAKESPEARE
Bloomsbury Publishing Plc
50 Bedford Square, London, WC1B 3DP, UK
1385 Broadway, New York, NY 10018, USA
29 Earlsfort Terrace, Dublin 2, Ireland

BLOOMSBURY, THE ARDEN SHAKESPEARE and the Arden Shakespeare
logo are trademarks of Bloomsbury Publishing Plc

First published in Great Britain 2021
This paperback edition published 2022

Cover design by Irene Martinez Costa
Cover image: The Goddess Ate, taken from *A Supplement to
the Plays of William Shakespeare* edited by W.G. Simms (1848)
(© University of South Carolina)

A catalogue record for this book is available from the British Library.

A catalog record for this book is available from the Library of Congress.

ISBN: HB: 978-1-3501-6334-8
PB: 978-1-3502-3282-2
ePDF: 978-1-3501-6336-2
eBook: 978-1-3501-6335-5

Series: Arden Studies in Early Modern Drama

Typeset by Deanta Global Publishing Services, Chennai, India

To find out more about our authors and books visit www.bloomsbury.com
and sign up for our newsletters.

CONTENTS

ILLUSTRATIONS

Figures

Table

ACKNOWLEDGEMENTS

My first thanks are to Lisa Hopkins and Douglas Bruster, my editors for Arden Studies in Early Modern Drama, for overseeing and guiding this work and to Lisa for seeing enough merit in the project to approach me in the first place. Huge thanks to Mark Dudgeon at the Arden Shakespeare for taking on the book, and to Lara Bateman for much patient guidance and enthusiasm in our search for a great cover image. This book is adapted from my PhD, carried out at the University of Roehampton under the rigorous and endlessly kind supervision of Clare McManus and Jane Kingsley-Smith. I couldn't have hoped for better mentors. The project was funded by the Department of English and Creative Writing. Many thanks to head of department Laura Peters for her support and subsequent careful mentorship in my post-doctoral Teaching Fellowship at Roehampton. Thanks too to my wonderful friends there, particularly those who gave their time to put me through a ruthless mock viva: Bea Turner, Morwenna Carr, Callan Davies and Dustin Frazier Wood; and to Ian Kinane for teaching *King Solomon's Mines* so I had time to prepare for the real thing. Thank you to my examiners, Andrew Hadfield and Andy Kesson, for a scrupulous yet far less harrowing actual viva, and for ongoing advice and support. The project originates from an essay written towards my MA in Shakespeare Studies at King's College London with Shakespeare's Globe Theatre. Without encouragement and brilliant teaching from the following, I never would have considered myself doctoral material: Farah Karim-Cooper, Sonia Massai, Lucy Munro and particularly Gordon McMullan, who advised that an essay on imaginary kings would be 'much more you' than my other suggestions. It was.

Thank you to Alixe Bovey, Margreta de Grazia, Tracey Hill, Paulina Kewes and Martin Wiggins, all of whom generously shared knowledge, conversation or work-in-progress on subjects ranging from pageant giants to pictorial timelines and university drama; also to Lisa Hopkins and Bill Angus for allowing me to see a pre-publication proof of *Reading the Road, from Shakespeare's Crossways to Bunyan's Highways*. And thank you to those who responded with lightning speed to a request to share successful book proposals: Jessica Chiba, Laurie Johnson, Trish Reid, Miranda Fay Thomas and Emma Whipday. A number of conferences and institutions have been kind enough to allow me to present my work at key moments in both the development of the thesis and its subsequent adaptation into an article and monograph, particularly multiple Britgrad conferences in Stratford-Upon-Avon and the 2017 Before Shakespeare conference at the University of Roehampton, hosted by my ever-inspiring friends Andy Kesson and Callan Davies. Thank you to Jakub Boguszak at Southampton University for inviting me to present my work on *King Lear*, and to Cardiff University's MEMORI group for giving me the opportunity to present a valuable close-to-the-deadline test paper on my final chapter. Thanks are also due to the editors of the British Shakespeare's Association's journal, *Shakespeare*, for permission to reproduce material from my article on *King Lear*, 'The Wonder Is He Hath Endured So Long', in Chapter 3. The final work on this book has been carried out while working as Disglair Lecturer in English Literature at Cardiff. My thanks to Ceri Sullivan for her support and for literally putting a roof over my head in Cardiff, and to Martin Willis, head of School for English, Communications and Philosophy for giving me the time and security to complete the book. Thank you to Derek Dunne, a great tutor back at the Globe, a great colleague at Cardiff and a friend throughout.

I came into academia quite late in life, and thanks are due to Sara Lodge, who offered vital encouragement. It has been a revelation and a huge joy to have been welcomed by the most supportive, fun and generous community I've ever encountered. Many of us convened in occasional and fitfully scholarly research meetings entitled Shakesposium: thank you to Sally Barnden, Matt Blaiden, Robbie Hand, Nicole Mennell, Sarah O'Malley, and all others kind enough to join in. Particular thanks to Lana Harper, co-founder of Shakesposium and a wise, constant friend who continues to surprise. And thanks to Amy Lidster, my co-traveller in picking apart the history play (or whatever we can agree to call it) and whose friendship, conversation and reckless agreement to co-organize the 2019 Changing Histories conference at KCL has shaped my work and academic life.

Beyond the early modern, sanity was often sustained by my three-or-more-decade friendships, by Ivan and Sophie, Alex and Julia, Ian and Lucy, Rich and Mez, Kielan and Kate, Lucas, Amy and Mark, and Nick and Sara. A few steps ahead, Nick gave sage thesis and book advice along with heavy riffs. This book, and the journey that brought me here, would not have been possible without the encouragement, example and wisdom of my partner, Maeve Rutten: the cause, companion and destination of the adventure. Thank you for the triumphal duck – it was a long time coming and, if I wavered, you never did. In *The Art of English Poesie*, George Puttenham tells his readers that one of the purposes of reading history is that men might become ennobled by studying the 'liuely image of our deare forefathers, their noble and vertuous maner of life'. I am fortunate, and needn't look so far back. I look instead to my mother, Anna Gilchrist, from whom I've learned more than I could from a chronicle's worth of forefathers, and to whom this book is dedicated.

NOTE ON TEXTS

All quotations from early modern texts use the original page references, spelling and, where possible, layout. Early modern 'v/u', and 'j/i' have been retained. Long 's' and 'vv' have been modernized. Quotations from Shakespeare use original spelling but comparative references are given for the relevant Arden Third Series edition of each play. For this study's two key Shakespearean texts, *King Lear* and *Cymbeline*, references are given for both the Arden and original early modern versions. This is because, in several cases, I draw upon the 'unediting' methodology pioneered by Margreta de Grazia and Peter Stallybrass (1993), Leah Marcus (1996) and others. As such, my analysis depends upon close attention to the original spelling and page layout of these texts. For this reason I consider it important that readers are able to both see the original spelling and reference the original texts themselves via online facsimiles.

Many characters from the Brutan histories appeared in multiple guises in medieval and early modern historiography, drama and wider culture, and each re-telling is different. In some versions a character survives war, in another they die; in one they are an exemplar, in another a tyrant. As such, rather than treating all versions of, for example, *King Lear's* Cordelia as iterations of the same figure, I will treat each as a different character. To emphasize this variety on the page, I have retained the original spelling of names from each text quoted. Thus the youngest daughter of Lear appears as Cordeilla in Geoffrey of Monmouth's *Historia Regum Britanniae*, Cordella in the anonymous play *Leir* and Cordelia in Shakespeare's play.

Introduction

The dissolution of created things is but a resolution of one thing into another.

HELKIAH CROOKE, *Mikrokosmographia* (1615: f. 198).

A Variety of Leirs

The Brutan histories encompassed more than a millennium of British antiquity, reaching from the island's conquest by the Trojan exile Brute around 1180 BCE to the early years of the Roman occupation of Britain. In between, Brute's descendants reigned. They included such still-famous rulers as Lear, Cymbeline and Lud. These were mighty, if not always wise, monarchs whose acts and lives were woven into the English national consciousness. There was just one problem. In reality, the Brutan histories were the invention of a medieval writer named Geoffrey of Monmouth, recorded in his incalculably influential book, the *Historia Regum Britanniae* (*c.* 1135).[1] Geoffrey's motivations for writing his *Historia* are obscure and disputed although the work was certainly shaped by the conflicts of succession and political turmoil of the mid-twelfth century. In an extraordinary twist, however, the *Historia*'s narratives endured to become almost universally accepted by the English and Welsh as the definitive account of Britain's ancient history and origins. Its tales spilled out into national culture and across the ensuing centuries via anonymous manuscripts, poetry, drama and oral tradition. Eventually, however, doubt began to eat away at the Brutan histories. Doubt was triggered in part by the sceptical Italian

Polydore Vergil who, commissioned by Henry VII to write a history of Britain, questioned the historical reality of almost everything Geoffrey claimed had occurred before the arrival of the Romans.

The early modern performance of characters and episodes from these Brutan histories tells us much about how the early modern English imagined their own origins. These performances can also be seen as reflecting the cultural process by which these histories were gradually abandoned as a legitimate account of those origins. The Brutan histories and the manner of their erosion should be understood in terms of the affective and cultural usefulness they held for the early modern English, factors that often determined the possible effects and reception of Brutan drama. The ways in which these effects made themselves felt, and by whom they were felt, were in part determined by questions of social class, literacy and textual community. Exploring these performances as a category allows well-known texts such as *King Lear*, *Cymbeline* and *Gorboduc* to be understood as existing within a continuum of Brutan performance the duration of which has not been fully recognized. To begin, a particular instance of Brutan drama – a performance of the anonymous play *Leir* – provides a useful introduction to these multiple receptions. One actor may have played Leir, but there were many dissonant and conflicting Leirs available to spectators depending on their profession, social status and location.

On 6 April 1594, and again on 8 April, two playing companies came together to stage what must have been a spectacular, or at least crowded, performance of a play about the ancient British king Leir. The play was performed at the Rose playhouse on Bankside by Sussex's Men and the Queen's Men. The previous afternoon the companies had performed Robert Greene's *Friar Bacon and Friar Bungay* which, like *Leir*, belonged to the repertory of the Queen's Men. On 9 April, they performed a Sussex's Men play, Christopher Marlowe's *The Jew of Malta*. Sandwiched between Marlowe's savage satirical tragedy and Greene's genre-defying extravaganza of battling magicians,

Leir must have appeared relatively wholesome, bringing to life an exemplary British monarch and his beloved heir, Cordella. The story was well known: the ageing Leir divides the kingdom of Britain among his three daughters but exiles the youngest, Cordella, when she refuses to express her filial love in suitably lavish terms. He soon discovers, however, that his remaining daughters are less than dutiful. Indeed, they arrange to have him murdered, an ordeal he survives only through a well-timed crack of divinely intervening thunder. Leir escapes to Gallia, where he is joyfully reunited with Cordella in a long scene of tearful and mutual forgiveness and kneeling. Together with Cordella's husband the Gallian king, father and daughter invade Britain, retake Leir's throne, and all ends happily. For those in the audience who knew their chronicles, however, the play's joyful conclusion may have felt bittersweet. After all, while Leir would rule for five more happy years before the throne passed to Cordella, the Brutan histories told that she would in turn be usurped by her nephews Morgan and Conidagus. Despairing in captivity, she would finally take her own life. Those who could afford John Higgins's 1574 prequel supplement to the *Mirror for Magistrates* may even have read its moving account of Cordella's fate, written in her own voice.

For those without access to literature or literacy, Leir's story could still have been familiar from oral tradition. Some may have had only the vaguest sense of Leir as a king who had once lived in a generalized time 'ago', yet he might have still inspired a sense of personal or national pride and meaning in the present. Other non-readers may have had a more precise sense of Leir's placement in time, derived from the chronologies of British kings printed in the early modern period's ubiquitous astrological almanacs. If you couldn't read, many public spaces such as barbers' shops and alehouses pinned almanacs to their walls, and the barber, at least, could be relied upon to read aloud their mixture of meteorological prognostication, medical remedies and key historical events (Fox 2000: 39).

Even without getting a haircut or tooth pulled, it was easy in 1590s London to encounter ancient British history and to understand that Leir was important not only as an individual king but also as part of a vast and glorious story of national origins. Books of British history by the chronicler John Stow were constant sellers, and while some editions may have been prohibitively expensive, there was a tiny sextidecimo edition that was affordable and slipped easily into the pocket. In this way, Londoners could learn that Leir was the tenth king descending from Brute, the Trojan exile who had landed on the island of Albion, slaughtered its resident giants and named the place Britain after himself over 2,500 years before the reign of Elizabeth I. Brute was an especially potent ancestor for London, having founded the city as Troinovant, or New Troy, entwining its foundation with that of Britain itself. The name-change came later, when Brute's descendant, the good king Lud, re-fortified and edified the city and renamed it Lud's Town, which in time became London. When they left the city and headed west, Londoners passed beneath statues of Lud and his sons set upon the eastern façade of Ludgate, which Lud had originally built. He was said to be buried under the gate itself. Indeed, Sussex's Men had staged a play about Lud in January 1594, also at the Rose, only a few weeks before they played *Leir*. Performed figures of ancient history often evoked and interacted with the places they were said to have founded.

Leir, too, was a founder, having built Leicester, a city the Queen's Men frequently visited on their regional tours. They would do so again that autumn of 1594, and we might imagine that if *Leir* was performed during their visit then the play would have had special resonance. City authorities had long known the symbolic power of bringing their ancient founders, as it were, back to life in the cause of civic dignity. In 1486 the conquering Henry VII had visited York following his defeat of Richard III. He was greeted by an actor playing York's founder, Ebrauk, Brute's great-great-grandson, who reminded the young king of his and the city's shared ancestry and of Ebrauk's seniority within that genealogy. Among the audience at Leicester Guildhall in 1594 may have been the young man who would, as an elderly steward serving at a local inn in the

1630s, take pride in informing a group of visiting soldiers that the city had been founded 'by the British king Leir, near 1000 yeeres before Christ' (Fox 2000: 231).[2]

Many spectators at the Rose would have been lawyers or law students from the Inns of Court. Lawyers had a professional investment in the Brutan histories: many English laws derived their lustre and dignity from having been founded by Mulmutius Dunwallo or Queen Marcia, more of Brute's descendants. Dunwallo had reunited Britain after five decades of ruinous war following the catastrophic decision by Gorboduc to divide the kingdom between his two sons. Lawyers of a more advanced age might even have remembered seeing the famous play *Gorboduc*, which had been shown before Queen Elizabeth in 1562 and in which she was warned to learn the lesson of history, get married and secure the succession. Anyone not old or well-connected enough to have been at Whitehall that day could, however, still read the play, which had been reprinted only three years previously. Those visiting the Rose a few years later in 1598 and 1600 would have been able to see a new play about Mulmutius and another of Gorboduc's sons, Ferrex and Porrex, on the same stage on which *Leir* now played. But there were also reasons for those who knew their histories to feel uneasy while watching *Leir*, and this raises the question, central to this book, of what it meant to 'know' history and to watch it staged.

For those lawyers and students, access to knowledge and documentation beyond the reach of other Londoners not only deepened knowledge of Britain's ancient Trojan ancestors, it could undermine them too. Those able to read Latin may have encountered Camden's *Britannia*, published in 1586, in which the historiographer appeared to endorse a view that had previously been expressed only by foreign, and therefore naturally jealous and unreliable, writers. These writers maintained that the entire history of Britain before the coming of the Romans in 52 BCE had been invented wholesale in the twelfth century by an unscrupulous lay priest named Geoffrey of Monmouth. Camden didn't *quite* say it – he demurred from taking responsibility for other men's patriotic beliefs – but he didn't defend Brute either. Those with the social capital to get access to Camden's work and ideas could no longer be sure that Mulmutius, Gorboduc, Leir or Brute had ever existed. These ideas and doubts were slowly spreading beyond elite, Latinate textual communities. Corrosion of faith in the Brutan histories was acutely troubling as there was no alternative account with which to replace them, only the impenetrable void of an antiquity that had left no textual traces.

What, then, and who, were the players on the Rose's stage representing that day in 1594, and what did their spectators believe they were seeing? Were they embodying and bringing into the present an ancient British king and his daughters, setting them among the great figures of patriotic history who had been, as Thomas Nashe put it in *Pierce Penniless*, 'raised from the Graue of Obliuion' on the same stage (1592: sig. F3r)? And if not that, what was Leir? Was he an echo of a half-lost truth, a fiction, a nothing? For those with doubts, Leir and all the others oscillated between different states, their solidity in the past and meaning in the present becoming dissonant and uncertain. To watch *Leir* in 1594 was to encounter a historical figure in the process of becoming eroded from history. Brian Walsh has described the performance of history as, more than other 'forms of history', providing the pretence of 'sensual contact with the vanished past through the bodies that move and speak on stage' (2009: 2), suggesting that drama affords an especially affective interaction with the past. Writing of the Brutan histories, Joseph Bowling has argued that performing the Brutan histories afforded playgoers 'a fantasy of ancestral contact' (2017: 82). This book builds upon and complicates this notion, asking in what ways this dialogue is changed, energized or compromised when the performed historical dead in question are revealed as never having lived: because the Brutan histories were, as those infuriating foreign scholars kept insisting, a none-too-subtle medieval invention that had nonetheless become the received history of Britain's ancient origins.

Accounts of British antiquity were transmitted into the early modern period via a medieval tradition of manuscript histories known collectively as the Prose *Brut*, so named for its chronicle narrative presenting Brute's founding and naming of Britain and the subsequent lives of his descendants. For reasons outlined further, I term these narratives the 'Brutan histories'. The *Brut* itself originated with Geoffrey's *Historia*, which extended from the life of Brute to that of the seventh-century Cadwallader, the 'last king of Britayne' (Stow 1565: f. 36r). By the early modern period, this conception of the past was a tradition undergoing sustained attack. On the one hand, the Brutan histories dominated as a habit of thought deeply embedded at all levels of English culture, sustained through the anonymous medieval manuscript *Brut* chronicles and their early modern print analogues, through elite genealogy, civic history, romance, *de casibus* literature and oral tradition. On the other hand, a growing number of sceptical historiographers and writers were uncovering this tradition's fictive and relatively recent origins. From the mid-sixteenth to the seventeenth centuries, this view slowly gained acceptance in scholarly and specialist circles while other communities – lawyers and livery companies, for example – seem to have remained indignant and resistant.

Eventually and unevenly, however, Brute and the generations of rulers that were said to have followed him up to the Roman era became accepted as mythic before disappearing from cultural usage altogether. Where other traditions were sustained as myths for far longer, the near totality of the cultural erosion of Brute and his ancestors raises, and is the result of, particular epistemological issues. Much myth, such as the ancient Greek traditions of narrative explored by Paul Veyne, could parse spurious accounts of ancient times as echoes of past events made fabulous over centuries of retelling, and therefore accommodate these into a vision of the lived ancestral past, a process termed 'euhemerism'.[3] Conversely, the tradition inaugurated by Geoffrey of Monmouth could be traced to a single author and was of far more recent date than the antiquity it claimed to recover. No one quite knew where the stories of ancient Troy originated, but it was comparatively easy to establish where the Brutan histories had started. They could not be 'myth', a poeticized account of otherwise lost truths, if they were manifestly fictive. The collective discovery of this fictiveness, however, was arguably delayed and challenged by the histories' cultural ubiquity, not least in their frequent theatrical portrayal.

Throughout the early modern period, narratives lifted from the Brutan histories were represented in drama and appropriated for civic and royal pageantry. These in turn were reproduced in manuscripts, playbooks and other textual records of performance. By 1612, Thomas Heywood in his *Apology for Actors* could write that plays had 'taught the vnlearned the knowledge of many famous histories', particularly 'the discouery of all our English Chronicles . . . euen from William the Conquerour, nay from the landing of Brute, vntill this day' (1612: sig. F3r), suggesting that the millennia of historical time covered by the 'English Chronicles' had been comprehensively mapped and reproduced by the industries of commercial drama. But the tradition of Brutan plays reached back further, to the Inns of Court play *Gorboduc* (1562), the first extant verse tragedy written in English, meaning that in 1612 Heywood was looking back over at least five decades of theatrical activity. In fact, Heywood was writing close to the end of this collective cultural 'discouery', contemporaneous to the performance of two of the last known Brutan plays, Shakespeare's *King Lear* (*c.* 1606; pub. 1608) and *Cymbeline* (*c.* 1611; pub. 1623). These two plays are, as might be expected, the Brutan dramas most frequently analysed by critics. However, their status as 'history' plays has been explored in only a few studies. More usually they are addressed as literary responses to questions of 'Britain' and 'Britishness' in the years following the accession of the Scottish king James VI to the English throne in 1603. Plays of Brutan drama *as a category* have been addressed in only a single article in the last twenty-five years, which takes as its premise the notion that early modern dramatists consciously struggled to produce persuasive representations of 'non-history' (Curran 1999: 1). However, there is clear evidence that the ahistoricity of the Brutan histories was far less apparent than Curran suggests; equally, even if the dramatists may or may not have viewed their material in this way, this does not speak to the works' possible effects in reception. As such, these dramas can be better understood if seen as emerging from a culture in which the assumed historicity of their material provides the base point from which their cultural effect is considered. To achieve this, the Brutan tradition itself, as well as the earliest evidence of Brutan performance, should be taken seriously as a site of collective and accumulating meaning and affect. Only in this way can the cultural impact of that tradition's erosion, and the effect of this erosion on perceptions of Brutan drama and national origins, be explored and assessed.

This book thus provides the first comprehensive study of Brutan drama from the first extant records in 1486 to the Caroline era.[4] It does so via the historiographic shifts outlined earlier: these texts, events and performances were paid for, witnessed and read by audiences whose understanding of their national origins was undergoing a process of long-term and deepening doubt and dissonance even as those origins were frequently invoked for ideological and propagandistic purposes. Before embarking on this study of ancient British history that was in fact neither 'ancient', nor 'British', nor 'history', it is necessary to re-examine some key terms, beginning with those for which, I suggest, 'Brutan histories' offers a productive replacement: 'Galfridian', and 'the British History'.

Questions of Terminology

When addressing representations and accounts of pre-Christian and pre-Roman Britain traceable to, but independent of, Geoffrey of Monmouth's *Historia*, I will adopt the term

'Brutan histories'.[5] This has several applications and aims to address and incorporate two problematic critical terms: 'Galfridian', which equates the tradition solely with Geoffrey of Monmouth, and 'The British History', a term implying a monolithic or secure sense of 'Britain'. The words 'Brutan', and 'Brutaine', among many spelling variants, were used to describe Britain and the British – usually, if not always, considered by the English as synonymous with England and the English – throughout the medieval and early modern eras. For example, John Stow mentions in his *The Chronicles of England from Brute vnto this Present Yeare of Christ* that 'some Englishe writers aboue an hundred yeares since, vsually doe name [the British Isles] *Brutan*' (1580: f. 18). Thus, 'Brutan histories' creates an etymological connection between these narratives and early modern conceptualizations of the British Isles' antiquity, their ancient inhabitants and their founder. In contrast, the term 'Galfridian' semantically reduces five centuries of cultural history to a single author and his book.

In the prologue to the *Historia*, Geoffrey noted that he had found nothing in previous chronicles touching on 'the kings who lived here before Christ's incarnation' (2007: 4). He addressed this omission with reference to a 'certain old book', or '*liber vetustissimus*', written in an ancient British language and translated into Latin by Geoffrey himself (2007: 4). The 'old book' was, as a growing number of early modern writers were discovering, an enabling fiction that had given Geoffrey a *tabula rasa* from which to concoct the pre-Roman invasion portions of his work *ex nihilo*.[6] Geoffrey's extraordinary invention, the *Historia*, was to enjoy enormous influence and be accepted almost universally by the English as an authentic account of their origins for almost five centuries. As such, it might seem natural that the term adopted by many critics for figures and narratives derived from the *Historia* is 'Galfridian', indicating an origin from a single author and text. However, the use of the term occludes the ways in which, almost from the publication of the *Historia* itself, Geoffrey's narratives escaped and mutated into vernacular and non-literate cultures, principally via the Prose *Brut*, described by Tamar Drukker as 'any of the chronicles of British history beginning with Brute' (2003: 451). *Bruts* often provided substantial material for chronicle and historiographic texts printed in the early modern period: the very first of these, William Caxton's *Cronicles of Englond* (1480), was in fact a print edition of a manuscript *Brut*. While Geoffrey was cited in many of these texts, his *Historia* itself was never published in English or in England in the early modern period.[7] The term 'Brutan histories' thus prioritizes the role of the wider *Brut* tradition and that of Britain's Trojan founder; it accommodates the huge variety of texts and the variant narratives those texts contained – 'histories', plural – that the tradition encompassed, each bringing its own quirks, additions and variations. Perhaps most importantly, 'Brutan histories' addresses the fact that most early modern English encountering these narratives would not have done so via the *Historia* itself but through vernacular, performed, or oral tradition. The term 'Galfridian', on the other hand, presents a monolithic sense of a single author and his text which is unrepresentative of the Brut tradition's collaborative anonymity and its function as a historical record that, being for so many 'true', did not need, indeed repelled, a sense of authorial origin. Thus many of the Brutan moments outlined at the beginning of this Introduction – the Leicester inn attendant's understanding of his own civic history, or the models of history available to the spectators of *Leir* at the Rose in 1594 – are testament to an experience of history drawn directly from the Brut tradition without any of the spectators or participants having ever heard of Geoffrey of Monmouth or his book.

'Brutan histories' also engages with another term that is often still used by critics, 'the British History', one which as far back as the mid-twentieth century Thomas Kendrick could adopt 'in accordance with . . . custom' (1950: 6). This custom reaches back at least as far as the phrase's appearance in Richard Grafton's *Chronicle at Large* (1569: 38).[8] The term raises questions of what – now, and in the early modern period – constituted 'Britain', and for whom. This is particularly apposite when we consider that the Brutan histories essentially served as the official English account of the past, bolstering English interests and competing with a rival, and amusingly different, Scottish account of ancient Britain.[9] For a long time, critics' failure to reflect upon the usage of 'the British history' prevented alertness to the complex issues raised by the word 'British'. The phrase's uses and function were challenged in the 1970s when John Pocock made an influential call for a new 'British history', that is, for new methodologies that questioned the Anglo-centric nature of historiographic approaches to the region Pocock termed the 'Atlantic archipelago' (1975: 603), and which also recognized the complex interrelationships within and between the territories familiarly known as England, Scotland, Wales and Ireland. In turn, this has produced much literary criticism focusing on the distinct and dissonant representations of British territories and regional cultures in early modern literature. For example, Andrew Hadfield has argued that at this time 'English intellectuals saw their nation in danger of dissolving' (2004: 138). The perception of, and resistance to, the erosion of the Brutan histories runs concurrent with these 'British' cultural anxieties and frequently interacts with them. In short, I suggest 'the British History' is far too entangled with outmoded critical tradition *and* recent progressive critical discourse to sustain independent meaning as a term for the fictionalized period of antiquity sustained by the Prose *Brut* and its myriad cultural expressions.

Additionally, the word 'Britain' in the medieval and early modern periods had very different, and equally ideologically inflected, meanings. Alan MacColl, exploring usage of the terms 'Britain' and 'British' in the medieval to early modern periods notes that texts such as the Prose *Brut* 'either do not refer to "Britain" at all or use it as a synonym for England' (2006: 257). Thus, much of what is described as 'Britain' in English culture of the time is in fact 'English', and this has the effect of eliding the island's other cultural identities. For example, the entertainments at Henry VIII and the Holy Roman Emperor Charles V's entry into London in 1522 included a 'pageaunte off [i.e. of] an ylonde betokening the Ile off [i.e. named] englonde compassed all abowte wt water made in silver' (Kipling 1997: 161). This might be cited as one among many examples of one party or another – but almost always the English – exploiting the blurredness between the two concepts. Here, a material representation of the landmass comprising England, Scotland and Wales functions in an English pageant as the 'isle of England' alone, subsuming Scotland and Wales into an 'English' monolith. This representational strategy reflects ways in which the Brutan histories themselves had long served English interests. In 1301, Edward I wrote a letter to the Pope defending the English right to invade Scotland on the basis that the kingdom had been established by Brute, whose son Locrine had been king of Britain *and* Loegria (England); thus the king of England, being also king of Britain, was the rightful king of Scotland (MacColl 2006: 257; Mason 1987: 60). The same tactic was applied in the sixteenth century, underwriting Henry VIII's 1542 *A Declaration Conteynyng the Just Causes and Consyderations, of the Present War with Scotts Wherin alsoo Appereth the Trewe and Right Title that the Kings Most Royal Majesty Hath to the Soveragntie of Scotlande.* The *Declaration* was followed in 1548 by a similarly themed 'epistle or exhortacion' from Edward Seymour, the Lord Protector (Robinson-Self 2018: 121). This is also the logic behind the English-facing rhetoric of James VI and I's project to 'reunite' Scotland and England. Abandoning the term 'the British History' reminds us that the Brutan histories represented an English tradition and asserted a sense of English primacy. Brutan drama was thus, in fact, a tradition in which the English performed their favoured account of their own history and origins, largely for themselves.

Another issue raised by the notion of a singular 'British History' is that it assigns a secure meaning to the word 'history' that is unreflective of early modern usage. In the medieval and early modern periods, the word 'history' was semantically insecure, suggesting almost any form of narrative, fictional or otherwise. Daniel Woolf has explored the varied and contradictory uses of the word, noting that, while the term had been 'problematic and fluid', in the Elizabethan era it gradually became used more often 'to distinguish between history proper, a truthful account of real events, and poetry or fable, the account of the verisimilar or fabulous' (1987: 19). However, acceptance of this extreme ambiguity can alert us to the multiple and dissonant meanings that early moderns may have had in mind, consciously or otherwise, when using or encountering the word. For example, writing in his *Suruay of London*, John Stow describes the playhouses in which were performed 'Comedies, Tragedies, enterludes, and histories, both true and fayned' (1598: f. 69). From Stow's syntax it is impossible to tell whether it is the comedies, tragedies, interludes and histories that are both 'true and fayned' – that is, derived from both accepted historical accounts and fictional sources – or whether only the histories themselves were both 'true and fayned', meaning that Stow is using the word 'history' in its sense of denoting any narrative, 'true' or otherwise. Attendance to this type of syntactical slipperiness alerts us to its presence at the level of early modern cognition, especially when addressing questions of what did, and didn't, constitute or denote historical truth.

This generic blurredness is significant at several stages of the process of cultural production, beginning with writers who, like plays, should not be securely categorized. An individual could produce works in many fields, making terms such as 'poet' or 'historian' misleading in ways that obscure the multiple and intersecting media through which 'history' was received. Historiographic texts were used as sources by writers of poetry, political and religious texts, and plays; and many of these writers in turn produced historiographic texts of their own. As Paulina Kewes has observed, early modern 'poetry, drama, and prose historiography . . . were often written by the same people' (2006: 7–8). For example, Samuel Daniel wrote plays and poems, but also wrote *The First Part of the Historie of England* (1612). To refer to him as a poet is to suggest that he was a poet writing history, a context which subtly compromises our sense of the seriousness with which his historiographical work – and thus its authority as an account of the past – might have been received by his readers. The fluidity between poetry and history, as well as the rhetorical value of material with uncertain or insecure truth value, was accommodated and systematized under the rubric of 'poesie historical'. George Puttenham's *Art of English Poesie* (1589), for example, supported this tradition of giving poetic accounts of figures and events believed to be historical so that they could provide exemplary or admonitory examples in the present. The term was defined by Puttenham as the poetic means by which readers might 'behold as it were in a glasse the liuely image of our deare forefathers, their noble and vertuous maner of life' (1589: f. 31). Poesie historical created a zone wherein flexibility was permissible and even expected in addressing such material, as well as in creatively reworking accepted historical accounts for didactic purposes. The moral 'truth' and exemplary function of these narratives was valued above their putative historicity:

> These historical men neuerthelesse vsed not the matter so precisely to wish that al they wrote should be accounted true, for that was not needefull nor expedient to the purpose, namely to be vsed either for example or for pleasure: considering that many times it is seene a fained matter or altogether fabulous . . . works no lesse good conclusions for example then the most true and veritable. (1589: f. 32)

A poetic treatment of history allowed that not all should be 'accounted true', as the point was to provide both 'pleasure' and models through which to evaluate personal and political conduct; this is, as its title suggests, the primary function of *A Mirror for Magistrates* (1559). As such, approaching early modern attitudes to historical truth in terms of a binary model of those who 'believed' or 'disbelieved' is insufficiently nuanced. This is especially true when addressing the Brutan histories, whose uncertain and shifting status as history provoked much doubt, will-to-believe, equivocation and frustration. Addressing the complex territories between belief and doubt in ancient Greek attitudes to religious and historiographic narratives, Paul Veyne finds evidence for 'modalities of wavering belief', marked by a 'capacity to simultaneously believe in incompatible truths' (1988: 56). Arthur Ferguson argues that Veyne's theories are also applicable to early modern attitudes to the remote past (1993: 2). Adopting Veyne's fluid 'modalities' allows for models of 'belief' in the Brutan histories that occupy a dissonant state between this will-to-believe and discomfiting doubt once the 'crisis of belief' in their historicity (Ferguson 1993: 26) was encountered. We might detect undercurrents of doubt in the most vociferous endorsements, such as Richard Harvey's *Philadelphus* (1593), or traces of nostalgia or regret in those writers such as William Camden, whose work contributed so much to the process of etiological erosion.

Today, such dissonant material – ahistorical narratives which serve and feed the story a culture tells about itself – is usually termed 'myth', and thus accommodated within Veyne's modalities. Indeed, 'myth' is a term almost universally adopted by critics engaging with Brutan history and drama. This is understandable, and an accurate term for a fiction that is believed and culturally utilized, as the Brutan histories were throughout the medieval and much of the early modern periods. However, I suggest that 'myth' – while perhaps applicable to the latter phases of the Brutan histories' reception, when their doubtful historicity was admitted but their rhetorical and propagandistic function sustained – fails to accommodate their status once they were abandoned. Roland Barthes defines myth as '*a type of speech* . . . a message . . . a mode of signification, a form' (1993: 109; author's emphasis); that is, something that must be expressed, given, received and used. Myth, in order to *be* myth, must be active and exchanged, characterized by a certain cultural usefulness, mobility and status. The mid-Jacobean period saw an intensification of the process by which the Brutan histories were disappearing from English culture. In Barthes's terms, the Brutan 'type of speech', whether historiographic or poetic, gradually ceased to be spoken, both figuratively and actually. It thus arguably ceased to be myth and entered an uncertain category of dead texts, or to repurpose a phrase from Harvey's *Philadelphus*, 'books of nothing' (1593: sig. H3r). The Brutan histories survived materially as manuscripts, printed volumes, statuary and other cultural records but had largely been silenced in terms of English culture, speech and reception. I will argue that this latter process, by which Brutan 'history' becomes myth, and then less still than that, can be mapped onto Jacobean dramas such as *Cymbeline*. Thus, an acknowledgement of the blurred boundaries among textual genres, modes of history and conceptions of truth demands that the performances, texts and events under discussion be examined not only within the Brutan tradition *in motion* as it erodes but also within their specific cultural and political contexts.

Performed History and Historiography

For its cultural resonance and reception to be more fully understood, Brutan drama must be resituated within the models of historical understanding determined by the 'social realities that define the world of the individual reader or listener' (Woolf 2003: 325). However, if an imagined early modern spectator is the only arbiter of what might constitute historical 'truth', then almost any early modern drama can be argued to have been received as representing the lived past by someone, somewhere. Of course, discrimination between fact and fiction was exercised by audiences and readers, albeit according to wildly differing standards of proof. This book considers the reception of Brutan drama by particular social groups, or textual communities, using as evidence the texts and historiographic traditions with which those groups might have identified and to which they had access.[10] This requires careful consideration of the availability and nature of the elite and popular sources through which a playgoer or reader might understand 'history'. As such, my approach to the performance of history is to work closely with both written historiographic materials and more popular and widely accessible modes of representing the past.

The foregoing discussion, which expands and complicates notions of what might be considered 'history' in the early modern era, raises the question of what to call the performances and texts considered in this book. The familiar term 'history play' is hardly sufficient for a tradition of performing the Brutan histories that incorporates not only narrative drama but also royal entries, court masques, civic pageantry and, I suggest, the communal reading aloud of historiographic material. In critical usage, the limitations of the term 'history play' derive from scholars' use of Shakespeare's English 'histories' as sequenced and defined by their appearance in the 1623 folio of his work (F1) as a benchmark of the genre (Lidster 2017: 19). F1 has thus established a model of the form's generic characteristics against which other works are compared in order to be categorized (2017: 19). Paulina Kewes has challenged the solidity of the Folio as a benchmark (2005: 185). Further, Kewes has persuasively argued against critical restrictions to the 'history play' genre that go beyond Shakespeare but limit the term to plays of medieval English history: 'If we want to understand the place and uses of history in early modern drama, we should be willing to consider any play, irrespective of its formal shape or fictional element, which represents, or purports to represent, a historical past, native or foreign, distant or recent' (2005: 185). Amy Lidster has compiled a chart of some 255 playbooks containing material that could be considered 'historical' (including reprints), published between 1584 and 1642 (2017: 298–324). The effect of Lidster's work is to demonstrate the extent to which the critical term 'history play' has come to exclude the vast majority of early modern dramatic texts purporting to represent in some way the lived past, such as 'foreign history, biblical history, classical history, and citizen-orientated history' (20). In response, I suggest the term 'performed history', to accommodate this multivalence. The Brutan figure Ebrauk, performed before Henry VII at York in 1486, could never be described as 'a play about . . .', yet Ebrauk is nonetheless an example of the embodied past, or performed history, as much as are the events and characters of Shakespeare's *Henry V*.

The notion of the 'history play' also creates a false barrier between the cultural reception of drama and historiographic texts as sources of historical knowledge. Indeed, the Jacobean Master of the Revels Sir George Buc explicitly complained about 'the ignorant, and never-understanding vulgare; whose faith (in history) is drawne from Pamphlet and Ballad, and . . . the stage' (1982: xxii), giving us clear, bad-tempered evidence of the divisions between elite and popular modes of history. Buc shows us that performed history was, for many spectators, a species of historiography and a source of historical truth. This is especially significant given Heywood's comments on the comprehensiveness of the London repertory of performed history and the fact that drama offered one of the most widely experienced versions of history available, being the 'genre that appealed to perhaps the broadest cross-section of Elizabethan society' (Woolf 1988: 348). For many, performed history *was* history.

This wider conception of performed history also extends in the direction of the historiographic text itself. The performance of history was not restricted to drama because reading history was not a silent, private act. Woolf notes that early modern writers 'thought of their works not as silent artefacts' but as texts with the potential to be spoken aloud (1986: 159–60). Early modern encounters with historiography could thus be performative and communal. Anthony Grafton and Lisa Jardine have influentially argued that the reading of history was often 'carried out in the company of a colleague or student; and was a public performance, rather than a private meditation' (1990: 31). This brings the reception of historiographic texts into the same zone of embodiment and shared experience as

that occupied by drama, especially if the text to be read aloud
might include first-person speeches and dialogue, as did the
Mirror for Magistrates, or the many accounts of Leir's reign
from Geoffrey's *Historia* onwards. Jennifer Richardson and
Richard Wistreich pursue this line further, arguing that in a
'hybrid culture where ballads were heard on streets, plays
audited in the London theaters, and the Bible read in homes
. . . the full realization of any written text would have been
dependent on its being vocalized, or at least on imagining that
it was', asking provocatively 'what would happen if we were to
assume that all early modern writers worked within a paradigm
of vocality?' (2019: 9). We should therefore be less confident
in drawing too-precise categorizations between texts usually
considered as chronicles and those considered as dramatic.
Here is Cordeilla's response to her father Leir's demand for a
display of love, as given in Holinshed's *Chronicles*:

> I protest vnto you, that I haue loued you euer, and will
> continuallie (while I liue) loue you as my naturall father.
> And if you would more vnderstand of the loue that I beare
> you, assertaine your selfe, that so much as you haue, so
> much you are worth, and so much I loue you, and no more.
> (1587: I *Hist.* 13)

The first-person perspective forces whoever was reading aloud
to adopt Cordeilla's voice and rhetoric – 'I protest vnto you' –
and thus, momentarily, to embody her. To read this passage
aloud in company, I suggest, constitutes performed history as
much as, if not more than, the act of reading the playbook
of *Leir* silently alone might do: the reading of historiographic
texts could be performative, theatrical performance could be
received as an authoritative account of the past, and published
dramas could be read as historiographic texts. The notion
that performed history made a powerful contribution to the
historical consciousness of early modern England is integral to
this book. Within this tradition of performed history, however,
the Brutan histories' underlying fictiveness poses a unique

set of problems in terms of their contribution to 'British', or rather English, etiology. Not only were they a fiction, but there was no alternative account of British antiquity with which to replace them.

   Attacks on the veracity of the received account of British antiquity often focused on the tales of King Arthur, which Geoffrey had fabricated and inserted into more numerous, and therefore verifiable, accounts of Saxon Britain by writers such as Bede. Polydore Vergil's *Anglica Historia* was particularly sceptical of Arthur, and as such he was the focus of defences such as John Leland's *Assertio Inclytissimi Arturii Regis Britannia* (1544). However, the pre-Roman era, which I term 'Brutan', was a blank. I am engaged here not only with accounts of individual kings, queens and their dynasties but also with the fictional macro-temporality that contained them, the notional expanse of time that Geoffrey created in which to house his epic, classicized vision of British origins. While King Arthur could be removed from the historical account without existential damage to the wider Saxon period in which he was said to have lived, the pre-Roman period as presented in the *Historia* could survive only, as it were, on its own authority. As such, to question the historical truth of Brute, or his descendants Lud, Lear or Gorboduc, was to undermine the integrity of pre-Roman British culture and origins as a whole, characterized as a civilization of cities, temples, conquering armies and universities and presented as the equal of any nation in the classical world, long predating Rome.[11] Thus the Brutan histories' sheer cultural *usefulness*, along with the vertiginous lack of anything with which to replace them, energized those that resisted their erosion. Around 1618, the Jacobean writer Edmund Bolton expressed his concern that to give up on this era would leave a 'vast Blanck upon the Times of our Country, from the Creation of the World till the coming of Julius Caesar' (1722: sig. Cc2v–3r).[12] I am interested in this notion of a historiographic tradition of centuries collapsing into nothingness, and I suggest that signals transmitted from the heart of this 'vast blanke' would have been perceptible in such plays as *Leir*, *King Lear* and their contemporary Brutan drama *No-body and Some-body* (*c.* 1604; pub. 1606). This book is, then, an account of the ways in which the Brutan histories returned to the nothing from which they had come and how this may have been perceived in early modern performance.

Brutan Drama in Performance and Print, 1486–1634

Table 1 outlines this corpus, which accommodates records of performance and playbooks addressing characters and events from the 'landing of Brute' to the reign of Cymbeline. Cymbeline's reign was positioned at the historical moment when the incompatible Brutan and Roman histories overlapped, providing a suitably dissonant case study for the moment when one model of history is challenged and, eventually, superseded by another.

Table 1 is indebted to the table of pre-Conquest drama provided in Gordon McMullan's 'The Colonisation of Britain on the Early Modern Stage' (2007: 139–40); however, I focus here only on Brutan figures of pre-Roman Britain, rather than drama which draws upon Roman, Arthurian or Anglo-Saxon accounts. I have also expanded the range of texts and performances, incorporating the post-Bosworth civic pageants and texts such as Milton's *A Masque* and Townshend's *Albions Triumph* (1632), that feature Brutan figures in more allusive states. For example, in *A Masque*, the Brutan figure Sabren appears transfigured as the river goddess Sabrina, while in *Albions Trivmph*, Charles I performed the allegorical figure of Albanactus, derived from Albanacht, Brute's son and the first ruler of Albany-Scotland.

This establishes the corpus to be examined, and the foregoing material has argued for the contribution made by performed history to the formation of early modern historical consciousness.

TABLE 1 *Brutan Drama in Performance and Print, 1486–1634*

Text / event (source noted for texts not published in print editions)	Perf. / Pub.	Company and performers; venue	Author(s); first publisher
Henry VII's entry at York (text recorded in Cottonian MS. Julius B. xii)	perf. 1486	'Diverse personage and minstrelsies'; performed at Micklegate Bar, York	Devised under the direction of Henry Hudson
Henry VII's entry at Bristol (text recorded in Cottonian MS. Julius B. xii)	perf. 1486	Unnamed citizens of Bristol; performed near St John's Gate, Bristol	Anon.
Elizabeth I's royal entry at London (performance recorded in BL: Cotton MS. Vitellius F)	perf. 1558	Unnamed London livery company members; performed at Temple Bar, London	Anon.
Gorboduc (text extant)	perf. 1562 pub. 1565	'Gentlemen of the Inner Temple'; performed at the Inner Temple and Whitehall Banqueting House	auth. Thomas Sackville and Thomas Norton; pub. William Griffith
The Joyful Receiving of the Queen's Most Excellent Majesty (text extant)	perf. 1578; pub. 1578	Passages performed by Sir Robert Wood, Mayor of Norwich, 'and others'; performed in the vicinity of St Stephen's Gate and later the marketplace, Norwich	auth. Bernard Garter and Thomas Churchyard; pub. Henry Bynneman

(Continued)

TABLE 1 *(Continued)*

'King Ebrauk with All His Sons' (performance recorded in BL: Harley MS. 2125, f. 43*)	perf. 1589	Performers unknown; performed at Chester before the Earl of Derby	Anon.
Locrine (text extant)	perf. *c.* 1590 pub. 1595	Unknown	auth. anon.; pub. Thomas Creede
'Guthlack' (Cutlack) (recorded in Philip Henslowe's *Diary*)	perf. 1594	Admiral's Men; Rose playhouse	Anon.
Leir (text extant)	perf. 1594 pub. 1605	Queen's Men	auth. anon.; pub. John Wright
'King Lude' (Henslowe)	perf. 1594	Sussex's Men; Rose playhouse	Anon.
2 Seven Deadly Sins[a] (plot recorded in Dulwich College, MS xix)	perf. *c.* 1597	see note	Anon.
'Mulmutius Dunwallow' (Henslowe)	perf. 1598	Admiral's Men; Rose playhouse	William Rankin
'The Conqueste of Brute' (Henslowe)	perf. 1598	Admiral's Men; Rose playhouse	John Day and Henry Chettle
'Brute Greenshield' (Henslowe)	perf. 1599	Admiral's Men; Rose playhouse	Anon.

TABLE 1 *(Continued)*

'Ferex and Porex' (Henslowe)	perf. 1600	Admiral's Men; Rose playhouse	William Haughton
The Triumphs of Re-United Britania (text extant)	perf. 1605; pub. 1605	Lord Mayor's Show (sponsored by the Merchant Taylors' Company)	auth. Anthony Munday; pub: William Jaggard
No-body and Some-body (text extant)	*c.* 1604; pub. 1606	Queen Anna's Men; Unknown	auth. anon.; pub. John Trundle
King Lear (text extant)	perf. 1606; pub. 1608	The King's Men; Globe playhouse and Whitehall Banqueting House	auth. William Shakespeare; pub. Nathaniel Butter
'Belynus (&) Brennus' (recorded in Add MS 27632, f. 43r)	unknown; before 1609	The reference appears in a list of playbooks owned by Sir John Harrington, compiled *c.* 1609	Anon.
Cymbeline (text extant)	perf. *c.* 1611; pub. 1623	King's Men; Globe playhouse and Whitehall Banqueting House	auth. William Shakespeare; pub. Edward Blount and Isaac Jaggard
Fuimus Troes (text extant)	perf. *c.* 1611–32; pub. 1633	'Gentleman students'; Magdalen College, Oxford	auth. attributed to Jasper Fisher; pub. Robert Allott
Albions Trivmph (text extant)	perf. 1632; pub. 1632	'The King's Majesty and his lords' with Queen Henrietta Maria; Whitehall Banqueting House	auth. Aurelian Townshend; pub. Robert Allott

(Continued)

TABLE 1 *(Continued)*

A Masque Presented at Ludlow Castle (Comus) (text extant)	perf. 1634; pub. 1637	perf. by members of the Bridgewater family and household; Ludlow Castle	auth. John Milton; pub. Humphrey Robinson
'Madon, King of Britain' (Madan?)	perf. unknown; Stationers' Register entry: 1660	Unknown	Attributed to Francis Beaumont[b]

[a] The dating and company attribution of this manuscript 'plot' of players' entrances and exits surviving in Philip Henslowe's papers (Dulwich College, MS xix) is controversial; see Kathman (2004), Gurr (2007). Wiggins follows Kathman in dating and company attribution (2013: 3, ref. 1065).

[b] This attribution is doubtful, given that the same Stationers' Register entry contains several unlikely ascriptions, including plays assigned to Shakespeare (Wiggins 2014: 4, ref. 1608).

Within this model, each text should thus be historicized not only according to its embeddedness within the wider Brutan tradition but also in relation to the specific cultural moment of its production. To stress, as I will do, the strange similarities between these texts – between, for example, performing Ebrauk at York in 1486 and Lear at Whitehall in 1606 – without acknowledging the gulfs of time, culture and dramaturgy that separate these moments, would be to render any comparison meaningless and misleading. These 'moments' should be addressed not only via the sociopolitical preoccupations of a particular textual community at a given time, or via the development of the 'crisis of belief' in Brutan history, but also via the shifting modes of early modern dramaturgy. Thus *Gorboduc*, a Senecan drama written by lawyers and concerned with the importance of good counsel and the rule of law to establishing a secure royal succession, cannot be separated from its early Elizabethan Inns of Court origins, just as *Cymbeline* is manifestly a product of dramaturgical trends in the years 1609–11 and James VI and I's irenic foreign policy.

It is apparent that several of these performances took place in the presence of English monarchs, from Henry VII to Charles I, and thus were shaped by a desire to influence, appease and aesthetically please those monarchs; however, it is equally apparent that many of these performances, particularly those represented by the 'lost' repertory of 1590s Brutan drama performed at the Rose playhouse and recorded in Philip Henslowe's *Diary*, seem to have been a commercial response to popular tastes. The Rose grouping, in fact, suggests an overarching sense of intertextual design and repertory planning in which these performances were absorbed into the larger cultural project of staging 'English chronicles' (as Heywood termed them) as a whole, reaching backwards into antiquity via the plays of Trojan history also performed within the same repertory (Teramura 2014: 128). Further, these can be seen as interacting with Shakespeare and his company's dramatic sequences of post-conquest English history, allowing Brutan drama the potential to provide a foundation for, and thus authorize, a collective London-wide, even national, dramaturgy of English history and etiology from the level of performances spoken directly to a reigning monarch to the spectators that crowded the Rose.

The integration of Brutan drama into these wider repertories of performed history asserts its potential to disturb and unsettle once awareness of its origins as a medieval forgery spread glacially outwards from historiographic circles into popular culture. To present a narrative that moves, thematically at least, from the reception of Brutan drama by those for whom it represented lived history to those experiencing historical dissonance, this book applies a degree of diachronic exclusion to the texts examined in a given section or chapter, in order to broadly reflect the materials available to those encountering the text or event under discussion. For example, analysis of

Locrine (perf. *c.* 1590; pub. 1595) might make reference to *Gorboduc*, or the lost play *King Lude* (perf. 1594), but not to the Jacobean *No-body and Some-body*. However, the Elizabethan *Leir*, performed at the Rose in 1594 yet not published until 1605, will be examined as a Jacobean playbook and therefore in the context of James VI and I's project to unite Scotland and England, allowing for it to be discussed alongside *No-body and Some-body* and *King Lear*. This approach creates a sense of the cultural accumulation of these dramas as the era progressed and also provides an opportunity to explore how they may have existed, like *Leir*, 'out of time' from their original composition and performance.

Finally, a disclaimer. In essence, my approach broadly follows the accepted notion that the cultural drift in these years was from belief to disbelief in the Brutan histories. Therefore, each chapter addresses a particular question relating to the experience of etiological erosion and does so via case studies of specific Brutan texts and performances. This should not, however, be taken as fully representative of the variety and complexity of thought and belief at the historical moments in question. I also work to resist the creation of a secure teleology, the misleading idea of a smooth and one-way transition across the period. For example, those with dwindling belief in Brute towards the end of the Elizabethan era may have had their faith reinvigorated by the outpouring of Brutan imagery and panegyric that accompanied James VI of Scotland's accession to the English throne. And while my narrative addresses *Cymbeline* and Milton's *A Masque* as texts resonant with the final erosion of Brutan time from early modern cultural usage, I should also note that when Geoffrey's *Historia* was finally translated into English and published in 1718, its translator Aaron Thompson dedicated his substantial preface to reassessing the arguments for and against the truth of this account of 'this most material point of Brutus': Thompson asserted the 'almost universal Content and Confirmation that ... learned men have given to it; from the Time this history was first published till the beginning of the last Century, and several of the last Century also' (1718:

f. cvii). As Thompson asserts, many were still willing, or hoping, to believe in Brute long after the historical era covered by this book.

Chapter 1 outlines the creation of Geoffrey's *Historia Regum Britanniae* and the subsequent forms in which the Prose *Brut* was transmitted across the medieval period into the early modern era. The breadth and duration of this tradition demonstrates its central importance to any discussion of Brutan drama as a representation of the lived past, doubtful or otherwise, as a key component of the story that the English told about themselves and their origins. In the early modern era, I outline the key texts that reproduced, progressed, or challenged this tradition, including works by William Caxton, John Stow, Raphael Holinshed and William Camden and poesie-historical works by Edmund Spenser, William Warner, John Taylor and others. The chapter concludes with a case study of *Gorboduc* as a play emerging from this historiographic tradition and upon which it was also dependent for its affective and rhetorical force. I argue for *Gorboduc* as a species of performed historiography that also enables the 'pretence of sensual contact with the vanished past through the bodies that move and speak on stage' (Walsh 2009: 2). That is, the authors of the first extant work of English narrative tragedy in blank verse chose a Brutan subject to confront their elite audience with a warning from history that derived additional affective power from its recourse to shared national ancestry.

Chapter 2 delves deeper into the question of what it might have meant to watch or read drama portraying the Brutan histories for an audience believing themselves to be descended from the figures depicted. Addressing the notion of Britain's ancient Trojan roots via Marian Rothstein's research into the early modern concept that 'origin defines essence' (1990: 332), I argue that Brutan figures were often considered typologically intertwined with the cities and territories they were said to have founded. The importance of this principle to figures of British etiology, whether Brute as founder of Britain or his progeny and descendants, is demonstrated to have been at the core of the earliest recorded instances of Brutan drama, the civic performances given before Henry VII in 1486. When connected to later accounts from the London playhouses, this evidence supports the idea, as expressed in Thomas Nashe's famous description of the slain Talbot in *1 Henry VI* as appearing before an audience that 'imagine they behold him fresh bleeding' (1592: sig. F4r), that the performance of history could be imagined as bringing the audience into a kind of sensory or affective contact with the historical dead. Applying this to *Locrine*, which performs the original foundation and division of ancient Britain, I argue that the Brutan founders are configured as troublingly alien, being Trojans of Near Eastern heritage and therefore typologically intersecting with English ideas of the early modern Turk. Further, *Locrine* diverts from the chronicles in re-imagining many of its deaths as suicides, and the chapter explores the effect this has upon the model of British foundation and origins with which the play confronted audiences. The chapter's second case study employs methodologies relating to 'lost' plays, those for which evidence of performance, but no dramatic text, survives, to explore a 1594 performance of 'King Lude' at the Rose playhouse. King Lud was the Brutan rebuilder of London, said to have renamed the city after himself. In addressing 'King Lude' I focus on the performed presence of Lud as a synecdoche for London, a reading which is then localized with reference to the Rose's repertory at the time of the performance and ways in which Lud as a celebrated civic rebuilder might have been received in that moment, when the city was in the midst of long-term plague outbreaks.

Chapter 3 asks what it might mean to watch or read drama portraying the Brutan histories for an audience experiencing doubt regarding the historical reality of the figures depicted. It thus addresses the concept of historical dissonance – the creeping uncertainty regarding the historicity of Britain's ancient origins – within the early Jacobean moment. Iconography relating to Brute as founder of a unified Britain was re-energized by the propagandistic needs of James VI and

I's project to unite Scotland and England in a single kingdom. The chapter traces James's historiographic background as rooted in the work and influence of his tutor, George Buchanan, and in Scotland's own fictive etiology, to argue that the English edition of his *Basilikon Doron* (1603) utilized Brute's narrative explicitly for an English readership and that this text may have influenced Anthony Munday's Lord Mayor's Show, *The Triumphs of Re-United Britania* (1605). Whereas Chapter 2 focuses on the performance of origins, this chapter principally addresses drama in print and the ways in which reading might trigger a sense of doubt and etiological erosion. Three playbooks are examined: *Leir*, an Elizabethan play published in 1605, is explored via the combination of its anachronistic Christian setting and the inclusion of the disruptive villain Skalliger, who shared his name with the era's foremost scholar of world chronology. *No-body and Some-body*, I argue, disrupts and undermines the perceived historicity of its Brutan king, Elidure, by subordinating his narrative to the play's comic subplot, centring on the character Nobody. The play's relentless punning on the word 'nobody', as well as the character's onstage presence, creates a semiotics of negation and nothingness that compromises the reality of the play's purported historical characters. Finally, *King Lear* is presented via a reading in which the character of Lear might be perceived as physically experiencing his own historical extinction, or *Historica passio*, an interpretation of particular resonance given that the text appeared in the years following the failure of James's union project and the death of his youngest daughter, Mary.

Chapter 4 explores what it meant to watch or read drama portraying the Brutan histories for an audience that has accepted the histories' fictiveness. It asks what happens to 'history' that is no longer admitted as a record of the lived past, a status usually defined as 'myth'. I read *Cymbeline* through its publication as the concluding play in the 1623 folio, asking what that volume's, and the play's, sense of resolutions and endings might mean for its ancient British setting, and as a setting for the end phase of etiological erosion. I have suggested, via Barthes's definition of 'myth', that the term 'myth' is insufficient for iconography that is no longer in cultural use. Resisting alternative terminology and instead embracing the post-mythic Brutan histories' multivalency, I examine *Cymbeline*'s engagement with endings and the confounding complexity and resonance of the play's character names, including those such as 'Imogen' that invoke Brutan history even as they seem finally to dissolve it within the play's oversaturated semiotic field. The chapter's final section complicates this sense of apparent finality and teleology through a survey of texts published or performed in the 1630s that express a continued engagement with Brutan historicity or iconography. These are the Oxford University play *Fuimus Troes*, the only extant drama to explicitly cite Geoffrey of Monmouth as a source, John Milton's *A Masque Presented at Ludlow Castle*, which reconfigures a foundational Brutan figure as a goddess of the river in which she was drowned, and the masque *Albions Trivmph*, in which Charles I himself performed the Brutan-derived figure Albanactus. The concluding section examines the ways in which a single seventeenth-century book collection, that of Frances Wolfreston (1607–77), can be seen in microcosm to demonstrate many of the models of readership and interaction between Brutan historiography and drama for which this book argues.

Cumulatively, this evidence argues that from the 1486 progress of Henry VII embodied Brutan figures served as a means by which English institutions might navigate their relationships with English monarchs until these Brutan founders were co-opted and, eventually, absorbed by the iconography of the monarchy itself, effectively muting this dynamic exchange between the past and present. More widely, this book argues that the performance of Britain's ancient origins should be approached via its embeddedness in a 500-year tradition that pervaded English culture across all social degrees. I argue that records of early modern drama present a singularly dynamic account of the ways in which audiences and readers were not only confronted with the physical presence of those origins but through which they may also have experienced their erosion into what Richard Harvey, in his 1593 defence of those origins, *Philadelphus*, unwittingly termed 'books of nothing'. It is with Harvey, then, and his mockery at the hands of Thomas Nashe and Christopher Marlowe, that Chapter 1's account of the Brutan histories' cultural and textual transmission begins.

1

Geoffrey of Monmouth and Etiological Erosion

Brutan performance was received within the context of a polyvocal and intertextual narrative tradition that dated back to the twelfth century. From their inception the Brutan histories had been disseminated not only through expensive manuscripts and specialist historiographic books but also through popular forms such as ballads, narrative poetry and almanacs. This complex transmission resulted in multiple, sometimes conflicting, accounts of Britain's origins. The production and reception of these, as shown in the Introduction, were determined in part by issues such as literacy, religion and social grouping. In the early modern era, the Brutan histories were being more frequently questioned by writers from Polydore Vergil in the 1530s to William Camden in *Britannia* (1586); however, support for the traditional account of pre-Roman Britain was continually shored up via a steady flow of defensive chronicles and treatises, as well as texts and events that endorsed Brutan historicity simply by failing to acknowledge its doubtfulness. This shoring up is also visible in the continued early modern popularity of medieval prose histories in print and in manuscript. Beyond the readers who encountered this textual tug of war, however, it is unlikely that many people were even aware that there was anything to doubt. Understanding this, I suggest, is essential for understanding the dramatic performance of Britain's ancient past, particularly in terms of its reception.

This chapter outlines the transmission of the Brutan histories from the twelfth to the seventeenth centuries and their gradual, uneven disappearance from historical consciousness. This process has been mapped by previous scholars and my account is in large part conventional and indebted to these.[1] However, accounts of this erosion are often presented as overly linear – the early modern doubt being sown by Vergil and eventually consolidated by Camden and John Speed. While this is also, broadly, the narrative that needs to be outlined, Daniel Woolf has noted that '[t]he study of popular culture and the influence of postcolonial theory have also made us deeply aware that perceptions of the past are not necessarily uniformly shared at all levels of society, nor uncontested' (2005: 36). And, in relation to the Brutan histories, Andrew Griffin has recently challenged this overly tidy account of historiographic progression as a 'narrative of methodological supersession' that 'occludes a more complicated and stranger story' (2019: 93). I will therefore pause along the way to challenge and complicate this picture by offering brief case studies that place better-known Brutan and anti-Brutan texts alongside contemporaneous, but critically overlooked, texts such as William Warner's *Albions England* (1586) and Thomas Deloney's *Garland of Goodwill* (*c*. 1593). Even as the Brutan histories were being challenged, many of these works endorsed and further disseminated Brutan material in other milieux, often beyond the secure textual record into the realm of wider, non-literate, popular culture. If the 'stranger story' argued for by Griffin is to be told, then forms such as the ballad must be considered alongside works that have left a more secure footprint within critical tradition, such as the pragmatic historiography of Camden, or Spenser's poesie-historical appropriations. Drawing attention to both the intertextuality and contradictions between these Brutan works invites reflection on the historical dissonance that exposure to such a variety of material might have provoked. My attentiveness to lesser-known texts is particularly revealing of attitudes to Brutan historicity in the later Jacobean and early Caroline periods when, contrary to the traditional account, in which Camden's *Britannia* is viewed as representing something of a 'case closed' moment for Brutan historiography, we see, if anything, a new burst of Brutan engagement into the 1630s, including Charles I's performance as 'Albanactus' in the masque *Albions Triumph* (1632). This chapter's final section returns to performance, using the preceding material to establish the first known Brutan drama as the outcome of centuries of Brutan confluence, that of the ancient British king known variously as Gorbodian, Gorbodug or Gorboduc.

Before beginning this survey of the Brutan histories' transmission, I would like to offer, as I did with the performance of *Leir* at the Rose playhouse in 1594, an initial case study of the ways in which the Brutan histories were deployed, debated and encountered across an intersecting range of textual communities. The central figure in this instance, rather than the unfortunate though fictional Lear, is the unfortunate and very real Richard Harvey, brother of the better-known Gabriel. Reading Harvey's 1593 defence of the Brutan histories, *Philadelphus*, in the moment of its publication, allows us to glimpse a culture of teeming Brutan perspectives.

Philadelphus catalogues the vices and virtues of the Brutan rulers while asserting their historical truth. Following a dedication to the Earl of Essex and a letter to his brother Gabriel, this short book launches into Harvey's impassioned, yet carefully argued, refutation of George Buchanan's *Rerum Scoticarum Historia* (Edinburgh, 1582). Like Vergil's *Anglia Historia* (Basel, 1534) – at which Harvey also takes occasional swipes – Buchanan questioned Brutan historicity: 'Yet neyther seuen *Polydores* more, nor ten *Buchanans* shall perswade me, that this Genealogy is a fabulous Tale' (1593: sig. C3r). Evidence from another text suggests that Harvey's Brutanism was intense and long-standing. Certainly, he was mocked for it. In an episode reported by the Harveys' frequent adversary-in-print Thomas Nashe, in *Have with You to Saffron Waldon*

(1596), Christopher Marlowe characterizes Harvey's advocacy of Brute as a kind of derangement:

> [T]hat Dick, of whom Kit Marloe was wont to say, that he was an asse, good for nothing but to preach of the Iron Age . . . Dick the true Brute or noble Troian, or Dick that hath vowd to liue and die in defence of Brute, and this our iles first offspring from the Troian, Dick against baldnes, Dick, against Buchanan. (1596: sig. N3v)

Nashe's use of his friend's insults demonstrates several things.[2] First, the likelihood that these comments predate the publication of *Philadelphus*, Marlowe having died in May 1593. Second, the overheated voice Marlowe attributes to Harvey offers clues to the tonality in which *Philadelphus* might be read. *Have with You* is a highly partisan and satirical text – principally, it's an attack on Gabriel Harvey – and it backdates this complex network of rivalries to the participants' time as students at Cambridge. Richard Harvey, we are told, was awarded the extraordinary distinction of having a play staged about him by his fellow students, '*Duns furens*' or 'Dick Haruey in a frensie' (1596: sig. N1r). In response to the play, Nashe recalls, Harvey 'broke the Colledge glasse windowes; and Doctor *Perne* (being then either for himselfe or Deputie Vice-chancellour), caused him to be fetcht in, and set in the Stockes till the Shew was ended' (1596: sig. N1r). Nashe's portrait of Harvey, partisan as it is, associates the defence of Brute with a particular kind of personality: ridiculous, violent, unpopular even with the deputy vice-chancellor, who appears to have wanted to finish watching 'Duns Furens' in peace. Yet, via *Have with You*, Harvey is also obliquely connected to one of the Brutan histories' most wide-ranging and popular manifestations.

Readers of *Have with You*, on turning the page to read of 'Dick the true Brute', would have just encountered a reference to Thomas Deloney, the 'Balleting Silke-weauer', and his *Garland of Good Will* which, like *Philadelphus*, seems to have been published in 1593, when it was registered with the Stationers' Company. However, the earliest extant copy dates from 1626, suggesting both that its popularity was enduring and that the book was read to pieces on a large scale. Among its twenty-seven ballads, *Garland* includes one on Estrild, the unfortunate mistress of Locrine, the first king of Britain and son of Brute. The companion of Humber, who invades Britain only to be defeated by Locrine, Estrild is ensconced by the British king in a subterranean boudoir before being made his queen. Enraged, Locrine's current queen, Guendolen, raises an army of Cornishmen, defeats Locrine in battle and has Estrild and her daughter Sabren bound and thrown into a nearby river. Deloney was 'the leading ballad maker' of the era (Marsh 2019: 128). Many of *Garland*'s ballads had been previously printed as broadsides (Carpenter 2006: 139). This means that their circulation and popularity were even more comprehensive than already attested by its impressive republication rate. Here, Nashe's textual community of rival pamphleteering graduates opens up to include a London artisan famous for ballad-making. As Tessa Watt has noted, 'there was theoretically no man, woman or child who could not have access to a broadside ballad, at least in its oral form, when it was sung aloud' (1991: 13). Deloney's Brutan ballad of the 'Dukes Daughter of Corwal' can thus be situated as a source of self-performance and communal song within the broadest possible textual community. It allowed Estrild's tragic story to be taken up alongside *Garland*'s many other songs of mistreated and tragic royal mistresses, asserting her place within popular, self-performed history.

Ballads were hugely popular even as writers and elite consumers of the era fretted over the form's perceived 'low' cultural and literary status (Carpenter 2006: 140–1). One of these writers was Thomas Lodge, who in 1579 had attacked ballads and those who wrote and sang them as 'odde rymes which runnes in euery rascales mouth' (1979: f. 20). In 1593, Lodge had, like Deloney, published his own version of the story of Estrild, 'The Complaint of Elstred', included in his collection of sonnets and poems, *Phillis*. *Have with You* thus offers a snapshot of intersecting Brutan dialogues and cultural uses in mid-1590s print, in which the artisan-class writer of a Brutan ballad appears on the same page as mockery of the author of an impassioned Brutan defence and, according to Marlowe, self-proclaimed 'true Trojan'. Both texts were published in 1593, the same year in which a university-educated critic of ballads, Thomas Lodge, saw his own 'Complaint of Elstred' into print. The defence, the ballad and the poem of 1593 all speak to the circulation of the Brutan histories through multiple literary factions and textual communities. Yet, as indicated by Nashe's mockery, there was also dissonance and doubt. These undercurrents can perhaps be detected in even the most ardent of Brutan defenders: Richard Harvey himself.

One point of apparent weakness in the received account of Brutan history was a sequence of approximately twenty-four kings, about whom the source text of these histories, Geoffrey's *Historia*, offered no information and regarding whom Holinshed's *Chronicles* (1577; expanded edition pub. 1587) admitted to 'great diuersitie in writers touching the reignes of these kings, and not onlie for the number of yéeres which they should continue in their reignes but also in their names' (1587: I, *Hist.* 22).[3] That is, the silence regarding the events and duration of these reigns raised uncomfortable questions regarding the historicity of the larger narrative in which they were embedded. In *Philadelphus*, Harvey offers an extraordinary range of justifications for this unsettling lacuna. For its sustained energy and the resourceful invention of his reasoning, the passage is worth quoting at length:

They were now I may well say kinges Abstracts: that they did it no where, either incomprehensibly like Gods, or metaphisically like strange men . . . . A king cannot possibly be without his excellencies, and memorials. Now I diuine modestly, heere were actors without recorders of their actions, patrons of learning, but no learned men: or, they were of both sortes, but their studies came to no effect, by some force: or, they were very old when they came to the Crown, and could do nothing: or, the furies and helhoundes raged so extreamely, that the Muses and Graces coulde not bee quiet for them: or, their actes were wrought in needleworke onely, and so worne out: or, the senses, and senslesse desires so ruled them, that theyr liues were not so short as their actes: or, the Histories were written in some strange kind of polygraphy and steganography, and coulde neuer yet be read, but remaine in some obscure place: or, they made little account of writers, and these set as light by them: or, they that take most pains at their booke, were not most regarded: and thereupon studied to themselues: or, some infortunate and maleuolent configuration of mouable skies and starres, and spirites remoued all Histories out of the way: or, the Kinges and People agreed among themselues, to bee remembred by being not remembred, wishing to haue their time called *The vnknowe Regiment,* adiudging secrecie greatest wisedome: or, our Countrimen listened so much after other Noble Actors in the earth, that they had no leisure, to doe any thing themselues: or, they disdained to haue them theyr iudges after their death, whom they would scorne to haue their iudges in their life: or, some outlandish enuy destroyed the rowles and registers of our Histories, to make vs seem barbarous: or, the Vniuersitie men of *Stamford* had by some Priuiledge got them wiues, and so forth: and had no leisure to do any thing but liue: or, before the kings were crowned, they were worthy men, and after theyr coronations they fell to make books of nothing . . . it was not thus, or so: perhaps, neither this, nor that, but some other way, I cannot tell howe, nor I care not greatly, for feare I may bee thought neither idle, nor well occupied. (1593: sig. H2v–sig. H3v)

Harvey appears both moved and disturbed by Buchanan's attacks as he accumulates contortions and paradoxes. Each proposed scenario tumbles into negation. There were actors but no action; patrons of learning but an absence of 'learned men'; general chaos – 'furies and hellhounds' – is invoked; the materiality of recorded time is found wanting as these rulers' acts were recounted in long-perished textiles; strange codes may have been used; the absence is so extraordinary and unaccountable that it must have been cosmically induced by malevolent astrological configurations of 'mouable skies and stares'. Harvey imagines the nature of the rulers themselves, suggesting they experienced a kind of urge for historiographic eradication, a desire to be known only as the 'vnknow[n]e Regiment', or unknown regime. Nothing is solid in Harvey's visions. Everything from the materiality of texts to the character of kings to the heavens themselves is characterized by entropy and annihilation. Yet, perhaps more troubling still, neither do any of these suggestions seem adequate, and Harvey moves from one to the next into literary breathlessness: 'it was not thus, or so: perhaps, neither this, nor that, but some other way, I cannot tell howe'. Of the many possibilities that Harvey proposes, he refuses the most glaring: that these kings were invented by Geoffrey of Monmouth. His suggestion that the kings 'fell to make books of nothing', however, seems to me an inadvertent gesture towards this possibility, an incipient doubt. If the *Historia* was disproved, then that is what the first millennium of British history would amount to, along with the thousands, even millions, of pages of chronicle material, typological exegesis, ballads and, latterly, plays, that sustained and repeated them: books of nothing.

Harvey, while not perhaps 'in a frenzie', nonetheless, appears to be responding emotionally to a historiographic problem and process: the gradual, evidence-based, elision of Britain's ancient origins from accepted history, or etiological erosion. The depth and breadth of this tradition, and therefore the intensity of feeling with which its erosion might be felt and resisted, can only be fully appreciated when it is understood as a habit of thought and collective self-understanding that had endured for almost five centuries.

Geoffrey of Monmouth and the Brutan Histories in Transmission

The question of why Geoffrey of Monmouth wrote the *Historia Regum Britanniae* has long preoccupied medievalists. Much criticism has been dedicated to identifying political factionalism from Geoffrey's dedications to Robert, Earl of Gloucester, and Waleran, Earl of Worcester. These 'have generally been interpreted and dated by the shifts in political allegiance precipitated by the civil war' that began in the 1130s and continued until Henry II's accession in 1154 (Crick 1991: 5). The projected sequence in which these appear on manuscripts is speculative and 'there is no consensus about their order' (Howlett 1995: 34). However, I am to a large extent bypassing the question of Geoffrey's possible motivations. The question of the Brutan histories' twelfth-century production can tell us little about their early modern reception in drama and performance. By the late fifteenth century they had, outside the confines of historiography at least, almost entirely broken free of their originator. Nevertheless, as this was the foundation from which the Brutan histories emerged and mutated, it is useful to briefly consider the conditions in which the *Historia* was composed, to reflect upon its initial readerships and therefore its subsequent transmission.

Most critics testify, happily or otherwise, to the monumental reach and effects that Geoffrey of Monmouth's text achieved. The *Historia*'s popularity can be tracked through its survival in more than 200 extant manuscripts (Tolhurst 1998: 3). The *Historia* was, in Francis Ingledew's words, 'the exemplary historiographical work of the Middle Ages' (1994: 669) and was accepted as authentic by generations of chroniclers (Keeler 1946: 24). Importantly, the *Historia* was also a key influence and source for writers of romance, presenting the first sustained narrative of King Arthur, and in this capacity it serves as the opening text in Helen Cooper's magisterial study of the romance genre (2004: 23). In these ways, it not only authorized itself as history but spread outwards in multiple directions, interweaving fiction and lived history so thoroughly that historiographers would be unpicking the fabric for centuries.

Geoffrey of Monmouth 'was a secular canon of St George's in the castle at Oxford' (Davies 1996: 3). His was, in some ways, a liminal position, operating as part of the church infrastructure but not within the monastic tradition (Robertson 1998: 50). The *Historia* was produced just as England stood on the threshold of a civil war provoked by the disputed succession of Henry I. Geoffrey's principal, or at least traceable, sources – aside from the mysterious 'old book' – were Gildas's sixth-century national jeremiad *De Excidio Britanniae*, Bede's *Historia Ecclesiastica* (*c.* 731), and the *Historia Brittonum* (*c.* 830) attributed to Nennius, and origin of the first, albeit brief, account of Brute as national founder. Connecting national origins to figures of classical antiquity was not new and had been practised from the sixth or seventh centuries (Jones 1994: 237). Indeed, the Normans themselves appear to have sometimes claimed Trojan ancestry (Tyler 2013: 3). This suggests the intriguing possibility that one of the *Historia*'s functions was to fuse the origins of Britain's founders with those of the new conquerors. Where Geoffrey innovated was in addressing, and filling, the existentially disturbing temporal void in British history prior to the arrival of the Romans. The earliest accounts of Britain were sparse, unedifying and 'did not record a single event which antedated [Julius] Caesar's expeditions' (Leckie 1981: 30). The *Historia*, then, offered to the twelfth-century Anglo-Norman English an account that competed with the histories of continental kingdoms for dignity and antiquity, bestowing structure and continuity, as well as heroic glamour, upon a previously inaccessible past. In filling up the dark millennia unexplored by previous historians, the *Historia* had 'conquered time' (Davies 1996: 4). It granted the story of the British people an antiquity capable of interconnecting, running parallel to, and sometimes even predating, the key episodes of classical and biblical history. It dignified the origins of the island the Normans were increasingly considering home.

Innovation – and, of course, forgery – invite scepticism as well as enthusiasm. And although the *Historia* was disseminated and accepted as historical in the ensuing centuries, it is important to note that there was also a trend, exploding finally in the early modern period, of resistance. However, William of Newburgh and Gerald of Wales, both writing in the 1190s, 'were virtually the only two critics to voice scepticism of Geoffrey throughout the Middle Ages' (Robertson 1998: 51). More powerful was the appeal to the landowning Anglo-Norman gentry for whom, Ingeldew has argued, the *Historia* valorized lineage and dominion by 'colonizing time [and] tenanting the past with nonexistent ancestors' (1994: 675). The appeal to power was only one use to which the Brutan histories could be turned. But it would be a function utilized not only by the provincial gentry but also by English royalty from Edward I to Henry VII and his son, and by James VI and I, who promoted his accession to the English throne in 1603 as the reunification of a single British kingdom, ruled from the south, that had been both founded and divided by Brute.[4] In terms of readership, Tatlock notes that the *Historia* seems to have broken free from the social circles expected to have access to, and make use of, such a text, speculating that Geoffrey's work, having been written for the 'upper-class laity', eventually 'came more and more to appeal to those for whom it was not designed' (1950: 395). This becomes increasingly significant as the Brutan histories are assimilated by anonymous producers of medieval manuscripts, who translated, rewrote and adapted the narrative for an ever-broader audience.

As good a description as can be found of the transmission of historiographic texts in manuscript across the medieval period comes from Daniel Woolf:

[C]hronicles were copied, borrowed, and paraphrased. They often grew more by gradual accretion than by conscious

> design or systematic composition. . . . But this was precisely
> what kept the genre alive, allowing it to grow and change to
> suit the purposes of generation after generation of writers.
> (1997: 351)

It was in this culture that the Brutan histories, rather than
Geoffrey's original text, seem to have become the pre-eminent
account of British etiology, expanding into the vernacular via
Wace's Francophone verse adaptation, the *Roman de Brut* (*c.*
1150) and Laȝamon's early-thirteenth-century *Brut* (Bzdyl
1989: 11). Only surviving in two manuscripts, Laȝamon's
work must be approached cautiously when considered in
terms of wider trends. With that caveat, however, W. R. J.
Barron's research into Laȝamon's possible patronage proposes
the dissemination of that text throughout a landowning
household incorporating 'extended *familia*' of 'household
retainers', associated artisans and servants, as well as the
landowner's spouse and others who may have, as is possible
with all iterations of the Brutan histories, gathered to hear
texts such as Laȝamon's read aloud (2002: 173). Reading
was often a communal activity, carried out aloud for the
purpose of analysis or debate, meaning that a text could be
transmitted far beyond its owner and reader (Woolf 1986:
159–60), suggesting a diverse, yet interconnected, audience
for tales of national history, and the potential for a degree
of oral dialogic response to those narratives among listeners
of different social rank and profession. This model both pre-
empts and establishes the idea of an early modern theatrical
spectatorship able to enjoy and analyse performances of
the Brutan histories, to interrogate their meaning but not,
necessarily, their historicity.

Wace influenced Laȝamon, but his popularizing effect was
far more direct; the *Roman de Brut* served as the source for
the first half of the anonymous Prose *Brut* (Marvin 2005:
283), the Oldest Version of which postdates 1272, where its
narrative concludes. The Prose *Brut* was an ever-extending
text, providing the foundation for a 'national historical

consciousness' (Marvin 2006: 4). From the Oldest Version, the Prose *Brut* was radically unmediated:

> [The original author] provided it with no title, no dedication to a patron, no self-identification as author, no prologue describing how hard he worked, how many sources he used, and why his book was worth reading, and no request for a reward, position, or even the prayers of his audience . . . (Marvin 2017: 1)

Each new version updated the foregoing narratives to the present moment. In this way the Brutan histories always flowed into the present. The Prose *Brut* was the Brutan histories' most significant repository, surviving in its Middle English version in more copies than any other Middle English text except the Wycliffite Bible (Lamont 2010: 286), with 250 manuscripts extant in total (Marvin 2017: 2): 50 in Anglo-Norman, 180 Middle English and 20 in Latin (Marx and Radulescu 2006: xiv). Crick suggests that the Prose *Brut* must have been inescapable in the fifteenth century for anyone connected to the book trade from 'scribes, illuminators, binders, and booksellers' to 'librarians, readers, hearers, and owners' (1991: 9). Yet it was also, effectively, authorless; not 'a singular text but a fluid, collaborative, and ongoing project' (Gillespie and Harris 2012: 142), attributed in some manuscripts to a polytemporal authorship of '[m]ani dyvers goode men and grete clerkes and namely men of religion'.[5] The notion of a collaboratively assembled, yet anonymous, text draws attention to the limitations of the term 'Galfridian'. The Brutan histories belonged not to an author but, in effect, to those who read it or heard it read aloud.

The Prose *Brut* was an interactive text in which readers and household members recorded thoughts, comments and annotations. Many of the Prose *Brut*'s readers added their own genealogies to household copies (Radulescu 2006: 192). In this way they were passing down and inscribing their identities upon an account of British history that led back, via Brute, to the creation of the world. Early British history and British origins, then, were for some readers neither as remote nor abstract as many sixteenth-century writers of historiographic texts would characterize them. Rather, they were a wider context in which to situate and dispute familial, national and spiritual identity and continuity; they were proof of consequential origins. Amy Noelle Vines places the Middle English Prose *Brut* as central to 'the family as a medieval textual community' (2006: 72). Vines describes a fifteenth-century manuscript, bequeathed to one Esabell Alen by her uncle, a Salisbury vicar, inscribed with a request that she pray for his soul (2006: 75–6). Here, the Prose *Brut* appears to serve as a devotional text, suggesting the function assigned it by Marvin as a 'species of Old Testament' (2006: 6–7) anchoring present events – war, family bereavement – to a shared antiquity. Tamar Drukker's 2006 study of marginalia supports the possibility that this example is not atypical, and that Bruts were often included in the household miscellanies that worked to 'construct and preserve the collective memory of the household' (Hardman 2003: 27; qtd in Radulescu 2006: 192). Setting these texts within Richardson and Wistreich's 'paradigm of vocality' enables the additional speculation that Prose *Brut*s may have served as a repository for the aural memory of a household's assembled voices, the marginalia as evidence of spoken interactions or tonal cues for the reader-aloud.

Annotators seem to have favoured material relating to the British kings, their wars, and 'natural disasters'. Annotation is often denser in the opening chapters – the material relating to the Brutan histories – and, while Drukker appears disappointed by the 'surprisingly unoriginal' and near-identical nature of much marginalia between manuscripts (2006: 99–102), this evidence suggests that the Brutan histories may have received consistent readings in diverse regional locations. The similarity between annotators' responses thus supports the possibility of widespread, even national textual communities, communities with the Prose *Brut* as their secular fulcrum. Over centuries, these conditions produced a historical consciousness that by the late sixteenth century was predisposed to encounter Brutan performance without experiencing, or even being aware of, the 'crisis of belief' taking place in some more scholarly circles.[6] Indeed, much Prose *Brut* marginalia was made by sixteenth- or seventeenth-century readers (Bryan 2006: 131), showing not only the exceptional duration of these books' utility, but that, for many, the oldest and most familiar history remained the most dependable.

Between the twelfth and fifteenth centuries, the Brutan histories were repurposed and repeated, adapted, altered and extended, creating a network of vernacular, poetic and historiographic traditions that lionized a single national origin. This network was pervasive enough that, for non-specialist readers, the Brutan histories offered so definitive an account of the national past that scepticism or further enquiry may have seemed unnecessary, in the same way that few early modern readers would have felt compelled, or even authorized, to question the historicity of, for example, King John or the biblical David. The sixteenth century, however, witnessed the erosion of the Brutan histories in certain textual communities even as they were, arguably, further disseminated and reinforced in others. Traditional models of historiographic practice, along with the texts they had produced, were under increasing scrutiny. Assessing the accuracy of received historical accounts proved difficult in part because the only recognized authorities were textual, and therefore anyone attempting to write or assemble a historiographic text 'was at the mercy of the judgment (or lack of judgment) of his predecessor' (Kretzschmar 1992: 523). Not only the Brutan histories, but the very means by which the historicity of people and events had been determined were also being revealed as essentially fragile. Thus the controversy over Brutan origins was characterized less by clear positions of belief or disbelief and more by what Ferguson describes as 'a typically Renaissance state of ambivalence' (1993: 26), or, by Veyne's 'modalities of wavering belief'.

In the following paragraphs, while sketching the narrative that shows early modern historiography moving from belief to disbelief through the work of writers such as Camden, John Speed and John Selden, I will also foreground those texts that resisted or ignored the developments in historiographic technique. These were also often highly successful in print and, through affordability or tone, appealed to textual communities resistant to anti-Brutan arguments. As well as the national network of households connected by the Prose *Brut*, these communities might include the lawyers of the Inns of Court and the complex urban networks that radiated outwards from the London livery companies. For both these groups, Brutan figures loomed large as founders of nations, cities and laws. In fact, the first decades of English print culture saw a wider and more sustained dissemination of the Prose *Brut* and Brutan histories than ever before, driven by William Caxton, who appears to have recognized a thriving interest in, and therefore a large market for, the Brutan histories.

The story of the Brutan histories' transmission from manuscript to print culture is one of continuity, expansion and mutation. The first historiographic text printed in English was Caxton's *Cronicles of Englond* (1480), a reproduction of the Prose *Brut*, extended by Caxton to include material up to 1461 (Tonry 2012: 171 n. 4). Woolf frames Caxton as a 'businessman rather than a scholar', aiming to meet his customers' interests (1999: 187). Caxton seems to have identified a pre-existent market for national history, and Brut texts in particular, a possibility strengthened by his decision, within two years of the *Cronicles*, to publish Ranulph Higden's fourteenth-century *Polychronicon*, and his own *Liber Ultimus* (Tonry 2012: 171 n. 4). Both texts incorporated the Brutan histories, the latter integrating these with more recent material taken from London civic history for a readership of 'well-informed mercantile Londoners' (Tonry 2012: 179). London, in its guise as Troinovant, was central to Brutan power structures. *Cronicles* was popular, frequently reprinted up to 1528, and its readers' attentiveness is attested by copies containing marginal notes and annotations (Crick 1991: 23). The influence of *Cronicles*, and thus of the Prose *Brut*, continued to the seventeenth century, serving as the foundation for William Warner's eclectic and digressive verse history *Albions England* (Marvin 2005: 303), a hugely successful work that received ten editions between 1586 and 1612. The endurance of the Prose *Brut*, then, is visible in the era of Camden's *Britannia* and John Speed's *History of Great Britain* (1611). This is important, as Camden and Speed's works are often cited as marking the end of the Brutan tradition in a process of erosion that began with Polydore Vergil, whose work initially provoked rage among English polemicists and historiographers.

Vergil, an Italian scholar working in the court of Henry VII, was commissioned by the king to write the *Anglia Historia*, which was finally published well into the reign of Henry VIII (Basel, 1534). Vergil's work effectively triggered the controversy over accounts of history deriving from the *Historia Regum Britanniae*, principally the *Historia*'s presentation of pre-Roman Britain and the reign of King Arthur. Vergil was not the first to express doubts, but his foreignness and Catholicism particularly upset his detractors, meaning that supporters of the Brutan histories, especially in the mid-sixteenth century, would often be associated with English Protestant nationalism (Crick 1991: 24–5). One of the most vocal of Vergil's critics was John Bale, who accused the Italian of 'polutynge oure Englyshe chronicles most shamefullye with his Romishe lyes' (1544: f. 5r). There were other, nationalist, reasons to resist Vergil. In *A Chronycle with a Genealogie Declaryng that the Brittons and Welshemen are Linealiye Dyscended from Brute*, Arthur Kelton attacked Vergil's 'slanderous stile' (1547: sig. C3v). Kelton defended the Brutan histories in order to protect the special status they conferred upon the Welsh as descendants of the original British, pushed west by the Saxon incursions.[7] It is typical of the historical dissonance associated with the Brutan histories that, while commissioning Vergil's sceptical history, Henry VII had also highlighted his own descent from Brute; he exploited this association, naming his eldest son Arthur 'that in his person the "return" of a British Arthur might be accomplished' (Parsons 1929: 398).

Another reason for the venom with which he was repudiated may have been that Vergil critiqued not only the Brutan histories, as well as King Arthur, but also those who believed in them:

> There is nothing more hidden, nothing more uncertain, nothing more unknown than early deeds of the Britons . . . by which the unschooled common run of men (for whom novelty always counts more than truth) seem transported to heaven with wonder. (2005)

In referring to the 'unschooled common run of men', Vergil gives valuable information on the textual community that was, in his view, most likely to champion the Brutan histories. Prior to the Reformation, prior to Bale, Vergil sees his only obstacle to truth as being an apparent popular tradition driven by a lack of specialized education ('the unschooled') and an appetite for the fantastical, a description that might be applied to the textual network that sustained the Prose *Brut* and Brutan histories in the medieval era and which both motivated and rewarded Caxton's decision to publish. Due in part to Vergil, an account of the past that was uncontroversial at the turn of the fifteenth century was, by the middle of the sixteenth, subject to pressures that may have triggered doubts even in those, such as Bale, whose apparent belief was inseparable from his acutely nationalist brand of Protestantism. From the mid-sixteenth century the Brutan histories were further disseminated not only in an increasing variety of historiographic works but also in exemplary, nationalistic and poetic contexts. This vibrant and combative print culture saw writers and stationers with Brutan interests – or, at least, perceiving Brutan interests in the readerships they targeted – producing work in a variety of genres and collaborative combinations. By joining the dots of this lively intertextuality, the historical consciousness of a particular textual community can be glimpsed. The following case study demonstrates the attitudes of a particular London coterie with close links to mechanisms of English state power.

FIGURE 1 The title page of Richard Grafton's *A Chronicle at Large* (1569), showing Brute and his sons positioned in parallel with biblical patriarchs. © The British Library Board (C.15.b.5).

The output of stationer and author Richard Grafton provides a mid-century establishment view of the Brutan histories. Grafton had published the first official English bibles and was king's printer to Henry VIII and Edward VI (Devereaux 1990: 34). In 1569, he published his vast *Chronicle at Large*. Dedicated to William Cecil, the text's frontispiece boldly aligns images of Brute and his sons with Moses, King David, King Saul and others: a telling juxtaposition in light of Marvin's description of the Prose *Brut* as a 'species of Old Testament' (Figure 1). To place Brute and Moses side by side in the reader's visual field is a striking statement of confidence in Brutan iconography and, thus, British origins.

In its front matter, the *Chronicle* included a letter 'to the Reader' from the lawyer Thomas Norton. Norton writes that Grafton 'hath brought things vnknowne from darknesse', protecting English readers, particularly 'princes', from the 'slaunderous reportes of foreyne writers', a probable reference to Vergil (1569: unpaginated). Seven years earlier, in 1562, Norton had, with Thomas Sackville, co-authored *Gorboduc*, the first recorded play in blank verse, the first to use dumbshows and the first recorded Brutan drama. Norton and Grafton's sustained engagement with Brutan material in such public arenas suggests that to do so was, as with Harvey's 1593 dedication of *Philadelpus* to the Earl of Essex, compatible both with a certain kind of community identity and with considerations of patronage and advancement that would have preoccupied stationer and up-and-coming lawyer alike. In other words, the Brutan histories were still, at this moment, establishment histories.

Norton's co-author on *Gorboduc*, Thomas Sackville, had contributed episodes and an introduction to a 1563 edition of the *Mirror for Magistrates*, the multi-authored verse text in the *de casibus* tradition. By 1574, the *Mirror* had acquired an additional 'First Part' by John Higgins, the extended title of which announced itself explicitly as running 'from the comming of Brute to the incarnation of our sauiour and redemer Iesu Christe'. Higgins acknowledges in his Introduction that the traditional account was 'uncertaine & briefe', yet appears to blame this on a lack of industry on the part of chroniclers, who with some research might still 'fetch our Histories from the beginning, & make them as ample as the Chronicles of any other Country or Nation' (1574: unpaginated). Indeed, he notes that the older texts he has studied include more detail and material than the 'great tome engroced of late by Maister *Grafton*' (1574: unpaginated). In turning to the Brutan histories, Bruda suggests, Higgins was repositioning the *Mirror*'s potential readership away from the 'originally targeted political authorities to the urban citizenry' and 'reacting against contemporary trends in English historiography' (1992: 3–4). However, these 'political authorities' arguably included figures such as Grafton, Sackville and Norton. Thus Higgins's additions to the *Mirror* may be seen not as redirecting its appeal but expanding it, inviting the 'urban citizenry', the very group perhaps alluded to by Vergil, into the textual community that, through events such as *Gorboduc* and books such as Grafton's *Chronicle*, had also endorsed the Brutan histories. Between and among these texts, London's citizenry and its legal and political class appear to exhibit an enduring attachment to the Brutan histories in the face of acknowledged dissonance. The citizenry also represented a connected, yet distinct, market that was eager for affordable works that integrated ancient and civic history, a market dominated by Grafton's younger rival, John Stow.

John Stow was 'the most prolific writer of history of the Tudor age and, if numbers or editions both cheap and expensive can be the measure, the most widely read' (Gillespie 2004: 1). His *Summarie of Englyshe Chronicles* (1565) was only one of several works by Stow that saw frequent reprints and revised editions. Being cheap and popular, these targeted a different market from large, expensive works such as those by Grafton and, later, Holinshed, thereby potentially providing the textual community served by Caxton and the Prose *Brut* since medieval times with newly affordable and portable Brutan texts. Yet by the 1570 edition, Stow was compelled to write in support of

Geoffrey of Monmouth, accusing sceptics of 'unthankfulnes' and asserting that, if Geoffrey's work might be sympathetically approached in the context of the age in which it was written, 'true Histories may of a skilful Reader be wel decerned from the false' (1570: unpaginated). Here, the reader is flattered by Stow as 'skilful' and recruited as an active collaborator and participant in the cognitive labour of rationalizing Brutan historicity. Despite appearing contradictory, even dissonant, this approach seems to promote acceptance of the Brutan histories by, as it were, any means necessary. Thus, as equivocal as it may now appear, the effect of Stow's comment on a readership that had traditionally accepted the Brutan histories, households that perhaps owned inherited manuscripts of the Prose *Brut* or ageing editions of Caxton, for whom those texts were material and domestic facts, may well have been a sustaining one. In fact, while many pro-Brutan texts may seem equivocal in admitting the doubtful nature of British etiology, they rarely outline the prosecuting case.[8] Further, critics of the Brutan histories such as Vergil and Buchanan wrote in Latin and their texts were never published in England, hugely limiting their accessibility. Thus, the majority of readers would only have learned of their criticism of the Brutan histories, and often not even the precise nature of that criticism, in texts that both contained and endorsed those histories.

Holinshed's *Chronicles* (1577) took a very different approach, including multiple and incompatible accounts of history produced by a syndicate of publishers and scholars who might also be said to represent the upper sectors of the book-buying public.[9] *Chronicles* included chapters on the physical appearance of the British, British chorography and ancient, pre-Christian British religion. Holinshed's stated ambition was that the work should not 'omit any thing that might encreace the readers knowledge' (1577: sig. ¶2r), an ambition that resulted in the largest book to be printed in England to that point (Kastan and Pratt 2012: 22).[10] *Chronicles* might be imagined as the material embodiment of an early modern English historiography primed to collapse under its own weight.[11] Holinshed's methodology meant that dissonance and controversy were absorbed and embraced rather than suppressed, but this could also result in a disorientating reading experience. Such potential to confuse is detectable in *Chronicles*' treatment of Samothes, a putative pre-Brute settler of Britain who had been added to later versions of the Brutan histories seemingly to connect ancient Britain and post-diluvian biblical history through his convenient descent from Japhet, a son of Moses. Samothes was integral to John Bale's conception of Britain's originary spiritual authenticity. The narrative of Samothes had been disseminated by Annius of Viterbo as the work of an earlier scholar, Berosus. Having read almost 7,000 words on Samothes as a historical figure, the reader of Holinshed's updated edition of 1587 finally reaches the editor's alienating announcement that 'I thinke good to aduertise the reader that these stories of Samothes . . . doo relie onelie vpon the authoritie of *Berosus,* whom most diligent antiquaries doo reiect as a fabulous and counterfet author' (1587: I, *Hist.* 6). Samothes was, in other words, a fiction. In such ways, a strategy designed to 'encrease the readers knowledge' may have had a bait-and-switch effect, disorientating those readers seeking a secure account of the ancient past by rewarding investment in complex and detailed historiography with countering evidence that such accounts were probably nonsense. Purchasers who had previously referenced the 1577 edition, which did not include this caveat, might have experienced particularly acute historical dissonance, as well as buyer's remorse. It is telling, however, that neither the story of Samothes nor an alternative tradition that pre-Brute Britain had been colonized by a princess named Albina, makes any appearance in the record of early modern drama, suggesting that considerations of historicity did play a part when assessing which versions of British antiquity were stageworthy. The discredited Samothes and Albina were excluded, while Brute and his descendants were frequently performed.[12]

A year previously, however, Brute also received what many modern critics consider to be his mortal blow in William

Camden's *Britannia* (1586). However, while *Britannia* is often presented as a seismic event, this picture changes – in the short term, at least – when the book is resituated within an intertextual moment that was anything but homogenous or conclusive. *Britannia* is often presented as the moment at which English historiography accepted that the Brutan histories were simply untrue and admitted, as Kendrick put it, 'that Polydore Vergil had, after all, been right' (1950: 108). To begin with, however, the language of Camden's demurral from tradition is exceptionally equivocal, endorsing Brute's historicity as if he had a gun to his head:

> [L]et no man commense actions against me, a plaine meaning man, and an ingenuous student of the truth, as though I impeached the narration of Brutus . . . let Brutus be taken for the father, and founder of the British nation . . . seeing that, as Plinie writeth, *Even falsely to claime and challenge descents from famous personages, implieth in some sort a love of virtue.* (1610: f. 8–9)

Camden tells his readers that Brute should be 'taken for the father', and that, even if a people lie about their descent from notable figures, this is symptomatic of an aspiration to virtue. His apologetic tone suggests that Camden knows he is risking substantial and influential resistance. Nonetheless, he proceeded to lay out the reasons for scepticism in a way no other English historiographer had yet done. It should also be observed, however, that *Britannia* was written in Latin, hugely limiting its initial readership.[13]

In contrast to Camden's modernizing intervention, new poetic texts such as William Warner's *Albions England* (1586), the full title of which refers to '*the Brutons their first aryuall in Albion*', and Spenser's *Faerie Queene* (1590; expanded edition pub. 1596) continued to adopt the Brutan histories. *The Faerie Queene* contained within its framing narrative a 'chronicle of Briton kings, / From Brute to Uthers rayne', named the 'Briton Moniments' (1590: II.IX, f. 324). That is, from Brute to the moment just preceding the time of the reader of the 'Moniments', King Arthur. Spenser had praised Camden in *The Ruines of Time* (1591), and thus may be seen as utilizing the Brutan histories in the exemplary mode of 'poesie historical'.[14] This might be argued as a way in which Spenser adopted Camden's appeal to 'virtue' as a trigger for his own use of the Brutan histories. *The Faerie Queene* features prominently in much critical work examining the construction of early modern nationhood and, as Bart van Es notes, has 'long been understood to shed light on Tudor historiographical practice' (2002: 21). Spenser, Ferguson argues, 'planned to transmute the national legends . . . into the more rarefied substance of myth' (1993: 123). Spenser's approach would engage works by later writers, such as Michael Drayton and Anthony Munday, that entangled the poetical and historical. Specifically, Spenser relates Brutan lineage to the Elizabethan present via the character of Britomart, one of *The Faerie Queene*'s analogues for Elizabeth herself, who learns that she is 'lineally extract: / For noble Britons sprong from Troians bold' (1590: III.IX, f. 538). This continues the Brutan histories' function as a means of configuring English monarchy as both ancient and representative of 'Britain' as a whole. However, it should be noted that Spenser's 'Briton Moniments' is an acutely adumbrated version of the Brutan histories that would have offered the reader, or the dramatist seeking adaptable material, far less detail and colour than was offered either by many of Spenser's sources or by less-examined contemporary texts.[15]

Both Higgins's 1574 additions to the *Mirror for Magistrates* and Warner's *Albions England* included instances of vivid physical description and dialogue ideal for lively communal reading and theatrical adaptation. Thus, while Spenser's use of the Brutan histories may have been influential, his poetic engagement with the narrative itself was comparatively cursory. *Albions England* was a verse account of ancient history derived, as previously noted, from the Prose *Brut* via Caxton. Warner's narrative leapfrogs through the Brutan histories but often favours episodes that would later be represented in playbooks published between 1590 and 1608, suggesting an interrelationship between *Albions England*, the playhouse and the criteria used by stationers when determining which plays to purchase for publication.[16] *Albions England* is as neglected as *The Faerie Queene* is ubiquitous in criticism of early modern poetics and poesie historical.[17] Yet Francis Meres in *Palladis Tamia* explicitly interconnected the two, citing Spenser and Warner as 'our chiefe heroicall Makers' (1598: f. 282v), and terming Warner 'our English *Homer*' (1598: f. 281r). Overlooking *Albions England* may cause the historical consciousness of many early modern readers and playgoers to be misrepresented. Therefore, while *Britannia* might serve as the moment at which the Brutan histories' rejection became, in intellectual terms, assured, it should be remembered that Camden's work was approximately coeval with *Albions England*, *The Faerie Queene*, a 1587 expanded edition of Holinshed, continuing iterations of Stow's works and other, smaller works arguing for and against the Brutan histories.[18] In addition to this, records from the 1590s onwards show that the Brutan histories were well represented in the repertories of the London playhouses, making those narratives available not only to those communities served by the stationers but also to those communities' non-literate employees and neighbours.[19]

Yet the textual form that perhaps most eloquently demonstrates the permeation and habit of popular belief in the Brutan histories is the almanac. These inexpensive texts included calendrical information, astrological prognostication regarding harvests and weather and, frequently, timelines of world history. The popularity of almanacs grew across the sixteenth and seventeenth centuries until they became 'arguably the most popular books of the early modern period', making them a useful means of assessing early modern 'assumptions and reading practices' (Chapman 2007: 1258–9). An almanac's timeline very often indicated the beginning of British chronology with the arrival of Brute, a practice that became more common after 1585 and often oriented Brutan

events via reference to parallel moments from biblical and
classical history (Capp 1979: 215–16). Daniel Woolf asserts
that almanacs were 'so plentiful that for the majority of Britons
they were the most accessible form of history lesson' (2003:
321). If so, it was frequently a lesson in Brutan history.

In *A Yorkshire Tragedy* (*c.* 1605; pub. 1608), the character
Sam returns to Yorkshire '[f]urnisht with things from London',
and describes himself as carrying 'three hats, and two glasses
. . . two rebato wyers vpon my brest, a capcase by my side,
a brush at my back, an Almanack in my pocket, [and]
three ballats in my Codpeece, naie I am the true picture of
a Common seruingman' (1608: sig. A2v). In other words, to
carry an almanac – and, incidentally, ballads – was integral to
the popular image, or 'true picture', of a 'common servingman'.
The Brutan histories' inclusion among the almanacs' bare,
'factual', data, the information through which readers sought to
situate themselves within metaphysical, seasonal and historical
time, argues that for many they were not something to be
'believed', or 'disbelieved', any more than were the weather
or the seasons. The almanac demonstrates the Prose *Brut*'s
permeation at a level deeper than any conscious consideration
of British antiquity. By the 1590s the Brutan histories should
be characterized not as a medieval hangover, fragile and
primed to be swept away by a few sensible, forward-thinking
historiographers, but as an enduring, collective and deeply felt
historical self-understanding that would only be eradicated,
and then only by glacially paced erosion, over the course of
the ensuing century. Nonetheless, as Harvey's *Philadelphus*
demonstrates, the controversy was spreading.

The beginning of the Stuart era famously saw a resurging
interest in 'British' history, or, at least, the rebranding of this
material in print as 'British', as opposed to English. As is
well known, this was triggered by James VI and I's symbolic
reunification, as he framed it, of Scotland and England, and
his energetic project to achieve the same in law. In adopting
and tacitly approving the use of the Brutan histories as an
'ideological weapon' in favour of union and against Scottish

sovereignty (Mason 1987: 62), James was rejecting the scepticism of his former tutor, and Richard Harvey's bête noire, George Buchanan, along with a competing Scottish etiology, the medieval *Scotichronicon* (Mason 1987: 63). Scotland's alternative history, unsurprisingly, conflicted with the Brutan histories' account of Scotland's foundation.[20] Graham Parry has characterized the controversy over the Brutan histories in the early Jacobean period as one of 'two competing versions . . . the Camdenian or authentically historical version, and the legendary version from Geoffrey of Monmouth' (1981: 158). Parry, I would argue, misrepresents the moment as a binary division. The short-term effect of the increasing availability of competing texts – including the 1610 English translation of Camden's *Britannia* – may have, like Holinshed's dizzying inclusivity, served to increase dissonance and confusion, rather than secure new converts to either faction. Parry's interest is in the poets to whom, he argues, the Brutan histories largely appealed by the Jacobean period. However, many 'poets' such as Thomas Heywood and Samuel Daniel also wrote historiographical texts, just as many who were not primarily poets wrote poems. In fact, Blair Worden has argued that 'the overlap' between poets and historians 'was more obvious than the divergence' (2005: 75). As with previous examples, when the interconnections rather than the distinctions between texts and writers are examined, the belief patterns of particular textual communities become both discernible and productively complicated. As noted, the legal profession appears to have held the Brutan histories particularly close. *Britannica*, a collection of Latin poems by John Ross of the Inner Temple (1607), demonstrates this sustained engagement, tracing a line back to the *Mirror for Magistrates* and *Gorboduc*. Historical and legal precedent was of especial importance to English legal culture, with lawyers' vested interest in the Brutan histories centring on Mulmutius Dunwallo. Dunwallo had reunited Britain after the decades of civil war following the disastrous succession of Gorboduc's sons Ferrex and Porrex, and as such he entwined legal precedent with a figure of national stability, legitimizing English law from deep antiquity. As will be seen in Chapter 3, even as John Ross endorsed the Brutan histories in his poems, he provided vivid and valuable evidence of the increasing controversy.

The years 1611–12 saw the publication of four new books that together characterize the various states of Brutan belief and scepticism. Samuel Daniel's *The First Part of the Historie of England* noted that 'with what credit, the accoumpt of aboue a thousand yeares from Brute to Casseuellaunus, in a line of absolute Kings, can bee cleared, I do not see' before proceeding swiftly to the Roman occupation of Britain (1612: f. 7). Emerging from London's civic institutions, however, Anthony Munday's *A Brief Chronicle* (1612) was dedicated to the City's mayor and the Merchant Taylors' Company. Munday's book endorses the Brutan histories, which is significant given Munday's long-standing role as a playwright and writer-producer of London civic pageants that often characterized the City as 'Troynovant'. Tracey Hill notes that Munday both drew frequently upon Stow's work and also updated Jacobean editions of Stow's *Survay* (2004: 145). Thus as editor, pageant-maker, historian and poet, Munday shaped works in multiple forms and genres for a community that held the Brutan histories especially close. Indeed, Munday's pragmatic approach is instructive. He had been both a playwright and author of antitheatrical works (McMillan and MacLean 1998: 4); he had 'hunted and betrayed Catholics professionally' yet 'showed no anti-Catholicism in his hagiographical play on Sir Thomas More' (Griffin 2001: 135). In other words, Munday seems to have exercised, to put it mildly, a degree of ideological flexibility where his work's marketability was concerned. His promotion of Brutan material therefore suggests a perception on Munday's part of a wide and receptive market. As such, *A Brief Chronicle*, rather than testifying to an authorial historiographical position, seems to indicate a strong perceived demand for pro-Brutan cultural products within the City. This is further suggested by the fact that Munday's work was printed by William Jaggard, 'Printer to the Honourable Citty of London', a post previously held by John Wolfe, publisher of *Philadelphus*.

Yet Munday's beloved Merchant Taylors' Company had also produced John Speed, whose *History of Great Britain* (1611) influentially rejected Brute as a source of national pride and, significantly, offered a conceptual alternative to the unnerving blank space left in the British Isles' prehistory, comparing the Romans' descriptions of the ancient British to contemporary accounts of the Native Americans. This new approach to the past was visually reinforced by illustrations in Speed's work which pictured the Native Americans, much as the ancient British had been described, as 'naked [and] painted' (Ferguson 1993: 79). Speed thus replaced the pagan and Trojan foreignness of the Brutan kings with a new, colonially inflected otherness that suggested, uncomfortably, that the Native Americans were to their European colonizers what the ancient Britons had once been to the Romans. This, perhaps, is the reality that the Brutan histories' most ardent defenders hoped to avoid. Famously, however, it is Michael Drayton's topographical verse history of the Isles, *Poly-Olbion* (1612), that most fully embodies the historical dissonance surrounding the Brutan histories at this time among the literate classes. By literally surrounding his Brutan narratives with marginal prose 'illustrations' by a sceptical John Selden, *Poly-Olbion* undermines their historicity even as they are celebrated, eroding them, in Anne Lake Prescott's striking image, 'like acid eating a book from its edges' (1991: 309). Selden addresses Drayton's endorsement of Brute with the simple, insistent point made by all sceptics that 'I should the sooner haue beene of the Authors opinion . . . if in any *Greeke* or *Latine* Storie authentique . . . were mention made of any such like thing' (1612: sig. C3r). In this way, *Poly-Olbion* materialized and interleaved in a single object the dissonance experienced by those encountering anti-Brutan arguments.

In 1950, Kendrick described Speed as 'the great antiquary who settled the matter for us' (124). For *us*, perhaps. Yet, as with Camden's *Britannia*, resituating Speed within other texts of his time complicates this to some degree. For example, if Speed had in fact settled the matter then no one told William Slatyer, sometime chaplain to Anna of Denmark, whose almost completely overlooked Latin verse response to *Poly-Olbion*, *Palae-Albion* was published in 1622, the same year as the extended second edition of Drayton's work. Dedicated to James VI and I, *Palae-Albion* continues the tradition of celebrating the English monarchy via its Brutan origins. In 1630, Slatyer published a supplement to *Palae-Albion*, *Genethliacon*, a pictographic genealogy of the rulers of what Slatyer, with copious inclusivity, terms 'Anglo-Scoto-Cambro-Britannica', or 'Great Britain' (sig. A1r). The only monarchs individually represented were Brute and his queen, Innogen, testament to their enduring, even enhanced, value in personifying and sustaining the putative and etiologically endorsed unity of the Stuart kingdom.

Enduring popular belief in the Brutan histories in the Caroline era can be found in John Taylor's doggerel history of Britain, subsequent editions of which, like many texts of the era, indicate a growing awareness of the controversy. *A Memorial of all the English Monarchs* (1622), which included brief verse biographies of British monarchs from Brute onwards, updated its 1630 edition with a full-hearted defence of Brute's historicity, concluding: 'I follow the common opinion . . . there was a BRVTE' (sig. B1r). Taylor's work targeted the gentry and 'urban, especially London tradesmen', although Capp notes that works such as *A Memorial* may also have targeted those unable to afford Holinshed or others (1993: 67). *A Memorial* included a dedication to the Lord Treasurer, and Taylor's appeals to women readers and the young, along with phrasing that suggests he anticipated his text to be heard as well as read (1993: 69–73). This shows Taylor serving as 'a point of contact between the elite and the urban tradesman' (1993: 54). Taylor's approach to the Brutan histories is thus useful when considering how, and to whom, they might still have appealed in the 1630s. *A Memorial* might be viewed as indicating a resurgence of interest in the Brutan histories in the context of the irenic 'cult of peace' that characterized the Caroline court during the early years of Charles I's 'personal rule', as opposed to the factual peace, which was 'contested, controversial and fragile' (Atherton and Sanders 2006: 3). Alternatively, it might simply be one work among many that continued to appeal to readerships divided not precisely by social degree, but by textual community.

In 1631, John Weever's *Ancient Funerall Monuments*, an antiquarian survey of English memorials, offered an account that provides evidence of sustained Brutan belief yet also treats this as a phenomenon distinct enough to be recorded. Addressing the question of Brute with specific reference to London, Weever quotes *Poly-Olbion*'s reference to the 'enuious world':

> Howsoeuer the Story of *Brute* be denied by some learned Authors, or not permitted but by coniecture; as Selden hath it in his Illustrations vpon this verse of *Michaell Drayton*, which now the enuious world doth slander for a dreame. Yet because I finde him, in our Annals, to haue beene buried here in this Citie, of his owne foundation, as both by reason and authority it is strongly argued by a most iudicious Antiquarie of the last age; I think it not amisse to speake somewhat of him (especially) in this place, as the truth of the storie is generally receiued. (1631: f. 374)

Weever appears to be acknowledging the 'learned' such as Camden and Speed, perhaps meaning by 'coniecture' approaches such as Camden's that allowed for the possibility of Brute's historicity while rejecting the argument that this could be proven through historiography. In turning to 'our Annals', Weever, like Higgins and Warner before him, prioritizes an outmoded historiographic form, the chronicle, over Selden's modernizing scepticism. History could still do the work one required of it, then, with recourse to a preferred 'authority'. Weever later notes the account of Brute as 'the vulgar receiued opinion' that has been brought into question by 'many of our learned authenticall writers' (1631: f. 377). In the 1630s, then, a near century after Vergil's *Anglia Historia* and a half-century after *Britannia*, the 'vulgar received opinion' of Vergil's 'unschooled common run of men' endured, despite a century of erosion and dissonance. Weever, who had travelled England in his research, notes that belief in Brute is 'especially' prevalent in London, home of the very institutions that, as has been shown, bound their rhetorical and historical identities particularly closely to a sense of Brutan origins. These included the livery companies, the Inns of Court and possibly the royal court itself, along with the more generalized audience for cheap texts and plays that George Buc had described as drawing their historical understanding from 'Pamphlet and Ballad, and . . . the stage' (1982: xxii). Buc himself, however, recorded having written dumbshows for a play on the life of Estrild (Sharpe 2013: 659), the same topic as Deloney's ballad and Lodge's 'Complaint of Elstred'. And, in his poem *Daphnis Polystephanos* dedicated to James VI and I, Buc had framed the accession as a resolution of the 'olde, and vnnaturall fewd betweene *Locrine*, and *Albanact*' that might return Britain to a unity established in 'the times . . . of Brutus' (1605: sig. B2v), signalling that educated impatience with historical inaccuracy in the playhouses did not equate antipathy towards the Brutan histories.[21]

Much like the almanac and ballad, however, it is an ephemeral document that speaks most eloquently to popular Brutan belief in the seventeenth century: *A Trve Chronologi of all the Kings of England from Brvte the First King vnto our Most Sacred King Charles Mo[n]arke of ye Whole YIes* (Figure 2). Published around 1635, this single-sheet broadside of 149 thumbnail portraits reproduced in pictographic form the history of the British, and subsequent English, monarchs. Upon reaching its present moment in the 1630s, the *Trve Chronologi* expands beyond its sequence of rulers, concluding not with a king but with portraits of Charles I's consort Henrietta Maria and their son Prince Charles, the royal heir (b. 1630). The pictographic schema is thus projected beyond the present monarch into an unbroken royal future. Yet these final images are manifestly the

additions of a later hand to an older, possibly Jacobean, brass
plate. The broadsheet's origin in a now-lost original is further
argued by the striking similarities between its thumbnail
portraits and the far cruder woodcut versions found in Taylor's
1622 *Memorial*, which seems to have appropriated the designs
from the *Chronologi*. The document's remarkable longevity is
further demonstrated by a copy surviving from 1674 entitled
*A Brief Survey of all the Reigns of the Several Kings of this
Isle*, which reproduces the *Chronologi* exactly but updates the
final figure to a portrait of Charles II. The 1674 version is also
more complete, being larger with a densely packed series of
regnal accounts surrounding the central images. The earlier
document has clearly been trimmed of this accompanying text.
The *Trve Chronologi*, then, for such an ephemeral document,

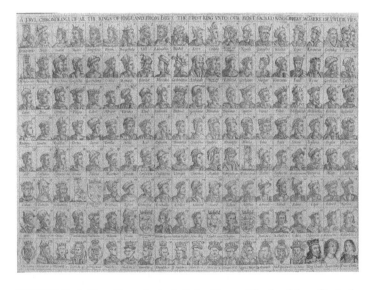

FIGURE 2 *A Trve Chronologi of all the Kings of England from Brvte the
First King vnto our Most Sacred King Charles Mo[n]arke of ye Whole YIes* (c.
1635). Reproduced by kind permission of the Syndics of Cambridge
University Library (Broadsides.A.63.5).

is a complex and temporally expansive artefact. Appearing within the market for ballads, coranto news sheets and pictorial representations of newsworthy events and religious themes, *A Trve Chronologi*, like almanacs, is evidence of a continued and popular market for Brutan material.[22]

The superficially ephemeral *Trve Chronologi* reproduces an account of the Brutan histories that appears unaffected by the upheavals and intellectual revolutions of the early modern era. It is only suggestive as one of the occasional traces of an otherwise obscured tradition of popular and oral historiography that I have gestured towards throughout this chapter. Nevertheless, I suggest that the survival of the Prose *Brut* in its manuscript and print iterations into the early modern era, and its adoption by households and particular institutions as a narrative from which their own origins could be drawn, attests to segments of the population for whom the Brutan histories remained an etiological *insula* relatively unaffected by erosion from newer accounts or scepticism. This *insula* was even, for a time, strengthened by resistance to scepticism. It was also sustained by recourse to the emotional resonance of tradition and intellectual habit. As Brian Stock notes, 'the textual community was not only textual . . . one of the clearest signs that a group had passed the threshold of literacy was the lack of necessity for an organising text to be spelt out, interpreted, or reiterated. The members all knew what it was' (1983: 91). It is from this paradigm, I would argue, that Brutan drama should be understood as emerging before the accumulating effects of disbelief and erosion are addressed. Therefore, it is through the lens of the Brutan histories as secure 'history' that I will address the earliest extant Brutan play: Norton and Sackville's *Gorboduc*.

Gorboduc

Gorboduc, called Gorbodogo by Geoffrey of Monmoth, receives only a single mention in the *Historia*, a comment that

serves both to situate him within the succession of Brutan
rulers and to state that he 'had two sons, called Ferreux and
Porrex', between whom he divided Britain (2007: 44). The
brothers' predictable and tragic struggle for primacy is the
subject of *Gorboduc*. Subsequent iterations of the Brutan
histories disagree as to whether Gorboduc split Britain between
his sons in his own lifetime or if they inherited it after his
death. Norton and Sackville's play shows the king dividing the
kingdom between his sons in his own lifetime, despite lengthy
counsel against such an action. However, the accounts of the
Brutan histories that would have been available to Norton and
Sackville, as well as their audience and subsequent readers,
focus wholly on the warring brothers and the actions of their
mother who, once the son she favoured was slain in battle
by the other, murdered the survivor in his sleep. The queen's
destruction of the line of Brute, and the fifty years of war that
followed, are the Brutan histories' principal concerns.

Somewhere between the Oldest Version of the Prose *Brut*
(*c.* 1272) and that employed by Caxton for the *Cronicles of
Englond*, confusion developed over the identities of the two
brothers, the Oldest Version noting that 'Porrez had an evil
heart and wanted, by treason or by trickery, to kill his brother'
(Marvin 2006: 95), and Caxton that 'Ferres had a felons hert
and thought thurgh treson to slee his brother' (1480: sig. B2v).
Such differences, when placed side by side in the early modern
period, may have presented a version of history that, while
unquestioned in its core historicity, was flexible enough in the
details to allow remoulding in the cause of a didactic, theatrical
treatment such as *Gorboduc*. Neither is there much agreement
over how, or why, the kingdom was divided between Ferrex and
Porrex, Caxton noting only that following Gorboduc's death
they 'werred [warred] to gedre for the land' (1480: sig. B2v),
while Robert Fabyan's fifteenth-century retelling, as published
in the sixteenth century, states that the brothers were 'ioyntly
made gouernours and dukes of Britayne . . . and contynued in
amytye a certayne tyme' (1516: sig. B4v). Several subsequent
texts repeat the notion of five years of peaceful co-rulership.

Fabyan also directly addresses the discrepancy between the two brothers in different texts, meaning he must describe the queen as killing 'whether [i.e. whichever] of them was lyuyng' by cutting him into small pieces to which, John Hardyng's *Chronicle* adds, she sets fire (1543: sig. D1v). The principal cause of the atrocities in the ensuing war between five kings, or barons, is identified by Hardyng as 'Defaut of lawe' (1543: sig. D2r). This may have provided a possible trigger for authors at the Inns of Court looking for a historical example wherein the failure of law, as well as succession, might be placed at the centre of a national disaster. These were the principal texts available at the time *Gorboduc* was composed and performed in 1561–2.

Gorboduc, then, simultaneously inaugurates extant Brutan drama and, more famously, English verse tragedy, by staging the annihilation of Britain's founding dynasty. Paulina Kewes has suggested that the play's Brutan setting probably reflects a 'decision not to seek the kind of immediacy that a dramatisation of national history could offer', the dramatists instead selecting a plot 'more distant in place and time' as a method of protecting themselves from the charge of commenting too forcefully on royal policy (2016: 180). Yet I see *Gorboduc* as reflecting quite the opposite impulse: not only is the play emphatically one of 'national' Brutan history, it also, as will be seen, works hard to diminish the distance 'in place and time' between the spectators and their putative Brutan ancestors. *Gorboduc* can therefore be read as a performance that positions the audience as witnesses to revived events from their own national story, part of a vast chronology within which they might consider themselves situated. Temporal and ancestral connectedness enhances the play's dire warning: that a line of rulers, having founded Britain and governed for approximately 700 years – twice as long as the Plantagenets, the longest serving English royal line – could be wiped out by one mishandled succession.

Gorboduc was performed by and for textual communities for whom the Brutan histories were widely still regarded as historical truth. It performed the actions of people who had once lived, people to whom an audience might consider themselves connected by blood and title. In fact, the play appears to have fed back to its source, leaving a mark on Brutan historiography. In the Brutan histories, no reason other than Ferrex or Porrex's villainous nature is given for causing their dispute, while in the play the influence of flattering counsellors is heavily foregrounded. Holinshed appeared to echo *Gorboduc* by claiming that the brothers were 'prouoked by flatterers' into conflict (1577: I, *Hist.Eng.* 22). This detail in *Chronicles* raises the possibility that a play, particularly perhaps a play associated with Sackville, by then an Earl and Member of Parliament, could be read as history, consciously or accidentally, by the compilers of the era's defining historiographic text. In *Philadelphus*, too, Harvey notes of the brothers' initially harmonious co-rulership that 'the comedie became a tragedie' (1593: sig. D4r). Harvey's theatrical reference, in its very *passingness*, shows the extent to which *Gorboduc* was understood as a species of performed historiography; an extension, rather than an alternative to or diminution of, ancestral truth. And this extension into the material field of embodied performance enabled a different kind of engagement with the past.

As noted, Thomas Sackville had also contributed to the *Mirror for Magistrates*, the framing device of which presents the reanimated historical dead recounting their tragedies for the moral instruction of the living. Woolf has noted of the oral component of historical transmission that 'English writers inherited and exploited the rhetorical practice of reviving the dead for conversation' (1986: 183). Further, Jessica Winston has identified a phase of 'intense interest' in the works of the Roman tragic dramatist Seneca in the 1560s and focused on the universities and Inns of Court, where students translated many of his works and 'performed a series of Senecan and neo-Senecan plays' (2006: 30). *Gorboduc* can be placed within a wider spectrum of historiographical and didactic strategies that allow it to be rendered as innovative within the early modern historiographic, as well as dramatic, genres. It is thus an engagement with British etiology inspired by, and structured according to, a Roman model.

Gorboduc's 1562 performances brought the Brutan dead into the room and made them speak. The play was first shown at the Inner Temple and then, a few days later, 'shewed before the *QVENES* most excellent Maiestie, in her highnes Court of Whitehall, the xviii. day of Ianuary, *Anno Domini*. 1561' (1565: sig. A1r). The didactic functions of its royal performance are attested by eyewitness accounts (James and Walker 1995). These addressed 'disrupted succession, the difficulty of attaining concord between monarch and council . . . civil war, and the impossibility of choosing a legal successor' (Axton 1970: 374).[23] James and Walker frame the play as presenting 'a direct intervention in the political controversy surrounding Elizabeth I's marriage plans (or lack of them) and the uncertainty of the succession' (1995: 109). This intervention, it has been argued, specifically promoted the matrimonial ambitions of Robert Dudley, a reading to which the account in the Beale MS explicitly alludes.[24] In doing this, Winston suggests that the play was a means by which members of the Inn 'claimed for themselves the authority to counsel the privy council' (2005: 12). Indeed, the play's language often insists upon the role of law. In the opening scene, Queen Videna bemoans Gorboduc's decision to divide his kingdom 'Against all Lawe and right' (1565: sig. A4v), suggesting that the ensuing tragic events are rooted in a disregard for law and tradition: legal values that, as shown, may have perpetuated an adherence to Brutan history within the early modern legal profession. *Gorboduc* specifies that its resultant civil wars will only be resolved, and peace established, by the great Brutan king and lawmaker Mulmutius Dunwallo (1565: sig. D5v). Dunwallo, as previously noted, was often cited as an ancient source of present legal authority. In this way, *Gorboduc* might be read as a prequel to the founding of English law itself, now embodied – to the satisfaction of the inhabitants, at least – by the Inns of Court.

In terms of performance, eyewitness accounts emphasize the visual over dialogue. The diary of London clothier Henry Machyn records that on '[t]he xviij of January was a play in the quen['s] hall at Westmynster by the gentyllmen of the Tempull, and after a grett maske, for ther was a grett skaffold in the hall, with grett tryhumpe as has bene sene' (1848: 275). The 'grett scaffold' indicates Machyn's perception of the scale of *Gorboduc*'s visual frame in performance; that is, the physical context into which the performers projected their vision of Brutan history. In other words, this was a spectacular, as well as rhetorically sophisticated, event. Complementing this, James and Walker note that the Beale MS focuses almost exclusively on the play's dumbshows (1995: 113). The opening mime contains several striking images: six 'wilde men clothed in leaues' enter, the first carrying a 'Fagot of smal stickes, whiche thei all both seuerallie and togither assaied with all their strengthes to breake' (1565: sig. A2v). The sticks cannot be broken but, in this physical enactment of a familiar metaphor, individual sticks are separated from the bunch by the wild men, who proceed to break them easily, indicating that 'a state knit in vnytie doth continue stronge against all force' (1565: sig. A2v). Following the unknitting of the British state, none of the principal characters survive into the play's fourth act, which brings onstage the British dukes Clotyn, Mandud, Gwenard and Fergus, each of whom represents a British region and who for 'fiftie yeares and more continued in ciuyll warre betwene the Nobylytie' (1565: sig. D4r). It is Clotyn who recounts the fates of Gorbduc and Videna:

> The people loe forgettyng trouthe and loue,
> Contemnynge quite both Lawe and loyall harte
> Euen they haue slayne their soueraigne Lord and Quene.

> (1565: sig. D4v)

The play's focus on the danger of division for the realm is brought home to its principal audience by brutal royal deaths at the hands of their own subjects. The play's Inner Temple context also reasserts itself once more: the people not only forget truth, love and loyalty, but 'Lawe'. The civil wars are triggered by the ambitious Fergus, Duke of Albanye (i.e. Mary Stuart's Scotland) who confides to the audience that he has 'strength in power aboue the best / Of all these Lordes nowe left in Brittaine Lande' (1565: sig. D8r). This reminds us that 'Brittaine Lande' is not a monolith but, like the wild men's sticks, a gathering of more fragile parts.

Gorboduc's opening image of wild men resonates with certain tensions that underlay an engagement with Brutan history. *Gorboduc*'s characters might not only be classicized exemplars of noble origins. They can also be perceived as wild, primal and even barbaric, their paganism and antiquity emphasized even as the play works to ravel in the temporal gulf between history and the moment of performance. *Gorboduc* makes frequent references looking back to Brute, condemning as disastrous his originary division of Britain between his three sons, asking 'how much Brutish blod hath sithence been spilt / To ioyne againe the sondred vnitie?' (1565: sig. B1r). This comment resonates not only within the play's temporality but also the Elizabethan moment. There are frequent invocations of Jove, and in the opening scene Videna references the pagan Gods, 'whose Aulters I / Full oft haue made in vaine of Cattell slayne, / To sende the sacred smoke to Heauens Throne' (1565: sig. A3r). All of this serves to remind the spectator that this is a pagan Britain of animal sacrifice and smoking altars, an orienting device later employed by Brutan plays from *Locrine* to *Cymbeline*. However, the closing lines of the play's fourth act gesture once more towards the future in which *Gorboduc*'s audience found themselves, and also towards that audience's future:

Blood asketh blood, & death must death requite
Ioue by his iust and euerlasting dome [i.e. doom]
Iustly hath euer so requited it
These times before recorde, and tymes to come,

Shall finde it true, and so doth present proofe,
Present before our eies for our behoofe.

(1565: sig. D4r)

Here, the Court of Whitehall accommodates a vast temporality reaching from the play's 'times before recorde', into the 'tymes to come' of the performance, two points enjoined in a 'present proofe' that could be either moment, or both. And perhaps the 'tymes to come' also take in a future beyond the performance. Here, *Gorboduc* works hard to bring together Brutan past, English present and English future. There were many exemplary episodes from classical and other sources that might be chosen to demonstrate the wickedness of envy, ambition and weak rule, but in presenting a catastrophic episode from the Brutan histories, *Gorboduc* places the audience, and the play's principal addressee, Elizabeth I, squarely within its projected temporalities. This is intensified with frequent invocations of 'Britain land', described with nationalist inflection as 'comen Mother of vs al' (1565: sig. C1r). Citing Benedict Anderson's notion of 'imagined communities', Jacqueline Vanhoutte addresses the play's appeal to British etiology, noting that '*Gorboduc* provides an emotional (as opposed to socio-political) basis' for national feeling (2000: 234). That is, by staging Brutan history rather than classical or international narratives, *Gorboduc* personalizes the rhetorical within a context of shared national and personal origins. As the inaugural moment of English verse tragedy, this suggests much about the Brutan histories' subsequent staging.

Conceived for a specific propagandistic function and audience, *Gorboduc*, once published, became accessible to multiple readerships and readings across a wider social range. It received its first edition in 1565, published by William Griffith, and a second in 1570 under the title *Ferrex and Porrex*.[25] The textual transmission of historiography from Inns of Court drama into print reveals the tensions implicit in the release of an elite text into the hands of more diverse textual communities. This is demonstrated by the subsequent 1570 edition of *Ferrex and Porrex*, published by John Day, the publisher of Foxe's *Actes and Monuments* and a key figure at the 'vanguard' of Protestant print since Edward VI's reign (Pettegree 2004). In an epistle to the reader, Day claims that Griffith had surreptitiously received the play 'at some yongmans hand that lacked a little money and much discretion, in the last great plage' and was published in a form that was 'excedingly corrupted' (1570: sig. A2r). This may be a stationer's typical and strategic belittling of previous editions in order to promote the new, and Day appears to have been happy enough to use Griffith's edition as his copy-text (Cauthen 1962: 231–2). Thus, Day's sense of excessive corruption might be found in the print milieu into which he felt *Gorboduc* had escaped. In the same year, he included the play in a volume of Thomas Norton's treatises. By reincorporating the play into the textual material of Norton's wider intellectual and political project, Day's editions assert its legitimacy. In a revealing editorial intervention, Day appears to have been concerned by the following question asked by the counsellor Eubulus in the 1565 edition: 'But how much Brutish blod hath sithence been spilt' (sig. B1r). Day amends this to 'Brittish bloud' (1570: sig. B4v). While 'Brutish' asserts the linguistic connection between the founder Brute and the kingdom he founded, the association of 'Brutish' and the meaning of 'brute' with which the opening dumbshow's wild men, and pagan antiquity in general, might be associated is perhaps revealed here as an underlying concern for Day who, through these cleansing strategies, reclaims *Gorboduc* for the elite textual community for which it was created. It would be another two decades before Brutan drama would emerge into the more anarchic discourses of public history, wherein its violence and brutality would become more fully realized in performance.

A third edition was published in 1590 by John Perrin, both 'annexed', as the title page terms it, to the *Serpent of Division* by John Lydgate, and also in a stand-alone edition. Perrin appears to have favoured Griffith's edition; he reinstates the original title *Gorboduc* and, for example, the blood spilled once again becomes 'Brutish' (1590: sig. B3v). The address in *Serpent* 'To the gentle reader' describes Julius Caesar's invasion of 'Brutes Albion, after called Brittaine, and now of late England' (1590: sig. A2r). It describes *Serpent* as an account of Rome's overthrow and suggests that if the reader 'compare our state with Romes', then England will be found 'to be no lesse in danger and dread' (1590: sig. A2r). Perrin's edition thus framed both the Roman and Brutan histories as parallel historiographic texts warning of present dangers, a striking juxtaposition considering that Roman histories were Exhibit A in arguments against Brutan historicity. It is, then, in printed form and in a didactic and historicized context that *Gorboduc* appeared within the 1590s' explosion of performed history and playbooks of performed history. However, as a stand-alone playbook this thirty-year-old play might be indistinguishable in the bookstalls from newer properties. These would have included not only another Inns of Court tragedy of ancient British history, Thomas Hughes's *Misfortunes of Arthur* (1587), but also Richard Jones's 1590 edition of Christopher Marlowe's amoral and hyperviolent *Tamburlaine*, a commercial context that John Day may well have considered 'brutish'.

In a piece of evidence that both extends *Gorboduc* back to the context of its original production and out beyond London into an English colonial context, William Chetwood's *A General History of the Stage* (1749) records evidence of a performance of the play given at Dublin Castle in 1601 by the Lord Deputy of Ireland, Baron Mountjoy (f. 51). *Gorboduc* had been performed on 1 September, Elizabeth I's birthday, thus reviving a warning of uncertain succession given in the first years of Elizabeth's reign in what would prove its waning months. Yet, as Chris Morash explains, Dublin in 1601 must have seemed frighteningly close to the play's final act, where Britain succumbs to anarchy from within and without:

[W]ith Hugh O'Neill, the Earl of Tyrone, in open rebellion in Ulster, and Spanish forces only a fortnight away from landing in Kinsale . . . Dublin Castle provided a common arena of intrigue for a number of competing groups: the Gaelic aristocracy, the Old English whose ancestors had come to Ireland during the Norman invasions . . . the New English of the Elizabethan plantations, and a constantly shifting cadre of English administrators and soldiers. (2001: 2)

Here, *Gorboduc*, through a dramaturgical sleight of hand, serves to bring Dublin within the temporal and territorial boundaries of 'Britain land', the play's 'common mother of vs all' (1590: sig. G2v). In this, its propagandistic function is revived and redirected; Morash suggests that Mountjoy was 'using the theatre to define the terms of war' (2001: 3). On the eve of the Scottish James VI's accession to the English throne, the associations between Brutan performance and English state power, even overseas, appear remarkably consistent.

The narrative of Ferrex and Porrex saw full public manifestation in a play performed at the Rose playhouse around 1600.[26] Philip Henslowe's *Diary* records a series of payments to William Haughton for 'a Booke called ferex & porex'.[27] Bullough has speculated that this lost 'Ferex & Porex' 'was probably a reworking of the material in *Gorboduc* with . . . a less didactic tone, and more action' (1969: 319). Martin Wiggins proposes an original piece by Haughton for which *Gorboduc* may nonetheless have served as a source (2014: 4, ref. 1244). Either is possible, although it is almost certain, given the emphasis on elaborate stage violence in Elizabethan tragedy, that 'Ferex & Porex' would have made spectacular much of the bloody business that in *Gorboduc* takes place offstage. The Henslowe commission also placed the play within the Rose's wider repertory of Brutan drama, allowing it to serve as both a kind of 'before' to the 1598 performance of the lost 'Mulmutius Dunwallow' and an 'after' to *Leir*'s account of Britain sundered and reunited. Performance at the Rose opens 'Ferex & Porex' more fully to the wider textual community gestured towards throughout this chapter. This community, economic and educational differences notwithstanding, would have shared, in grand sweep if not in detail, an account of collective etiology rooted in the Brutan histories. The minimal critical emphasis placed on the power these narratives may have held for early modern playgoers should emerge as an oversight when these plays are resituated within the centuries-long tradition from which they emerged, a tradition that remained embedded within early modern culture and historical consciousness long after the historiographical process of its erosion was underway. The following chapter explores some of the undercurrents and implications of these origins, and what it might have meant for early modern playgoers to consider themselves descended from ancient Trojans who had emerged, troublingly, from the pagan Near East.

2

Staging Brutan Origins
(1486–1600)

This chapter explores the Brutan histories in performance
from 1486 to the 1590s through civic drama and the plays
'The Conqueste of Brute', *Locrine* and 'King Lude'. These
performances confronted audiences with representations
of their civic and national roots embodied in the figures of
ancestors who had given their names to British towns, cities
and nations. This was not, however, a simple matter of noble
inheritance. To perform the Brutan ancestral dead carried
inherent typological and representational tensions, even as
these ancestors were used as symbols of civic and national
identity. Marian Rothstein has argued that a 'sense of the
living presence of the source is manifest in the Renaissance
treatment of words, things, individuals, and institutions',
which were thus imbued with the 'vitality of the source', the
initiating energy of the founder or inventor, a model that
shaped the early modern period's approach to history so
that, for many, 'origin define[d] essence' (1990: 332). This
also applied to the founding and naming of British countries,
cities and rivers, many of which were believed – mostly by
the English and Welsh – to have been founded by Brutans.
A founder, in giving their name to a territory, could even be
said to have undergone a metamorphosis similar to those of
classical myth which Holinshed describes as the 'translation

of mortall men into heauen' (1587: I, *Desc.* 21), by which 'he which had any starres or forme of starres dedicated vnto him, was properlie said to haue a seat among the gods' (I, *Desc.* 21). Something similar, if more earthbound, can be observed in the relationship between Brutan founders and the places they had founded. Jeffrey Jerome Cohen raises the possibility that the giant Gogmagog, whose defeat symbolized the conquest of Britain by Brute and his Trojans, would become 'immortalised as geography' through the naming of the site of his defeat as Gogmagog's Leap (1999: 35). The same could be said for Brute's naming of Britain after himself. Cohen describes this act of naming as a process through which the founder also becomes 'installed within the system of language' (1999: 35), a formula that applies to many of the Brutan figures performed in the early modern era, arguing for a complex entanglement of founder, name, place and player in the moment of performance. This symbiosis could provide a sense of noble inheritance, of reconnecting to what Joseph Bowling describes as an 'uncorrupted, native identity', thus enabling 'a renewal of ancient glory' (2017: 83). However, when the founder was a more complex or problematic figure, this could also invoke a troubling sense of corruption at the root, of disaster-bound fatedness.

In performance, these relationships are intensified and complicated. Brian Walsh describes performed history as 'a dialogue with the dead that is produced through real-time, embodied acts of ventriloquism' (2009: 21). If the historical figure performed was also considered a founder or originary figure, they might then also be perceived as representing not only the historical dead but also the city, region or nation they had founded and even the people indigenous to those places. Thus the performed presence of London's rebuilder King Lud, for example, might resonate not only with Lud's own history but also with the nature and destiny of London and Londoners: this instilled Brutan figures with a force of meaning that had the potential to reach into and influence the spectator's present moment. Performance reanimated Brutan figures as situated prior to, yet present within, the regions they both defined and preceded. This book is a study of etiological erosion and historical dissonance and Chapters 3 and 4 will engage with these factors as they might have manifested in the Jacobean era. However, to assert the potential meaning and cultural force of such doubts, it is essential to engage with the affective potential of Brutan drama as a source of collective self-understanding. The present chapter therefore approaches these texts and performances from the perspective of those spectators for whom the Brutan histories represented the lived past.

To demonstrate the longevity of the tradition of performing Brutan founders as synecdoches for their cities and regions, I begin with the pageants that greeted Henry VII on his first progress through England in 1486. These performances reveal the Brutan histories' perceived power to evoke community identity and autonomy in the face of national transformation and regime change. Performances given before subsequent English monarchs exhibit similar, and often surprisingly assertive, expressions of the Brutan founder-as-civic-protector. Incorporating these earlier performances into the record of Brutan drama provides a fresh perspective not only for critical contexts of performed history, in general, but also for later dramas such as *King Lear* and *Cymbeline*. Often, the 1486 pageants appear to engage with and spill over into the wider civic topography via associations with statuary and other material features of local architecture and landscape.

Moving from civic to theatrical performance I will then examine the first founder, Brute, via the lost play 'The Conqueste of Brute' (perf. *c.* 1598). Misha Teramura refers to Brute as a figure of 'historical transition' between the Trojan and British worlds (2014: 128). However, Brute's relative absence in the theatrical record may also reflect, or have created, his role as a paradoxically pre-Brutan figure, making him more representative of the 'Trojan' past than the 'British' future. In *Locrine*, Brute refers to himself, his sons and his followers as 'Troians' (1595: sig. B1r), while his son Locrine calls them

'Brittans' (sig. G2v). Yet as a national founder, Brute represented
what Rowland Wymer refers to as Britain's 'moment of primal
unity', even if this was indeed only momentary, superseded by
Brute's division of the island between his sons (1999: 5). This
was the meaning Brute assumed in the Jacobean era, when he
was revived as a propagandistic symbol of James VI and I's
project to 'reunite' the kingdom Brute had both founded and
sundered.

However, as noted, Brutan founders necessarily brought
with them sometimes troubling associations with their own
putative origins in the Trojan diaspora, and thus the dramatic
representation of national and civic foundation was often hard
to separate from the classical Trojan narratives of disaster and
destruction. Additionally, these characters' own lives were
rarely simple records of glory. Locrine, England's first king,
allowed his lust for Estrild to plunge Britain into civil war.
Further, *Locrine*'s stylistic similarity to popular dramas of the
late 1580s and early 1590s, such as *Tamburlaine* (*c.* 1587; pub.
1590) and *Selimus* (*c.* 1591; pub. 1594), which depict Near
Eastern despots, may have drawn uncomfortable associations
between Trojan Brutans, themselves products of the ancient
Near East and the alien 'other', specifically the early modern
Ottoman Turk. Further disturbance to the play's model of
Britain's foundation is caused by *Locrine*'s deviation from the
chronicle record in depicting its five central deaths as suicides,
meaning that the foundation of key British territories and
rivers is achieved through the spectacularly staged enactment
of self-killing, an action that was believed to both damn and
disenfranchise the suicide and their household. The superficially
ennobling concept of 'origin as essence' can, in *Locrine*, be
read as revealing Britain as a land infused with the essence
of aliens and suicides. Finally, I examine the lost play *King
Lude* (perf. 1594), which would have told the Brutan story
of London's rebuilding, fortification and renaming. *King Lude*
was performed in a brief respite between plague outbreaks in
London and as part of a repertory featuring biblical accounts
of civic destruction. These contexts of repertory and current

events may have challenged Lud's effectiveness as a figure of civic renewal, protection and regeneration.

Civic Brutan Performance

Before around 1592 – when the availability of Henslowe's *Diary* and a marked upswing in the publication of playbooks hugely expands the records of early modern drama – all evidence of Brutan performance save *Gorboduc* relates to civic pageantry. This asserts the importance of the Brutan tradition to medieval and early modern English identities, and that performed history was integral to the public display and assertion of this etiology. Alexandra Johnston notes that civic pageantry was a 'major tool of public propaganda in a period when the vast majority of the public were either illiterate or had received very little education' (2009: 21), and that pageantry was often used by civic authorities to define and negotiate the relationship between city and monarch (32). Again, this asserts that performed history could simultaneously address popular and elite spheres in a shared Brutan language. The language of these pageants often concerned themes of origin and essence. Lawrence Manley, writing on the myths of London's founding, defines this theory in civic terms: '[T]he notion of a founder implied that a city was not the product of organic growth but the result of a single decisive act . . . a sacred geometry was laid out at the moment of the city's foundation and fixed its identity for all time' (2014: 143–4).

As an extended narrative of origins, the Brutan histories were careful to assign to many British kings the foundation of towns and cities, such as Leir's founding of Leicester. Cities overlooked in the *Historia* often acquired founders in later iterations of the Prose *Brut* and other Brutan texts. These king-founders appear in records of civic pageantry throughout England, in ways that emphasize and ennoble the local site through association with ancient monarchy, often as a component of civic encounters with new regimes. Writing of Elizabethan pageantry, Rowland

Wymer has stated that 'although the myth of descent from Brute was a myth which was used to validate absolutist claims, the way it evolved in civic pageantry began to point instead to the limits of royal power' (1999: 5). The evolution of this trend in fact began much earlier. The earliest extant account of Brutan performance appears in the records of two royal entries at York and Bristol in 1486, the year following Henry Tudor's defeat of Richard III and the founding moment of the dynasty that would last until Elizabeth I's death in 1603. The new king's progress 'was that of a military conqueror' (Johnston 2009: 35) through a country where many of Richard's supporters were still at large and contemplating rebellion (Meagher 1968: 47). On his progress, Henry was frequently greeted with elaborate pageants that addressed the anxieties and tensions underlying the newly forming relationships between the monarch and his dominions. When these pageants featured performances of figures representing regional etiology and history, these were often enmeshed with local statuary and landmarks, allowing the performance to expand, figuratively inhabiting the wider civic topography.

At Hereford, Henry was to be greeted by a performer representing King Ethelbert, the sixth-century martyr and king of East Anglia, whose relics lay in the town's cathedral, of which he was also the patron saint (Attreed 1994: 223); at Worcester, Henry heard a speech by a performer representing Henry VI, followed by two short speeches from the saints Oswald and Wulstan, former bishops of Worcester whose shrines and tombs were present in the cathedral (Meagher 1968: 65). The performance of these figures created an immanent interconnection between the performed dead, civic memorial and the material remains of the historical dead themselves. At York, a permanent statue of Ebrauk, York's traditional founder and great-great-grandson of Brute, 'stood as a boundary-marker at the west end of St. Saviourgate', and an early fifteenth-century stained glass image of Ebrauk is still extant in the city's Minster, which Henry also visited (Meagher: 59). At Bristol, where Henry encountered a representation of the Brutan king Brennus, he passed through St John's Gate, on which are placed statues of Brennus and his brother Belinus, although these may post-date Henry's visit (Fleming 2013: 30). The performed founder simultaneously preceded, inhabited, embodied and represented their town or city. Such polytemporal presence is not consistent, however, and founders are presented as both eternally present within their cities and capable of a kind of absence, even neglect.

York was the seat of the dynasty Henry had defeated, and the city's loyalty to Richard III 'caused its officials distress' following his death (Attreed 1994: 219). In preparation for his visit, the civic authorities repurposed the machinery of their annual mystery cycle plays to create a pageant for Henry (Meagher 1968: 53). Framing this, the king is addressed by Ebrauk, described as York's 'begynner' (*REED* 1979: 2, 139; 1. 36). Ebrauk presents Henry with the keys of the city, 'thenheritaunce [the inheritance] of the said Ebrauk' (139; l. 38). He further establishes authority by declaring his own achievements as a conqueror, of ancient France rather than England, and subtly asserts his status as Henry's ancestor, reminding Henry of his right to the new king's 'remembrance / Seth that I am prematiue of Your progenie' (140; l. 20). At the beginning of his reign, Henry had accentuated his putative descent from King Arthur in order to strengthen his claim. Here, Henry is reminded that Arthur was in turn a descendant of Ebrauk, whose ancient authority is again emphasized later in the pageant by the figure of the biblical King David, who explains that he lived at the same time as Ebrauk (Meagher 1968: 58). Brutan origins, while, or because, they were 'prematiue', had a currency and historicity that could be supported and contextualized by figures from biblical time. This served as a reminder that ancient Britain, while troublingly pagan, existed within the same plane and temporality as sacred history. Ebrauk embodies York's antiquity, mirrors its present statuary and asserts the city's dignity in the face of a potentially hostile new ruler.

The final stop on Henry's progress was Bristol. Proceeding to the town gate, the king encountered a 'pageaunt with great melodie [a]nd singing' (*REED* 1997: 11; l. x), beginning a sequence of performances designed to highlight 'the town's recent decay and begging Henry to help restore their prosperity' (*REED* 1997: xiv). Then followed a player representing Bristol's ancient founder Brennus, who asserted himself as the voice of the city who had '[c]alled It Bristow In the begynnyng' (11; l. 20). At the same time as representing the city's beginning, Brennus implies a kind of after-presence, that as founder he is also capable of absence, and that this absence is harmful to the city's fabric and well-being: 'This Towne lefte I in great prosperitie', he tells Henry, but 'I haue ben so longe Awey / That Bristow Is fallen in to decaye' (11; 31–2). Brennus is presented as almost revenant-like, inhabiting a zone between antiquity and the present moment: where, and what, Brennus has been during his absence remains unspoken. Nonetheless, Brennus's return after 'so long' is enacted so that he might intercede with Henry on behalf of his decaying city. At a time of profound national transformation both York and Bristol initiated and negotiated their relationships with the new monarch via the public performance of Brutan founders. These were local figures of origin and foundation whose status as ancient rulers of Britain integrated the local into a larger national story, thereby asserting regional autonomy and dignity.

Like Brennus and Ebrauk, Norwich's founder Gurgunt could also be contextualized through the city's wider topography. Records of the order of events for Elizabeth I's 1578 entry into the city show that, while the city's aldermen and representatives trooped two miles into the countryside to greet the queen, the performer representing Gurgunt waited just outside the city wall at a spot where 'the Castle of Blaunche Flowre', which he was said to have built, 'was in most beautiful prospect' (*REED* 1984: 249). Gurgunt's meaning as a Brutan founder, then, was emphasized through his being positioned within a *verité* tableau of the city. In this way, the founder extends his presence outwards from the site of performance and becomes, figuratively, the castle and city themselves. Gurgunt's unfortunate punchline is that his star turn was never performed that day in Norwich. It is noted that 'by reason of a showre of raine' Elizabeth 'hasted away, the spéech not vttered' (1578: sig. B2v). However, as Matthew Steggle has observed, Gurgunt's unperformed presence in Norwich 'had a national profile' (2015: 69) and could participate in discourses of English and Brutan history beyond its local political function via the text's publication in 1578 as *The Ioyfull Receyuing of the Queenes Most Excellent Maiestie into Hir Highnesse Citie of Norwich* and its later inclusion in the 1587 edition of Holinshed's *Chronicles*. That this event only existed in a textual record of *intended* performance also speaks to the porous boundaries between historiographic modes. If spoken aloud in a company of readers engaging with Holinshed, the Norwich entry latterly becomes a species of performed history. Yet that which Gurgunt implied and never had the opportunity to speak was directly expressed later in the same pageant by another Brutan figure, Gurgunt's daughter-in-law Martia.

Following a parade of female biblical figures, Queen Martia is introduced by a performer representing the city of Norwich itself. She confronts Elizabeth as a self-proclaimed revenant and as one who can 'exceede' the living queen in grace (1578: sig. C2v). One of the few prominent Brutan queens, Martia was renowned as 'a woman expert and skilfull in diuers science' and, chiefly, as having 'deuised and established profitable and conuenient lawes, the which after were called Martian lawes' (Holinshed 1587: I *Hist.* 19). Martia had been described by John Bale as a 'lady excedyngly fayre, wyse, & lened in all the lyberall scyences', and as having 'redressed the commen welthe, refourmed the grosse maners of the people, and made most honest lawes, called of her name, Leges Martiane' (Bale 1548: f. 43r). Thus Martia was also a Brutan founder, having established and given her name to a legal tradition rather than a city or region. Bale's comments appear in the postscript to an English edition of a devotional poem by the one-time French queen Marguerite of Navarre. The poem had been translated by a teenage Elizabeth Tudor, whose work was published in 1548 and again with Bale's additions in 1590. Thus Martia was a figure with whom Elizabeth had been honourably compared in a commentary appended to her own published text. At Norwich, this textual entwinement, and Martia's exemplarity as a Brutan queen, were employed to assert the city's pre-eminence. While the Mayor's opening speech declares that the city enjoys its liberties through Elizabeth's 'only clemencie' (1578: sig. B2r), as a fellow queen and Brutan founder, Martia then navigates the relationship on strikingly different terms.

Martia explains that, prior to her arrival, a summons from Fame caused the earth to break and 'rend vp graues, and bodies raisde', after which 'eche spirite tooke his place'; that is, Martia and Gurgunt are freshly risen from the grave along with every 'Prince that erst had raigned here', and that each has 'receyvde againe his breath' (1578: sig. C2v). The purpose of this secular Judgement Day is then revealed. The collective Brutan dead – the princes 'that erst had reigned here' – were promised that any might live and rule again, receiving 'libertie to holde againe his place' if they can prove that they exceed Elizabeth in grace. Only Martia and Gurgunt succeed, while the others return to their 'caues [caves] agayne and there ful quiet lye' (sig. C3r). Thus, rather than mere obeisance, Martia's eventual bestowing of 'realme and right' upon Elizabeth is the magnanimous decision of a Brutan queen raised from the grave who, as proven by Fame, exceeds Elizabeth in grace and who, according to the terms of this raising from the dead, may 'hold again [her] place' should she choose. Martia's manifestation at Norwich appears to threaten an English monarch with usurpation by a revenant. This figurative threat to the boundaries between living and dead, between the authority of city and monarch, and of ancestral rights to reclaim a realm lost to death is unique in the extant records of Brutan civic performance.

Each of the English cities examined so far engaged with its own, regional, Brutan founder. It is telling, however, that

London's civic pageantry often invoked national, rather than civic, origins. As noted, for the early modern English, the name 'Britain' was often interchangeable with 'England'. For Londoners, both terms could be further subordinated to London's identity as a self-fashioned 'capital and epitome of Britain' (Manley 2014: 131). The use of the iconography of national foundation in London's pageantry has the effect of presenting London as a synecdoche for both England and Britain. It is telling, then, that a key element of this pageantry was Brutan. Throughout the early modern period – to the present day, in fact – London's royal entries and Lord Mayor's Shows have featured two giant figures, frequently referred to in account books and eyewitness testimony as Corineus and Gogmagog. Corineus was Brute's ferocious general, of 'incomparable strength and boldnesse' (Holinshed 1587: I, *Hist.* 9). Gogmagog was the leader of Albion's indigenous giants: Brute's conquest was symbolized by Corineus's defeat of Gogmagog in a mighty wrestling match.

The use of giants in civic pageantry across Europe was not unusual and, it has been argued, may have represented 'the imposition of culture and authority' upon the primal barbarity that preceded national foundation (Stephens 1989: 41; qtd in Manley 2014: 251–2). For many, the 'Trojan triumph over these bellicose monsters' marked 'the birth of the British nation' (Cohen 1999: 31). The material structure and nature of these two giants is, however, uncertain. Pageant giants are recorded, unnamed, as early as Henry V's triumph following the battle of Agincourt in 1415 (Cohen 1999: 29), when entries in the *Bridge House Weekly Payment Book* (the accounts book for London Bridge and its estates) record payments for a giant's head (1995: 257), for fitting head armour and buying two sets of garments and sixteen 'hoops' (1995: 265).[1] While these giants are not identified as Corineus and Gogmagog, they do offer insight into the longevity of the tradition of performing twin giants in London pageants, and their possible mobility and impressive scale in performance.

In August 1554, Mary I entered London with her husband
Philip II, the Spanish king. As recorded by John Elder in a
letter published the following year, 'when they came to
the drawe bridge', the royal couple encountered a 'fayre
table, holden vp with two greate Giauntes: the one named
Corineus Britannus, and the other *Gogmagog Albionus*'
(1555: unpaginated). The giants' surnames suggest their joint
function as a kind of 'before and after' of Britain's conquest.
Their presence together invokes remembrance of this process,
Gogmagog standing for the primeval Albion, Corineus for
the Trojan colonization of Britain. Alexander Samson has
argued that the use of the names Corineus and Gogmagog
in 1554 was an 'invocation of a British myth of origin' that
asserted 'English identity' (1999: 244) in the face of perceived
Spanish incursion-by-marriage. Richard Grafton, author and
publisher of the pro-Brutan *Chronicle at Large* (1569), was
'the alderman principally responsible for these pageants'
(1999: 245), suggesting that the naming of Corineus and
Gogmagog may have been motivated by an attachment to the
Brutan histories. The giants' performance extended beyond its
already huge public audience via a reference in Foxe's *Actes
and Monuments* (1570: f. 1654), embedding a record of Brutan
performance within that widely read historiography of English
martyrdom. Elizabeth I encountered Corineus and Gogmagog
when leaving London following her royal entry of 1558, as
recorded in the 'diary' of Henry Machyn: 'at Tempylle bare
[Temple Bar] was ij grett gyanttes, the one name was Goott-
magott a Albaon and the thodur Co(rineus.)' (1848: 186).
Ian Mortimer describes the manuscript's author as 'probably
the earliest instance in England of a poorly educated man . . .
recording the history of his own times' (2002: 983), making
this a valuable and early example of popular engagement with
Brutan performance.[2]

There is also some evidence that London's Gogmagog
was part of a wider, national performance tradition. The
Records of Early English Drama (*REED*) for Newcastle
reveal payments in 1591 and 1592 'for keeping of Hogmagog

this year' (1982: 79; 85) and a 1594 record of a payment
for 'keepinge hogmagoes koate and him self in licknes' (xv).
These effigies, then, were semi-permanent presences, sustained
and maintained between pageants. The Newcastle records
also echo a payment in Henslowe's *Diary* relating to 'The
Conqueste of Brute', for 'diuers thinges for to macke cottes
[coats] for gyants in brvtte' (2002: 100). Henslowe's note
strongly suggests that the play staged the wrestling match
between Corineus and Gogmagog, allowing the performance
to draw associations with the two pageant figures that were
such a consistent feature of London's theatrical landscape
and self-identity: the writers of 'Conqueste' were perhaps
invoking a familiar and resonant popular tradition. Corineus
also appears as a key character in *Locrine*, in which the
dying Brute speaks of having 'queld the giants', notably
Gogmagog, 'cursed Captaine of that damned crew' (1595:
sig. B1v). Indeed, Corineus and Gogmagog were long-
standing fixtures of London's iconography. Two large figures
of giants, also often referred to as Gogmagog and Corineus,
stood in London's Guildhall by the 1590s at the latest and
were still present in 1611, when Henry Peacham notes them
among London's antiquities and oddities and as 'toyes not
worthy the viewing' (Coryate 1611: sig. P1r); these may have
been the figures used in the royal entries and Lord Mayor's
Shows (Cohen 1999: 29–31; Stephens 1989: 40). If so,
this suggests a material practice similar to Newcastle and,
in figurative terms, they can be seen as operating similarly
to Ebrauk, Brennus or Gurgunt, waiting in the Guildhall
to be reanimated in performance, symbolically evoking the
'vitality of the source' with which Britain had been instilled
by their founding battle. It is one of the mysteries of this
study that Corineus and Gogmagog should have become
London's Brutan totems when there was a seemingly far more
obvious figure available: Brute himself, founder of London as
Troynovant. Yet Brute, despite his obvious pre-eminence in
the Brutan histories, presents a peculiarly insubstantial figure
in the record of Brutan drama.

'The Conqueste of Brute'

By making conquered Albion and its new inhabitants synonymous with himself, Brute permanently fused island and founder, instilling it with his 'living presence', as Rothstein terms it. As Holinshed told the story, Brute 'commanded this Ile (which before hight Albion) to be called Britaine, and the inhabitants Britons after his name, for a perpetuall memorie that he was the first bringer of them into the land' (1587: I, *Hist.* 11). We might then expect that, as the founding 'original', Brute should loom large in the record of early modern Brutan performance. This is precisely how Brute is represented in the Jacobean Lord Mayor's Show *Triumphs of Re-United Britania* (1605) in which he is returned to life so that he might celebrate the 'reunion' of Britain under James Stuart. Yet in Elizabethan drama we have only two records of his performance, *Locrine* and 'Conqueste', and both of these are in different ways equivocal.

The only evidence of a play concerning Brute and the adventures that led him to Albion comes from a reference in Henslowe's *Diary* to 'Conqueste', performed in 1598 or 1599 at the Rose. However, the evidence suggests a drama that compromised or fragmented Brute's story by including events from the reign of the later King Bladud, a confused picture that results from the multiple references to Brute in the *Diary*, which are both allusive and conflicting. First, there is a payment on 30 July 1598 to the writer John Day for a 'Booke . . . called the con-queste of brute wth the firste fynding of the bathe' (Henslowe 2002: 96). This is followed by five payments to the writer Henry Chettle between August and October towards a play named 'Brute' (98; 100). These payments are followed in December by the payment of twenty-four shillings towards the purchase of 'divers things for to macke cottes [i.e. coats] for gyantes in brvtte' (102). As noted, this raises the likelihood that the play included a spectacular battle between Brute's Trojans and Albion's giants,

including Gogmagog. Then, in March 1599, Henslowe made
two payments to the Master of the Revels 'for the lycensynge
of A booke called brute grensh*i*llde' (106). While this entry is
often taken to relate to a different play, one relating the acts of
a later king, Brute Greenshield, this is not as apparent as it may
at first seem and muddies the waters further as to what kind
of play 'Conqueste' was and, importantly, how much of Brute-
the-founder-of-Britain it actually contained.[3] The reference to
'the first fyndinge of the bath' seems to allude to the discovery
of the hot springs at Bath, an event traditionally ascribed to
King Bladud, father of Lear, who lived eight generations after
Brute. Geoffrey Bullough therefore suggests the play 'may have
summarized the reigns of Locrine . . . and others until Bladud'
(1969: 316). Alternatively, it may have attributed to Brute
actions that the Brutan histories assigned to others. In either
case, the evidence suggests that 'Conqueste' either truncated or
expanded the traditional account of Brute's life. Further, the
likelihood that the play featured the wrestling match between
Corineus and Gogmagog once again marginalizes Brute as an
onstage icon of conquest: it is Corineus, not Brute, who enacts
the mastering of Albion.

The evidence, then, suggests that Brute did have his
own play, or part of a play, in 1598–9, but that this play
incorporated episodes not associated with his life and, in terms
of its dramaturgy and action, foregrounded events in which
he was not the central figure. Similarly, when Brute appears in
Locrine's opening scene, it is as an ageing king on his deathbed
who recounts his past deeds before dividing Britain between
his sons. Thus, even when onstage delivering a hugely extended
monologue, Brute serves as an emblem of *pastness*, of a *pre-*
British epoch. Much of the Brutan histories' account of Brute's
life engage with his adventures prior to founding Britain,
including a highly stageworthy episode in which he prays at
a shrine of the goddess Diana, whose apparition steers him
towards Albion. Once on British shores, however, the symbolic
event of the conquest – Corineus defeating Gogmagog – and
the opening narratives of British history – the tales of Locrine

and his brothers – do not involve Brute. While it may be an accident of documentary survival, Brute's relative absence from the records of Elizabethan drama figuratively reflects the brevity of his moment of national foundation. It is in the aftermath of conquest, in the life and death of Brute's son, Locrine, that the full, painful shaping and division of Britain is enacted. In the anonymous play *Locrine*, the implications of Brutan origins become far more complex and disturbing than suggested by the civic pageantry explored thus far.

Locrine

Locrine is unique, being the only extant Elizabethan playbook of the Brutan histories as performed in a public playhouse, and the only extant early modern play to represent the foundation of Britain. Yet in other ways it is embedded within its moment and the practices of late-Elizabethan drama. The play's single print edition was published in 1595 by Thomas Creede, whose 'prominence as a printer, publisher, and enterer of plays in the 1590s can hardly be overstated' (Syme 2012: 28). Typical of this period is *Locrine*'s debt to *Tamburlaine*, an influence felt especially in the play's close relationship with the *Tamburlaine*-derived play *Selimus*, with which *Locrine* shares extended and identical passages (Gooch 1981: 5). The title page offers no information regarding theatrical venue or playing company, only that the text has been 'Newly Set Forth, Overseen and Corrected by W. S.' (1595: sig. A2r).[4] The question of the text's origins has also been complicated by a copy of the play annotated by George Buc, the Jacobean Master of the Revels, which ascribes *Locrine*, or perhaps another play on the same subject, to Charles Tilney, who was executed for treason in 1586 for his role in the Babington Plot supporting Mary Stuart (Gooch 1981: 5), and Buc himself seems to claim authorship of the play's dumbshows.[5] If Buc's note is accurate, then *Locrine* originated as an Inns of Court piece similar to *Gorboduc*; but even if this is the case, the text as published is manifestly an adaptation for the public stage by a playmaker 'whose head was filled with Marlowe and Spenser' (Berek 1982: 69).[6] To these can be added *The Spanish Tragedie*'s vengeful ghost, which seems to have influenced *Locrine*'s portrayal of the ghosts of Albanact and Corineus. The influence of the playhouse is also indicated by a substantial clown's role and several onstage deaths atypical of the Senecan model followed by Inns of Court tragedies such as *Gorboduc* and *The Misfortunes of Arthur* (pub. 1587). Also unlike the academic drama, it is hard to detect in *Locrine* a position coherent or timely enough for political or propagandistic uses. This is, in part, perhaps a symptom of its episodic and anarchic source narrative.

Having founded and ruled Britain, Brute awarded the island's south-western territory to Corineus – which he named Cornwall – and ended his reign by dividing the rest of Britain between his three sons, Locrine, Albanact and Camber. Locrine was the first king of the British territory of Loegria – later England – and was also, according to Caxton, over-ruler 'of alle the lande of Breteyn' (1480: unpaginated). Albanact was apportioned the northern territory and Camber the western region. Each was named after its new ruler: Albania, or Albany, for Albanact, Cambria for Camber. These were understood as being, respectively, Scotland and Wales. Brute's founding actions set the stage for Locrine's reign, and the beginning of *Locrine*, from which point events swiftly topple into chaos. In the chronicle accounts, Albania is invaded by Humber – described in Holinshed as being king of either the Huns or the Scythians; the play mentions both – and British unity is shown when Locrine and Camber raise armies to assist Albanact who, nonetheless, is slain in battle. Humber is driven back and drowns in a river while retreating; the river is subsequently named Humber. Travelling with the Huns is Humber's consort, Estrild, with whom Locrine immediately becomes enraptured. Before Brute died, however, he promised Locrine to Corineus's daughter Guendolen; seeing the young king beginning to backslide, Corineus menaces Locrine into marrying his daughter. Secretly, Locrine builds a subterranean chamber, where Estrild is hidden and where she bears him a daughter, Sabren. Upon Corineus's death, Locrine immediately divorces Guendolen and installs Estrild as queen. Guendolen retreats to Cornwall with their son Madan, raises an army and invades Loegria. Locrine is defeated in battle. Upon assuming the regency in Madan's minority, Guendolen has Estrild and Sabren drowned in a river, which she names after Sabren. The river's name transmutes over time into 'Severn'.

The story of Locrine, particularly its account of the tragic deaths of Estrild and Sabren at the hands of Guendolen, was of 'great significance' in the early modern period, being 'far better known than the story of King Lear' and coming 'second only to the feats of Arthur among the popular inventions of Geoffrey of Monmouth' (Schwyzer 1997: 26); this is shown in the treatment given to these episodes in Thomas Deloney's ballad, Higgins's *First Parte of the Mirour for Magistrates* (1574), William Warner's *Albions England* (1586) and Thomas Lodge's 'Complaint of Elstred' (1593). In the play *A Knack to Know a Knave*, the English king invokes Locrine's illicit relationship with Estrild as a warning against adultery '[e]uen in the lyfe time of faire *Guendolin:* / Which made the Cornish men to rise in Armes, / And neuer left till *Locrin* was slaine' (1594: sig. G2r). Given this narrative's wide dissemination, it is unsurprising that the economies of the London playhouses should generate a play of Locrine's life.

The play *Locrine*, however, makes several crucial changes to the traditional story: principally, five of the story's key deaths are restaged as suicides. For example, Locrine and Estrild take their own lives together and are discovered by Sabren who, too weak to slay herself with her father's sword, evades capture by drowning herself in the river that will bear her name. These suicides are unprecedented in any extant account of the Brutan histories. In making these changes, *Locrine*'s anonymous playmakers further toxify an already discomforting ensemble of Brutan founders. The play provides much evidence of stage tableaux, allowing insight into the staging of Brutan origins. This evidence allows us to explore what it might have meant to witness, rather than read about, Britain's foundation and fragmentation.

Jeffrey Jerome Cohen describes the Guildhall's Gogmagog and Corineus effigies and other material evocations of pre-Brutan Albion as having a 'haunting presence-in-death' (1999: 59): the dead are revitalized in the present through their remains and effigies. Cohen's term perhaps also articulates an implication of Brian Walsh's observation that of 'all the forms of history, performance alone supplies a pretence of sensual contact with the vanished past through the bodies that move and speak on stage' (2009: 2). The underlying suggestion in Walsh's formula is that the 'sensual contact' described is a physical interaction between the living and the dead. To perform historical figures is to enact a kind of embodied haunting, to invite the dead into the room. These are the terms in which Thomas Nashe conceives performed history in his famous discussion of Talbot in *1 Henry VI* in his *Pierce Penniless*. Defending plays against antitheatrical critics, Nashe invokes Talbot's exemplary effect, one similar to the role of poesie historical as argued by George Puttenham. He does this with specific attention to the performative aspect of the exchange, using imagery in which the character's onstage presence interconnects with the historical Talbot's relic-like physical remains 'raised from the Graue of Obliuion':

How would it haue ioyed braue *Talbot* (the terror of the French) to thinke that after he had lyne two hundred yeares in his Tombe, hee should triumphe againe on the Stage, and haue his bones newe embalmed with the teares of ten thousand spectators at least, (at seuerall times) who in the Tragedian that represents his person, imagine they behold him fresh bleeding. (1592: sig. F3r)

In suggesting that Talbot would experience great joy knowing that the performance of his death had been wept over by playhouse audiences two centuries after the event, Nashe invokes something polytemporal and potentially disturbing. Talbot's bones are oiled, or 'embalmed', by 10,000 weepers, an encounter enabled by his reanimation via performance from a body in a tomb to one both 'fresh bleeding' and able to relive and repeat his triumphs. Yet there is also something troubling, and cyclical, in the notion that Talbot has been raised only to die again, to die, even, 'at seuerall times', in performance after performance. Further, it can be asked if, while Talbot joys at his reception, others from history would be so happy to, as Nashe puts it, 'pleade their aged Honours in open presence' (1592: sig. F3r).

Locrine is, in several ways, a product of the dramaturgical moment that produced *1 Henry VI* and, as noted, popular plays of the Near East such as *Tamburlaine*. However, in relocating these tropes to ancient Britain, the play presents a singularly bleak enactment of British origins. One reason for this is that, by staging the figures said to have founded Britain, *Locrine* cannot avoid invoking the principle that equated the essence of the founder with the nature of the thing founded. Each of the play's key characters is the founding figure of a British region or river, and this fusion is often heightened by those characters' onstage deaths: the martial hero Albanact dies in Albany, Locrine in Loegria, and the characters Humber and Sabren drown in the rivers to which they give their names. *Locrine* thus confronts spectators with Rothstein's 'living presence of the source' and Cohen's 'haunting presence-in-death' as embodied in the performed, raised dead. Being founders and ancestral figures, these characters draw *Locrine*'s early modern audience of putative Brutan descendants, like that of *Gorboduc*, within the radius of its tragic schema. Most spectators could potentially derive a sense of descent from Brute and his Trojans, and all inhabited the territories founded by *Locrine*'s characters. Yet these characters are raised in performance only to die violent deaths, often through their own venality. Thus the characteristics with which they instil the landscape, territories and peoples to which they give their names are, in *Locrine*, those of Trojan suicides associated with the alien Near East.

Brute – Brutus in *Locrine* – exists uneasily as both a glorious national founder and a warlike invader. The dying Trojan is the central figure of *Locrine*'s opening scene, wherein he describes his life and the conquest of Britain, before dividing the island among his three sons. The founder of Britain dies at the moment of its division, unsettling the nature of his relationship with the land he has founded. The play emphasizes a sense of Brutus as disruptive, opening with a dumbshow representing him as a lion pursuing 'a Beare or any other beast' (1595: sig. A3r). Throughout *Locrine*, the dumbshows are presented and interpreted by a threatening and chaotic figure, Ate, the Greek goddess of 'ruin, folly, and revenge' (Bate and Rasmussen 2007: 76). Ate describes the lion, and therefore Brutus, in terms of savagery and disruption, as 'the terror of the world':

> A Mightie Lion ruler of the woods,
> Of wondrous strength and great proportion,
> With hideous noyse scarring the trembling trees,
> With yelling clamors shaking all the earth.

> (1595: sig. A3r)

Rather than a bringer of civilization, Brutus is introduced as a ferocious animal whose voice scares, or scars, and shakes the landscape. In *Locrine*, Brutus is described five times as a 'terror' to his enemies, an embodiment of violence and domination. The same word is used to describe Tamburlaine throughout Marlowe's *Tamburlaine* plays; he is also described five times as a 'terror of the world', the precise phrase used for Brutus, asserting him as a Tamburlaine-like conqueror, connecting the founder of Britain with Elizabethan tropes of both the classical and early modern Near East.

Corineus, Brute and their Trojans are colonizers and thus alien to Britain. They carry their own complex etiology as manifestations of the 'other'. Walter Stephens argues that the Brutan histories' account of Gogmagog offers 'a fully traditional portrait of the Giant as menacing cultural Other' (1989: 40). I suggest that Brute and his Trojans had the potential to appear similarly alien, emerging as they did from remote pagan antiquity. This is the view expressed by Thomas Fenne, who in 1590 wrote a treatise against the likelihood of the Trojans being the founders of Britain but, crucially, also testily asks why anyone should *want* them as ancestors. Fenne describes a 'wicked race, who alwayes were the chiefe cause of their owne destruction, and procurers of their fatall destinie by their periurie, vnfaithfull dealing, churlish conditions, and vnsatiable lecherie' (1590: f. 91r). If this is not a balanced view of the Trojans en masse, it will serve as a description of Locrine himself, a character whose play is indebted not only to the Brutan histories but also to the dramaturgical culture established by *Tamburlaine*, when unfaithful, churlish, insatiable and lecherous tyrants stalked the English stage. Yet something specific happens when these tropes are engaged in the service of a Brutan narrative. Just as the lion in the play's opening dumbshow terrorizes the landscape he inhabits, *Locrine* imagines the originary founding and division of Britain as the violent incursion of the Near Eastern Trojan 'other'.

This is established from the opening moment. *Locrine*'s dumbshows are extrapolated onstage throughout by Ate, and the figures they present are drawn almost exclusively from Greek myth. Ate had served as a prologue before, in George Peele's *The Araygnement of Paris* (c. 1581; pub. 1584), a play addressing the origins of the fall of Troy and, therefore, obliquely and coincidentally, serving as a kind of prologue to *Locrine*'s story of Trojan descendants. Ate opens Peele's play, coming 'from lowest hell', brandishing 'the bane of Troie' (1584: sig. A2v), an apple that Ate leaves to be discovered by the goddesses Juno, Pallas and Venus. The three divinities argue over the identity of the 'most beautiful' to whom it is addressed (Wiggins 2012: 2, ref. 751), selecting Paris as the judge. Paris chooses Venus as the winner, for which she rewards him with the world's most beautiful woman, Helen. Famously, this is the event that leads to the Trojan wars and thus, in the Brutan histories, to Brute's discovery of Albion. In *Araygnement*, then, Ate is the activating force of Trojan doom. In *Locrine* she resumes this role to oversee the ruin of Paris's Brutan descendants. This interconnection suggests a great deal about the resonance Ate's presence in *Locrine* may have had for audiences' perceptions of the play's Brutan figures who seem, as with Fenne's view of their Trojan ancestors, to be 'chiefe cause of their owne destruction'. However, *Locrine*'s characters, products of the classical Near East, will, over the course of the play, metamorphose and in turn be metamorphosed by the landscape they have settled. Albion becomes Britain, the Trojans become British. Yet Ate is nonetheless the presiding deity of this assimilation of founder and landscape, and her presence persistently draws spectators' attention back to the Brutan Trojans' shared origins in ancient Troy and its typologies of glory and destruction.

In *Untimely Matter in the Time of Shakespeare*, Jonathan Gil Harris explores notions of what he calls 'palimpsested time' (2009: 1), arguing that the historicist tendency to situate objects and events within synchronic space elides the complex and destabilizing ways in which the past interacts with the present. In other words, we should look not just to how a text interacted with the moment in which it was composed or performed but also the ways in which it invoked a sense of the past, even carrying that past into the present. References to Britain's Trojan origins in drama could have this effect, the Brutan founders being 'the bridge that linked England directly to the mythical Mediterranean of Homeric and Virgilian epic' (Teramura 2014: 128). Several plays appearing in the same theatrical moment as *Locrine* invoke Trojan origins. Peele's *Edward I* (*c.* 1592; pub. 1593) stages Britain as a network of territories in conflict: the Wales of Lluellan, Edward's England and Balliol's Scotland. Edward and his followers are described at the play's opening as 'Albions Champions, / Equiualent with *Trotans* auncient fame' (1593: sig. A2v), while Edward's rival, Lluellan, claims Brute for the Welsh, described as 'true *Britaines* sprong of *Troians* seede' (sig. C3r), thus presenting conflict between the Welsh and English as a conflict between those with shared ancestry. Similarly, in Thomas Hughes's *The Misfortunes of Arthur*, a messenger describes Britain as 'the stately type of *Troy*, / And *Brytain* land the promist seate of *Brute*' (1587: sig. B2v). In both cases, the Trojan inheritance is invoked in the context of martial excellence and international reach, all deriving from the source, essence or 'type', of Troy. That is, to be made in the image of Troy, of Brute, is to be typologically descended from the heroes of the classical world. However, Teramura, referencing *Gorboduc*, asserts the less desirable aspect of Trojan origins: 'In [*Gorboduc*] Trojan descent is not a claim to national prestige but a curse: the fall of Troy is not a typological antecedent to be redeemed, but a national trauma that haunts and indeed threatens the present' (2014: 140).

This sense of a curse, of perpetual haunting, is not only amplified by Ate's presence as the initiator of Troy's downfall but by the characters themselves. *Locrine*'s characters refer to themselves only as 'Brittains' and are named as Trojans only by Humber and by Brutus, when discussing his antecedents. *Locrine*'s Brutans thus seem to see themselves as British rather than Trojan, suggesting a sense of disconnection from their own origins. Yet, bemoaning Albanact's death, Locrine invokes the name of 'aged *Priam* King of stately *Troy*, / Graund Emperour of barbarous *Asia*' (1595: sig. A4r). His words, as with so much else in *Locrine*, echo *1 Tamburlaine*, in which the phrase 'emperour of Asia' (sig. B1r) appears multiple times. But Locrine's formulation draws an explicit association with Troy and the 'barbarous' Near East. As Andrea Cambini noted in his *Two Very Notable Commentaries*, it was understood that the early modern Ottoman Empire incorporated 'those partes where the citie of Troy once was' (1562: sig. A1r). To invoke ancient Troy was also to invoke a people whose blood and homeland were now associated in complex ways with 'barbarous Asia' and the putative enemy of Christendom. These associations could then be translated to Britain's founders.

At the beginning of his prequel-like additions to the *Mirour for Magistrates*, John Higgins, adopting what Paul Bruda calls 'the hoary tradition of the dream frame' (1992: 10), describes himself falling asleep while reading a previous edition of the *Mirour*. Awaking and encountering a Virgil-like figure, Morpheus, Higgins is led 'into a goodly hall / At th'ende wherof there seemde a duskish Ile' (1574: sig. A2v), wherein he encounters the revenants of the Brutan dead:

> Men mighty bigge, in playne and straunge atyre:
> But some with woundes and bloud were so disguisde,
> . . . .
> And eke their faces all and bodies were
> Destainde with woade, and turkish berds they had,
> On th'ouer lippes moutchatoes long of heyre:
> And wylde they seemde as men dispeyring mad.
>
> (1574: sig. A3r)

Aside from displaying wildness, despair and madness, Higgins's miserable Brutans seem to embody the themes of haunting and partial resurrection explored earlier, while their 'turkish berds' and woad-smeared bodies present them as both Near Eastern and anciently British. The woad derives from Roman accounts of first contact with British tribes (Curran 2002: 158), but the 'turkish berds', or 'moutchatoes', evoke the origins of Brutus's line in 'barabarous *Asia*'. The word 'moustache' is rare in sixteenth-century English print and very often appears in contexts relating to Turkishness, despotism and ancient Britain. Nicolas de Nicolay, in his *The Nauigations, Peregrinations and Voyages, Made into Turkie*, reports that the Turks 'suffered no haire to grow, but only the moustaches betwixt the nose & the mouth' (1585: f. 125). In Richard Knolles's *The Generall Historie of the Turkes* there is a detailed description of the facial hair worn by Selimus I, the tyrannical Turkish ruler and subject of *Selimus*, the play that shares passages and perhaps a playing company, the Queen's Men, with *Locrine*:

But in Selymus his sterne countenance, his fierce and pircing eies, his Tartar-like pale colour, his long mustachoes on his vpper lip, like bristles, frild back to his necke, with his beard cut close to his chin, did so expresse his martiall disposition and inexorable nature, that he seemed to the beholders, to haue nothing in him but mischiefe and crueltie. (1603: f. 516)

This description, incorporating a warlike nature with cruelty and capriciousness, is uncannily close to both Fenne's scathing analysis of the Trojan character and Ate's presentation of Brute as a lion and 'terror of the world'. The word also appears in an ancient British context in Thomas Hariot's *A Briefe and True Report of the New Found Land of Virginia* (1590). To illustrate that the ancient British were as 'barbarous' as the Native Americans encountered in Virginia, Hariot gives a description of a British tribe who 'did also wear longe heares, and their moustaches, butt the chin wear also shaued' (unpaginated). Some combination of this moustachioed antiquity combined with classicized Britishness also seems suggested in part by the sixteenth-century statues of a moustached King Lud and his sons that once stood upon Ludgate, whose hair is long, as in Hariot's description.

In these examples, English colonialism, Turkish otherness and ancient Britain interconnect in ways that further complicate *Locrine*. Those characters in *Locrine* who become, to paraphrase Holinshed, 'translated' into British territories will then infuse those territories with the inherited qualities of ancient 'barbarous *Asia*' and, through typological association, early modern English notions of Turkishness. As noted, *Tamburlaine* triggered a fashion for exotic locations and eastern despots and conquerors in plays such as *Selimus* and *The Battell of Alcazar*. *Locrine* participates in this trend through its presentation of Brute as a 'terror' alongside its Scythian invader, Humber. Daniel Vitkus names several characteristics of the 'Turk' as understood by the early modern English, including 'aggression, lust, suspicion, murderous conspiracy, sudden cruelty masquerading as justice, merciless violence rather than "Christian charity", wrathful vengeance instead of turning the other cheek' (2002: 2), all behaviours in which *Locrine*'s characters indulge themselves. Locrine himself embodies many of these vices, transforming from a noble young king to a lecherous and paranoid despot, exiling his queen, replacing her with his lover and threatening with death anyone who 'seekes by whispering this or that, / To trouble *Locrine* in his sweetest life' (1595: sig. I2v). The only key character who doesn't at some point call for revenge is the clown, Strumbo. The combination of putative Britishness and 'Turkish' intemperance may have seemed incongruous, even insulting, given the Brutan histories' frequent utilization in the cause of English national aggrandizement in pageantry and plays such as *Edward I*, particularly because, for 'London theatregoers, the Turk was not an imaginary bogey' (Vitkus 2000: 3) but a complex and topical cultural figure.

Elizabeth I had established diplomatic relations with the Ottoman Empire in 1580, partly, as Matthew Dimmock notes, due to a 'willingness in the post-Reformation environment to express the national identity and its allegiances in opposition to the over-arching power of Catholic Spain' (2005: 3). Dimmock shows that the Spanish authorities often referred to the English as 'turks' and that by the 1590s '[a]ttacks upon Elizabeth and her realm began to centre exclusively upon relations between England and the Ottoman Empire' (2005: 163). Conversely, there was a Protestant tradition going back to Martin Luther of parsing the Pope and the 'Turk' into two faces of the same satanic threat (Vitkus 2002: 8), a tradition that reached John Foxe, who could not decide 'between the Turk and the Pope as the ultimate expression of Antichrist' (Penny 1997: 256). In these ways, the Ottomans represented a dissonant combination of ally, antichrist and geopolitical threat, just as the Trojans were simultaneously ancestors, pagans and invaders. In appropriating tropes of the popular 'Near East' dramas of the time, *Locrine* invites polytemporal associations between the Brutan founders and an ancient, 'barbarous Asia' that has apparently endured in the form of the early modern 'Turk'. Yet the play is, in terms of its sense of place, very different from *Tamburlaine* and its offshoots. *Locrine* locates its complexly alien Brutans within a British landscape that is often evoked through the language of pastoral. One effect of this is to place the island and its inhabitants at typological odds. The interactions between the Brutan founders and the landscape through which they will be immortalized are frequently, indeed only, violent.

In *Locrine*, a sense of place and landscape is evoked through vivid and attentive descriptions of the fields, mountains and rivers that will become defined by the play's Brutan founders. Having arrived with Humber and his invading army and viewing Britain for the first time, Estrild describes this landscape:

> The plaines my Lord garnisht with *Floras* welth
> And ouerspred with party colored flowers,
> Do yeeld sweet contentation to my mind,
> The aierie hills enclosd with shadie groues,
> The groues replenisht with sweet chirping birds,
> The birds resounding heauenly melodie,
> Are equall to the groues of *Thessaly*,
> Where *Phaebus* with the learned Ladies nine,
> Delight themselues with musicke harmonie,
> And from the moisture of the mountaine tops,
> The silent springs daunce downe with murmuring streams,
> And water al ye ground with cristal waues,
> The gentle blasts of *Eurus* modest winde,
> Mouing the pittering leaues of *Siluanes* woods,
> Do equall it with *Tempes* paradice,
> And thus comforted all to one effect,
> Do make me thinke these are the happie Iles,
> Most fortunate, if *Humber* may them winne.

(1595: sig. C3r-v)

It is ironic that Estrild, as part of an invading force, initiates *Locrine*'s strategy of pastoral imagery, invoking Britain as 'the happie Iles', a phrase often used for Britain, including in the near-contemporary Rose play *A Looking Glasse for London and England* (1594: sig. I1v). As the play progresses, this language of topography becomes contaminated with imagery of slaughter and drowning. Albanact declares he will pursue the invading Scythians until 'all the riuers [are] stained with their blood' (1595: sig. D2r). A description of an encamped army is interspersed with images of 'murmuring riuers' that 'slide with silent streames', almost precisely repeating, and thus incanting, the 'murmuring streames' and 'silent springs' of Estrild's description, returning the spectator to the original unspoiled landscape even as its despoliation is underway (sig. D2v). The invading Humber prepares for battle with references to '*Abis* siluer streames / That clearly glide along the *Champane* fields, / And moist the grasie meades with humid drops' (sig. E3r). The British meadows, then, like the rivers, will soon be fed, made 'moist', with blood. The alien colonizers and invaders, Trojan and Scythian, inhabit the landscape and alter it with spilled blood, and this integration of the founding 'other' with the landscape is ultimately fulfilled via the performance of five suicides.

Like tropes of the ancient Near East, the representation of historical suicides would have invoked contemporary preoccupations. Macdonald and Murphy's study of early modern suicide outlines the cultural conflict: on the one hand, the Reformation had 'intensified religious hostility to self-murder in England' (1990: 2), while '[h]umanist intellectuals were inescapably aware of Roman customs and Stoic arguments in defence of suicide, and these views were given greater currency in the literature of the age' (86). In this context, the suicides of notable classical heroes were well known (87). Thus, as pagan characters emerging from the same classical antiquity as ancient Rome, *Locrine*'s suicides could be understood as Stoic and, therefore, in their way, exemplary. Folk tradition and the law, however, contradicted this. As shown in *Hamlet*'s portrayal of Ophelia's funeral, a suspected suicide could be excluded from the comforts of Christian burial in consecrated ground. Punishments for self-killing also extended to the suicide's family and heirs. Goods, leases and money were 'forfeited to the crown' (Macdonald and Murphy 1990: 15), and these laws were enforced with particular rigour in the sixteenth and early seventeenth centuries (116). The suicide was also feared as a potential unquiet spirit capable of reanimation. The corpse might be carried 'to a crossroads and [thrown] naked into a pit' with '[a] wooden stake . . . hammered through the body, pinioning it to the grave' (15). This punishment is reminiscent of earlier medieval practices where suicides 'were commonly disposed of in rivers . . . banished to parts unknown, so that their corpses might not become revenants' (Caciola 1996: 30). While this account is 'untimely' – Caciola is describing practices recorded many years before the 1590s – it is possible that the early modern burial methods described here bear witness to the survival, on a ritual level, of suicides as the 'dangerous dead', or potential revenants. Eric Langley, in a study of suicide tropes in early modern literature, paraphrases Hamlet in a digression on the punishment given to suicides in Dante's *Inferno*: 'The self-slaughterer dreams of liberation into infinite space, but is bound to bad dreams' (2009: 195). Dante's suicides are, like Ariel in *The Tempest*, bound into the trunks of trees, welded into agonizing materiality, an evocative and painful image when considering Brutan 'immortalis[ation] as geography', and the questions of origins and essence explored earlier. In terms of raising the ancestral dead through performance, their status as suicides further disturbs the 'sensual contact' between the living and performed dead proposed by Walsh. In a study of early modern stage suicide, Richard Sanderson observes that a suicide's 'last "communication" may include an image – consciously fashioned by the suicide – to be left behind in the minds of the suicide's survivors' (1992: 203). If playgoers might be included as the 'survivors' of a suicide as portrayed in performance, then attentiveness to the 'consciously fashioned' images of suicide in *Locrine* may tell us something about the play's possible effects.

One of the ways in which *Locrine* provides an encounter with history unavailable in any other form of early modern historiography is its inclusion of the clown Strumbo, who moves in and out of the action and whose subplot seems to parody the history's tragic developments (Gooch 1981: 10). Strumbo first appears in the play's fourth scene, comically lovelorn and, tellingly, contemplating suicide: '*Strumbo* kill thy selfe, drowne thy selfe, hang thy selfe, sterue thy selfe' (1595: sig. B4v). This list foreshadows *Locrine*'s five suicides, two of which are by drowning and one of which is, if not suicide by starvation, Humber's despairing response to starvation. Albanact is first to take his own life, stabbing himself to avoid capture by the invading Humber. Albanact is a heroic, martial figure, comparable with Talbot in *1 Henry VI*. His suicide appears valiant, infusing his territory of Albania with his rough, martial courage.[7] A further parallel for Albanact might be found in the Roman figure of Young Marius in Thomas Lodge's *The Wounds of Civil War*: overpowered in battle, Marius takes his own life onstage. Comparison to Young Marius would seem to position Albanact as a Stoic Roman hero. The two deaths are both interpolations by the playmakers upon their source materials, but in other respects they are very different. Marius dies mourning that the tyrant Scilla has created a 'world dispoyld of vertue, faith and trust', and pleads for his allies to kill Scilla to preserve the state, for 'gouernance is banisht out of Rome' (1594: sig. I1v). His concerns are political and, in promising to show 'a constant Romane die' (sig. I1v), his suicide is Stoical. Conversely, Albanact focuses his final words on personal glory, railing against 'Iniurious fortune', promising to 'finde her hateful mansion' (sig. E1r). This vaulting language of glory and honour is closely allied with that of *Tamburlaine* and the plays it influenced, while the suicide of Young Marius is Lodge's addition to the historical account of the wars between Sulla and Marius (Hadfield 2005: 96). Albanact's suicide presented spectators with a death that was heroic in its classicized context, spectacular in its Tamburlainian rhetoric yet troubling in that it stages the founding moment of Albany, later Scotland, in terms of military defeat by invading barbarians, feeding the landscape with its founder's suicidal blood.

Humber provides one of *Locrine*'s most acute compressions of founder and landscape: the invader declares that a river's 'siluer streames . . . shall be agnominated by our name / And talked of by our posteritie', wishing the waters red with his enemies' blood (1595: sig. F1r). Silver streams flow through *Locrine* and between its characters, punctuating its uneasy pastoral. Camber evokes the Iscan, where 'lightfoote faires [fairies] skip from banke to banke' and which is also the site of his encamped army (sig. E4v). The silver streams of the river Lee flow above the 'curious' subterranean jewelled grotto Locrine builds to hide Estrild (sig. H3v). In performance, Humber would have personified imagery of rivers and violence. He is described as 'arm'd in azure blew' (sig. D2v), with ensigns as 'banners crost with argent streames' (sig. G1r); that is, vivid blue armour or costume coupled with banners showing crossed silver streams, suggestive of rivers. While barely mentioned in the playtext, these martial accoutrements could be highly visible as props in performance, waving in the air like rippling or flowing water. This riverine presentation foreshadows Humber's 'translation' into topography via his drowning in the river that receives his name. In the Brutan histories this founding action is undertaken by the victors over Humber, who is driven into the river during battle. In *Locrine*, Humber drowns himself after seven years' near-starvation in the British wilderness. Humber's self-drowning appears, as far as I can establish, to be unprecedented as a stage effect.[8] I mention this possible innovation to emphasize the moment's potential impact in performance. The despairing Humber's decision to 'Fling himselfe into the riuer' (1595: sig. H4r), as the stage direction has it, presumably through a trapdoor, may have intensified the moment at which a foreign, barbaric invader, previously armoured in azure and waving a silver streaming banner, vanishes into and, through 'translation', becomes the silver streams of a British river. This suicide leaves the stage briefly empty, the next entrance being the ghost of Albanact, whose cry of 'leap earth, dance trees' (sig. H4v) calls for Humber's death to be physically celebrated by the landscape in which he has drowned and through which he will be immortalized.

At the play's climax the embattled lovers Estrild and Locrine kill themselves with Locrine's sword. One effect of this is to lessen Locrine's warrior-like status – he does not die in battle but in retreat, in his lover's arms. Estrild and Locrine are described in death as 'Clasping each other in their feebled armes, / With louing zeale, as if for companie' (1595: sig. K3r–v). Again, this is a passing image in the text but a striking tableau that would have remained on stage until the end of the performance, even as Sabren and Guendolen exchange lengthy recriminations. The inert players' embracing bodies suggest a British landscape that is a fusion of both Brutan king and foreign woman. Yet this synthesis is undone by Guendolen: Locrine will be buried in Troynovant, in 'his fathers tombe', absorbed into the landscape defined by Brutus, to whom, Guendolen states, 'we owe our country, liues and goods' (sig. K4v). Estrild, however, will 'lie without the shallow vauts, / Without the honour due vnto the dead' (sig. K4v), a fate identical to that of Tamora in *Titus Andronicus* (perf. 1592; pub. 1594), another woman alien to the culture into which she has, through captivity and perceived erotic currency, been absorbed; in that play's final lines, Tamora's body is ordered to be thrown 'to beasts and birds to pray' (1994: 5.3.197). Excluded from burial, Estrild is alone among the play's suicides in not giving her name to a British region or river. In this way, Guendolen erases Estrild from the dialogue of founder, place and essence. The Brutan future will be Trojan, determined by Queen Guendolen and her son Madan, grandson of Brute and Corineus.

However, perhaps *Locrine*'s most complex performance of the synthesis of British landscape and suicide is embodied in Sabren. This may have been intensified in performance in ways that are occluded on the printed page. Declaring that her 'virgins hands are too too weake' to kill herself with her dead father's sword (sig. K3v), the encircled Sabren escapes Guendolen's threats of violent death by leaping into a conveniently adjacent river with the lines 'And that which *Locrines* sword could not perform, / This pleasant streame shall present bring to passe' (sig. K4r). As with Humber, Sabren's self-drowning could have been enacted by the player jumping through a trap in the centre of the stage, merging her with the river that will be called, by Guendolen's decree, '*Sabren* for euer' (sig. K4v). Through the convention of stage doubling, this suicide may have further implications in performance that allow Sabren's suicide to ripple outwards into the play's overarching depiction of Brutan time and history.

   Examining the performance practices of the playing company the Queen's Men, McMillin and MacLean make a detailed study of the company's possible doubling strategies, particularly necessary when touring with a reduced company.[9] This includes assessing the minimum number of boy actors required, determined by the number of female or youthful male characters onstage at any one time, and those required for the preceding or following scenes (1998: 107). Attending to this suggests ways in which doubling was used for satirical or poetic stage effects that can, as McMillin and MacLean assert, be 'part of [a] play's beauty' (1998: 112). Adopting this methodology for *Locrine*, the play appears to require four or five boy actors, principally for the roles of Guendolen, Estrild, Sabren, Madan and, possibly, Thrasimachus, who describes himself as 'young and of a tender age' (1595: sig. I2v). This maximum number is suggested by the play's final scene, discussed earlier, in which all five characters appear onstage simultaneously. The scene is immediately followed by an epilogue spoken by Ate. By casting herself into the 'river' Sabren exits the stage nineteen lines before the end of the scene, making the boy playing Sabren the most likely candidate to reappear as Ate, the early exit affording time for the player to change costume and re-enter. If this is the case, it presents a strikingly poetic and thematically provocative use of doubling. Sabren is the play's most vulnerable and guiltless character. She was also, as previously shown, one of the Brutan figures most frequently referenced in early modern poetry.[10] Aside from a brief, silent appearance alongside her mother (sig. I2v)

Sabren does not appear again or speak until discovering her parents' bodies in the final scene, lamenting them with a call for sympathy antithetical to Ate's malevolence, asking 'What fierce *Achilles*, what hard stonie flint, / Would not bemone this mournfull Tragedie?' (sig. K2v). Her failed attempt to slay herself with Locrine's sword is directly followed by the entrance of her father's enemies Thrasimachus, Madan and a company of soldiers, led by Guendolen, who calls for Sabren, '*Locrines* only ioy', to be found so 'That I may glut my mind with lukewarm blood' (sig. K3r). This mass entrance would visually have overwhelmed the childlike figure. Yet Sabren commands the scene, speaking a third of its lines. Further, much of Guendolen's speech is used to threaten and describe Sabren, retaining the scene's focus on the child's distress, resilience and vulnerability. Sabren's lines are spoken in three uninterrupted speeches given by a child character surrounded by armoured enemies, their massed attention augmenting her presence and authority. She calls upon the spirits of the British landscape to mourn Locrine and Estrild:

> You mountain nimphs which in these desarts raign,
> Cease off your hastie chase of sauadge beasts,
> Prepare to see a heart opprest with care,
> . . . .
> You *Driades* and lightfoote *Satiri*,
> You gracious Faries which at euening tide,
> Your closets leaue with heauenly beautie storde,
> And on your shoulders spread your golden locks,
> You sauadge beares in caues and darkened dennes,
> Come waile with me, the martiall Locrines death.

> (sig. K3v)

Sabren invokes a dense, wild and dynamic pastoral. Nymphs that hunt savage beasts through the desert – dryads, satyrs and fairies whose 'heauenly' beauty is confined to night-time wanderings, and even bears lurking in caues – are called upon to mourn Locrine, whose name defines and demarcates the topography they inhabit. The speech is Sabren's first following the army's entrance, yet her grieving invocation goes uninterrupted, suggesting a performance of awed, or at least respectful, silence from the enemies surrounding her that gives space to this conjuration of a transformed British landscape in the moment at which the integration of founder and place is fulfilled. Attending to Sabren's onstage presence reveals a powerful and fearless figure of childlike loyalty and innocence. Yet if doubled with Ate, Sabren becomes physically, disturbingly, fused with *Locrine*'s hellish presenter. Ate opens the play 'with thunder and lightning all in black, with a burning torch in one hand' and, in contrast to Sabren, who can barely lift her father's sword, 'a bloodie swoord in the other' (sig. A3r). In this reading, the play's closing image is that of a boy player enacting Sabren's self-drowning and immediately reappearing as Ate. This is a complex synthesis, embodying in a single player a Brutan founder raised from the 'graue of oblivion' through performance only to re-enact her own suicide, through which she is translated into a British river; this player *also* and almost simultaneously embodies the pagan deity Ate who oversees *Locrine*'s tragic action and, as performed in *The Araygnment of Paris*, can be seen as the presiding spirit of the events leading to the destruction of Troy and, therefore, the creation of the Trojan diaspora that results in Brute's conquest of Albion. Even as it brings the Brutan ancestral dead into the room, this final synthesis also drags *Locrine*'s vision of British foundation back to the Brutan founders' own tragic, Near Eastern origins.

Collectively, these suicides present the interaction of landscape and Brutan founders as resulting from defeat, treachery and despair. Additionally, those spectators familiar with the Brutan histories would have known that the play does not necessarily represent a regrettable yet necessary cleansing that might clear the way for better rule, as *Gorboduc* could be argued to do. According to many medieval and early modern iterations of the Brutan histories, Locrine's heir, Madan, would become a lecherous, perverse and violent king whose crimes result in his being eaten by wolves. Even those for whom the Brutan histories represented the lived past may have left the playhouse with different understandings of the play's final image. For readers of Holinshed, Higgins, Stow and others, the play ends with a young king who will become a despot. For those who read Caxton, Hardyng, Higden, or Geoffrey, Madan was to become a good king who ruled in peace.

In its raw materials, *Locrine* is in many ways typical of its cultural moment, combining aspects of English Senecan tragedy familiar from *Gorboduc* and the popular post-*Tamburlaine* dramaturgy of Near Eastern tropes. However, in applying these to the Brutan founders, the play enacts an idiosyncratic fusion of 'barbarous' colonizer and pastoral landscape, from Humber's costume and language pre-echoing the British river he will become, to Sabren's pastoral eulogy for her father and subsequent riverine suicide-transformation. It is an unhappy and violent vision of Brutan origins. Slipping from the careful controls under which civic pageantry operated and released into the relative semiotic anarchy of London's commercial drama, the underlying tensions and contradictions of Brutan origins spring, like Ate, into full public view. This view was, of course, also shaped by the surrounding cultural moment. While this context is difficult to address through *Locrine*, for which no date of composition or performance records remain, possible interactions between Brutan drama and contemporary events can be explored through the lost play 'King Lude'. Unlike *Locrine*, which confronts its audience with the most unpalatable aspects of their often-celebrated Brutan origins, 'King Lude' may instead have been a celebratory drama overwhelmed by the unpalatable reality of London life *c.* 1594.

'King Lude'

Performed history opened up a discourse between the Brutan past and the early modern English by figuratively raising the ancestral dead in the presence of their descendants. But this discourse could be disrupted by contemporary events. It could also be complicated and challenged from the same stage by the playhouse repertory's competing narratives. Both possibilities are demonstrated by an examination of the conditions in which 'King Lude' was performed. Brutan time was a sequence not only of foundational moments but also of destruction and regeneration: the reigns of Gorboduc and his sons saw the end of Brute's direct dynastic line and the restoration of good rule by the Cornish duke Mulmutius; King Lud rebuilt crumbling Troynovant, the city founded by Brute. According to the Brutan histories, Lud restored Troynovant a few decades before Christ's birth and, in a quasi-foundational act, renamed the city after himself, making him the best-known exponent of these restorative energies. A play named 'King Lude' was performed at the Rose playhouse in January 1594. No text survives, but the titles of lost plays often suggest their possible content, and recent work by David McInnis and Matthew Steggle supports the study of these events: '[l]ost plays . . . should be regarded positively as witnesses to otherwise unrecorded theatrical events rather than as mere failures to preserve a literary text' (2014: 7). In this way, it is possible to explore how audience perceptions might have been shaped by Lud's resonance as an icon of London's capacity for renewal. As a symbol of Lud's regenerative force, the London gatehouse, Ludgate, which Lud was believed to have built, been buried beneath and upon which stood statues of the king and his sons, will be considered as a key 'text' through which spectators may have contextualized the king's onstage presence. Further, the precise dating of this performance of 'King Lude' allows questions of reception to include the cultural contexts in which this performance took place. 'King Lude' was performed at the Rose in a brief respite between extended plague outbreaks and playhouse closures. Additionally, it was performed in repertory alongside plays depicting civic destruction, which was often presented as divine punishment. These performances may have offered alternative typologies through which Londoners could imagine their city and its destiny, a consideration sharpened by the divinely punitive function often ascribed to plague. The Rose performance of 'King Lude' stages a celebrated Brutan founder at a moment when his value as a regenerative symbol may have been compromised or overpowered by the grim realities of plague-time London, a city often imagined as a new Jerusalem but which had – according to the Brutan histories – been founded as New Troy.

At the close of *Locrine*, Guendolen announces what is to be done with Locrine's body: 'Retire braue followers vnto *Troynovant* / Where we will celebrate these exequies / And place yoong *Locrine* in his fathers tombe' (1595: sig. K4v). Troynovant was believed to be the burial site of many Brutan monarchs. Their tombs were said to lie beneath familiar and ancient buildings, rooting the city's foundations in imagined Brutan bones. Elizabethan poetry made great use of Troynovant; it appears during the sequence in which the 'Thames doth the Medway wedd' (1596: IIII.XI, f. 156) in *The Faerie Queene*, a 'chorographic poem' embedded within Spenser's larger scheme that narrates a pageant of personified global rivers and cities that 'move from rivers "present" at the marriage to old and new histories' (van Es 2002: 59) relating to each river's origins and nation. Troynovant is described as 'wearing a Diademe embattild wide / With hundred turrets, like a Turribant', or turban (1596: IIII.XI, f. 164), the headgear seeming to emphasize once more the Brutans' classical Near Eastern origins.[11] Plays dealing with English history also evoked Troynovant. In *Friar Bacon and Friar Bongay* (*c.* 1589; pub. 1594), the medieval Bacon prophesies Elizabeth I as one day emerging 'here where Brute did build his Troynouant' (sig. I1v), and the second part of *The Troublesome Raigne of Iohn King of England* (*c.* 1591; pub. 1591) has the French dauphin refer to London as 'Troynouant, your faire *Metropolis*' (sig. I3v). But London had a second and subsequent Brutan origin, etymologically connected to its present name and topography. In the earliest extant printed text of a Lord Mayor's Show, George Peele's *The Deuice of the Pageant Borne Before Woolstone Dixi Lord Maior of the Citie of London* (perf. 1585; pub. 1585), a child representing 'London' declares himself 'New *Troye* . . . whome *Lud* my Lord surnam'd, / *London* the glory of the western side' (1585: sig. A2v). Here, Lud represents not a founder but a re-founder or renewer, bringing the city to a state of 'glory'. This role defers in typological terms to the essence determined by 'the authority of the foundation', meaning that while 'the mythical King Lud renews London's walls and gates and gives the renewed city his name' this cannot fully negate the city's dependence upon Brute's originating act as its source of essence and destiny (Manley 2011: 144). As we have seen, Troy could be perceived not only as glorious but also as corrupt and doomed. Thus, Lud's rebuilding is merely a stage in an ongoing process, the outcome of which is uncertain. Manley characterizes the rebuilding of London as representing, along with 'the acts of the lawgiver Mulmutius Dunwallo', the 'recoveries and renewals that sustain historic purpose amid the overwhelming disasters of British history' (Manley 2011: 192). One of these 'overwhelming disasters', as identified by Manley, was a series of plague epidemics between 1592 and 1594. Thus, while the 1594 performance of 'King Lude' appears to have brought onto the stage an embodiment of civic renewal, this occurred when that very city was experiencing sustained disaster, perceived by many as divine punishment. Yet Lud was a powerful symbol of the city's endurance and safety, manifested in the edifice of Ludgate, built by Lud to protect the city from attack.

While the Brutan histories' material on King Lud as the rebuilder of London offers narrative elements suitable for a play, the presiding emphasis is one of rebuilding and renewal, of increased civic pride and security. King Lud lived at the far end of pre-Christian time to Locrine, only seventy-two years before the birth of Christ (Holinshed 1587: I, *Hist.* 23). Fabyan's account is typical:

This man was honourable in all his dedes for he edyfyed new temples, and repayred the olde . . . in the cytye of Troynouant he causyd many buyldynges to be made and gyrde the sayde cityE about wyth a strong wall of lyme and

stone. And in the weste parte of the sayde walle he arreryd
a fayre and stronge gate, and commaunded it to be called
Luddys gate. (1516: f. 16v)

Ludgate is often the chroniclers' focus, revealing the
structure's significance for Londoners. Hardyng's fifteenth-
century chronicle, for example, states that 'Lud kyng of
Brytain buylded frome London stone [the site of modern-day
Cannon Street station] to Lud gate & called that parte Luds
toune, & after by processe, was called London by turnyng of
tongues' (1543: f. 35v). The effect of cultural and historical
change upon language is vividly captured in the phrase
'turnying of tongues', and shows that, despite this process, it
is difficult for Hardyng to name or describe London without
invoking Lud. Holinshed refers to the same process as that
of Lud's name being 'drowned in pronuntiation' (1587:
I, *Hist.* 23) and speculates as to which sites had once held
Lud's palaces and temples, called 'endlesse moniments' in
The Faerie Queene (1590: II.X, f. 338). Thus, the haunting
presence of a partially lost Brutan city might be overlaid upon
the present buildings in a kind of topographic palimpsest. Yet
Lud's shaping actions were inscribed not only on the City's
buildings and defences but also in less tangible structures that
nonetheless determined the parameters of Londoners' lives as
surely as a city wall. As has been seen in Manley's association
between Lud and Mulmutius Dunwallo as lawmakers, one
textual community for whom Lud had particular meaning
was the legal profession, for whom he represented a reformer.
Polydore Vergil seemed to accept that Lud 'reformed the
commonwealth. For he abolished some laws [and] put an end
to no few abuses' (2005). Lud is also cited as an example of
'the efficient and materiall cause' given in Abraham Fraunce's
The Lawiers Logike: 'the cause efficient either maketh or
destroyeth . . . and dooth either procreate or bring foorth
that which was not before, as God the worlde, king *Lud* the
Citie of *London*' (1588: sig. D3v). The perceived power of a
founder for early moderns is here expressed in striking terms:

for Fraunce, Lud's rebuilding of London is comparable with God's creation of the world. Lud was, Holinshed states simply, 'greatlie beloued of all the Britaines' (1587: I, *Hist.* 23) as a protector and a rebuilder, a synecdoche for London's ancient capacity for renewal.

In the absence of a playtext, 'King Lude' can be approached by attending to the possible receptions of Lud as a staged figure embodying the compression of topography, cultural resonance and the ancestral dead explored throughout this chapter. His onstage presence was a dramaturgical event in itself – character as stage effect, perhaps. That is, the physical presence of an iconic figure might be considered independently of dialogue and action as a means of entertaining, and conveying meaning to, audiences. The play was performed by Sussex's Men during a six-week residency at the Rose playhouse that began on 27 December 1593 (Wiggins 2013: 3, ref. 907). The company performed twelve plays between December and February, when the theatres were once more closed by the Privy Council due to plague. 'King Lude' was performed on Friday, 18 January, and was one of only two plays not to receive a repeat performance during this short season.[12] The receipts were twenty-two shillings, a middling level of success for the run but not so little as to deter the possibility of a repeat performance.[13] Regarding the play's possible content, Bullough cites historiographic texts to support speculation regarding narratives (1969: 304) while Wiggins limits his speculation and cites only Holinshed as a possible source (2013: 3, ref. 907). As shown, there were multiple textual, topographic and popular sources from which Londoners might draw a sense of Lud's meaning for their city, and thus 'King Lude' can be approached as 'a complex and multi-faceted cultural phenomenon in its own right', accessible beyond the written or printed record of its action and dialogue (McInnis and Steggle 2014: 6). Ludgate was the key reminder of Lud's association with the city, a symbol available to more Londoners than any written text. It was one of the City's western gateways, a site of defence and a prison.

Jonathan Gil Harris describes Ludgate as 'a vital component in the symbolic topography of London' having 'signifying power as a nodal point, connecting not only the City's inside and outside but also its past, present, and future' (2008: 17). It also, however, had meaning as a structure with its own inside and outside, having functioned since the fourteenth century as a debtors' prison although even here, as Harris notes, early modern accounts seemed to associate the site with protective containment as much as punishment, shielding unlucky defaulters from their 'rapacious creditors' (2008: 22–3). Ludgate was simultaneously a defensive boundary between London and not-London, between debtors and their creditors and between Lud himself and Brute's Troynovant. This sense of containment and stability is compromised in the years prior to 'King Lude' by the fact that, by the early 1580s, Ludgate's medieval structure was dilapidated and 'in no shape to be considered [in Spenser's term] an "endlesse monument"' (Steggle 2000: 36). The structure's decay extended to the statues of Lud and his sons, which had been defaced during the wider iconoclasm of Edward VI's reign and subsequently restored by Mary I (Harris 2008:16) through a process of 'setting new heads on their old bodies' (Stow 1598: f. 33). These statues were once again recontextualized for the Rose audience by an Elizabethan restoration programme that perhaps echoed Lud's most famous actions in the Brutan histories.

> In 1586, as the Queen's Privy Council made preparations for the expected Spanish Armada by extensively repairing the stonework of the gates and citadels in England's port cities, London's rulers likewise decided to rebuild the now dilapidated Ludgate wall as an expression of a militarized English patriotism. With funds levied from the citizens, statues of Lud and his two sons were installed. (Harris 2008: 16)

Stow's wording is unclear but suggests that, while Ludgate itself was rebuilt, the statues had in fact been preserved and then replaced 'as afore, on the East side' (1598: f. 33). Lud's survival in stone, then, was enabled by the enforced material investment of London's civic communities, for whom the Brutan histories had particular resonance. As Lud had restored the city, so the City restored Lud. For spectators to encounter Lud in performance and hear his name spoken may have conjured the statue's image, the renovation of which, Steggle argues, 'renewed, rather than destroyed, his legacy' (2000: 36). As echoed in the names of Ludgate and London, 'King Lude' would have evoked a shared, protective and Brutan topography that was said to incorporate the material remains of Lud himself.

In *Untimely Matter*, Harris examines John Stow's attempts to translate a Hebrew-inscribed stone unearthed by workmen during the 1586 rebuilding project (2009: 101). Stow, while fascinated by the stone, would also have been aware that these workmen were digging in the vicinity of Lud's reputed burial site. Fabyan noted that Lud had been 'buryed in his gate called Portlud or Ludgate' (1516: f. 16v). Stow adjusts Fabyan, writing in the *Summarie* that Lud 'was buryed nere to the same Ludgate, in a Temple whiche he there buylded' (1598: f. 18v). For some, to dig in the vicinity of Ludgate was potentially to disturb Lud's bones. Manley notes that 'Stow's archaeological impulse is inseparable from his spiritual membership of a community where the past was in a more or less continual state of disinterral' (1995: 41). In 1586 Lud was, figuratively at least, part of this 'continual state of disinterral', as potentially unearthed human remains. Yet in 1594 he was disinterred through performed history, another way in which the early modern English relentlessly raised their dead. A synecdoche for the restored defensive gate and London itself, Lud's onstage presence may have been celebratory in the tradition of those pageant Brutans Martia, Brennus and Ebrauk who had appeared to speak for, protect and celebrate their cities. However, 'King Lude' is complicated by its performance between plague outbreaks, harrowing conditions in which to perform the embodiment of the city's glorious regeneration.

Compounding this, the play appeared within a repertory at the Rose that included plays representing the destruction of cities to which London was also often compared, Jerusalem and Sodom. At a time of plague these competing typologies may have challenged and even inverted the affective potential of a play depicting Lud.

Plague outbreaks kept the playhouses closed for almost two years between 1592 and 1594 (Knutson 2010: 452–3). The outbreaks were eerily pre-empted and dramaturgically contextualized by multiple performances at the Rose of Thomas Lodge and Robert Greene's *A Looking Glasse for London and England*, a play that uses biblical civic allegory – the corrupt city of Nineveh – and repeated direct address to warn its audience that plague will be among the punishments meted out on London should its perceived moral decay continue. *A Looking Glasse* reveals something of the popular typological evocation of London in the months prior to both the playhouse closures and the moment at which the plague abated sufficiently for the theatres to be reopened in the winter of 1593–4. Using biblical typologies to configure London was not unusual. Beatrice Groves notes that one of 'Elizabethan England's most cherished beliefs was that "Israel" and "Jerusalem" were concepts which transcended race and geography' (2011: 150). London could thus be imagined as a new Jerusalem, providing a typological invocation that competed with London as Troynovant or Lud's Town. Tracey Hill notes that '[o]ne consistent theme of royal entries from the fourteenth century to the mid-sixteenth century . . . was the personification of London as a new Jerusalem' (2010: 28). However, in *Christs Teares Over Ierusalem,* a treatise written during the 1593 plague, Thomas Nashe expressed the troubling subtext of this association: 'As great a desolation as Ierusalem, hath London deserued. Whatsoeuer of Ierusalem I haue written, was but to lend her [London] a Looking-glasse' (1593: f. 78). Earlier, in 1592, biblical comparisons were unsparingly expressed at the Rose in *A Looking Glasse*, which relates Jonah's reluctance to obey God and preach to the decadent

people of Nineveh. The action is framed by regular addresses
to the audience by the figure of Oseas, a prophet from another
biblical era who, the stage directions indicate, is '*brought in by
an Angell . . . set downe ouer the Stage in a Throne*' (1594: sig.
B1r) and remains onstage throughout, observing the action and
admonishing sinful London, uncomfortably represented by the
playhouse audience themselves, with apocalyptic warnings:

> Repent all you that heare, for feare of plagues,
> O London, this and more doth swarme in thee,
> Repent, repent, for why the Lord doth see.
> With trembling pray, and mend what is amisse,
> The swoord of iustice drawne alreadie is.

(1594: sig. F1v)

The play ends on a hopeful note, with multiple Christian
conversions saving many characters from the spectacular
deaths, which include being struck by lightning, that have
afflicted others; but the play's polytemporal use of figures from
different biblical eras allows it to invoke the destruction of
Jerusalem lamented by Nashe: in the Old Testament, Hosea's
warnings are 'directed primarily at . . . Jerusalem' and, while
the Ninevites repented the Jews did not, and Jerusalem was
destroyed (Sager 2013: 59). Groves notes that *A Looking
Glasse* 'reminded its audience that their aspiration to build
Sion in their land was a precarious as well as a blessed
undertaking' (2011: 153). Four performances of *A Looking
Glasse* were recorded by Henslowe, 'twice at the Rose in
March 1591, again in April that year and later in June 1592 by
Lord Strange's Men' (Connolly 2007: 5). Taunting Londoners
with threats of imminent destruction was, clearly, no barrier to
box office success.

In the same period that *A Looking Glasse* was performed,
Henslowe records ten performances of another lost play, 'Tittus
& Vespacia', which almost certainly staged the destruction
of Jerusalem alluded to in Lodge and Greene's play (Manley

2014: 174–7). The two plays were twice performed on adjacent days, on 19 and 20 April and 7 and 8 June 1592, suggesting repertory design. One may wonder what the audience made of Oseas's admonitions such as 'London take heed, these sinnes abound in thee' (1594: sig. C1r) and 'Sin raignes in thee o London euery houre' (1594: sig. C1r). The word 'plague' is an incantatory presence in *A Looking Glasse*, spoken sixteen times and usually in direct address. As the year progressed, *A Looking Glasse* may have seemed prescient. As Alice Hall records, citing the Acts of the Privy Council, '[n]otice of increasing plague deaths appeared in 13 August 1592, when plague was described as "dailie increasing in London"', the September Thames Fair was postponed and the Lord Mayor's Show abandoned in October (2008: 96). This was only a few weeks clear of *A Looking Glasse*'s final performance, and the play never again appears in Henslowe's records. Sager has argued against the play's appeal as didactic material in favour of its value as spectacle (2013: 56); yet the two are not exclusive and, as institutions from the church to monarchies to city authorities were well aware, one can be used to intensify the other. Playgoers may plausibly have had Oseas's warnings ringing in their ears as the offstage plague deaths increased. Lodge and Greene, in a dramaturgical sleight of hand, had transferred Oseas to Nineveh, allowing the comparisons to London to end with the Ninevite conversions. But many in the audience would have known of Hosea's association with Jerusalem's destruction. London, whether as a new Troy or new Jerusalem, was locked into a typology of divinely authorized annihilation.

This was perhaps a frightening parallel in time of plague, even for the more sternly devout citizens welcoming God's wrath, and those fears are reflected in practical guides to surviving the outbreak, which provide evidence of beliefs and actions relating to the threat.[14] In Simon Kellwaye's *A Defensatiue Against the Plague*, Londoners and, finally, London itself become plague hosts. Kellwaye evokes the disease as being 'most commonly' spread

by accompaning our selues with such as either haue, or
lately haue had the disease them selues; or at least haue
beene conuersant with such as haue bene infected therewith.
But for the most parte it doth come by receauing into our
custody some clothes, or such like things that haue bene
vsed about some infected body, wherin the infection may lye
hidden a long time. (1593: sig. B1v)

Kellwaye's channels of infection quickly expand to include,
potentially, everyone, including those present only through
their discarded garments. The cohesive, contained London
body, symbolized by Lud and his gatehouse and walls, is now
threatened from within. Kellwaye's proposed 'second meanes'
of avoiding infection is to 'flye far off from the place infected'
(1593: sig. B2v). An official proclamation of 28 May warned
that 'the infection of the plague is at this present greatly
increased and dispersed aswel in the Citie of London and
Westminster' and throughout the country (1593a); another
issues the infamous instruction that 'the houses of such persons
out of the which there shall die any of the plague' should
be closed up for six weeks, including anyone still resident
inside (1593b).[15] Londoners could either flee the city or risk
horrifying imprisonment in their homes. For those leaving the
city at its western end, their last glimpse of home might have
included the statue of Lud, a rebuilder and protector seemingly
rendered powerless.

I have dwelt on *A Looking Glass* and the outbreak of
plague because it was a mere few weeks after the latter abated
sufficiently for the theatres to be reopened in the winter of
1593–4 that 'King Lude' was performed. Drama depicting civic
debasement, however, may have fallen closer still to the moment
of performance. On the day before, 17 January, Sussex's Men
performed a lost play of 'Abram and Lotte' (Henslowe 2002:
21) which, if it followed the biblical accounts of Abraham
and Lot accurately, would have included God's destruction of
the sinful cities of Sodom and Gomorrah (1568: Gen. 19.24–
28). The play is likely to have included the dramatic moment

when angels appear to Lot and urge him to take his family and leave the city before God destroys it: 'And when the mornyng arose, the angels caused Lot to speede him, saying: Stande vp, take thy wyfe, and thy two daughters which be at hande, lest thou perishe in the sinne of the citie' (1568: Gen. 19.15); This angelic intervention almost precisely echoes Kellwaye's urging of Londoners to 'flye far off from the place infected'. 'Abram and Lotte' was performed three times in three weeks and drew higher receipts than 'King Lude', making fifty-two shillings on 9 January and thirty shillings on the 17. The play's repeated performance and good box office further amplifies the reception of narratives and experience of civic destruction preceding and challenging King Lud's onstage presence as a figure of protection and renewal.

Unless, and it is possible, 'King Lude' eschewed all narrative possibilities provided by the Brutan histories, the play's performance on 18 January 1593–4 would have addressed Troynovant's celebrated renovation, fortifying and renaming as Lud's Town. The Brutan histories' account had recently been echoed in Ludgate's 1586 restoration and its repaired statues. But with 'King Lude', these narratives of endurance, performed by and embodied in the figure of Lud himself, took place at a time of crisis. Before its 1592 closure, the Rose had staged repeated performances of A Looking Glasse and 'Titus & Vespacia', one of which warned that plague is a punishment for sinful cities and alluded to the destruction of Jerusalem, the other play almost certainly enacting that destruction. In 1593, Londoners had been told to flee the city and to fear their peers, even their empty clothes, and that the principal cause of the epidemic, as Kellwaye noted, in terms similar to A Looking Glasse, was 'a iust punishment of God' (1593: sig. B1v). In the winter of 1593, this narrative was given biblical re-enactment in 'Abram and Lotte', which may have included a scene wherein angels warn a family to leave a doomed city. Only weeks after the Rose had reopened, this staged destruction of Sodom confronted audiences with a reminder – if one was needed – of the punishment that had befallen decadent cities in the past, a biblical event they appeared to be directly experiencing. The following day, King Lud was raised from oblivion to rebuild and rename ancient Troynovant.

King Lud, then, as the Brutan embodiment of London's capacity for regeneration, was performed in a context that could forcefully negate his meaning and function, or render it ironic. Lud may have been welcomed as representing and heralding great endurance and antiquity, embodying London's ludic regeneration at the reopened Rose. However, particularly given the comparatively high receipts achieved by 'Abram and Lotte' and that play's repeat performances, it is also possible that Lud at the Rose fell short as an icon of urban protection and resurgence. He simply provided insufficient comfort from, or context for, the reality of plague, a Brutan figure typologically overwhelmed by competing associations of London with the annihilated cities of Jerusalem, Sodom and Gomorrah, and also even by his own origins in 'Barbarous *Asia*'. That is, if King Lud carried less authority than the biblical analogues presented at the Rose, then he also, as a rebuilder rather than founder, could not escape the etiological source of all Brutan typology: the doomed city of Troy, imprinted onto the landscape by Brute's original foundation of Troynovant. The performance of Brutan founders had always resonated with troubling semiotic undercurrents. It brought English audiences and monarchs face-to-face with the raised ancestral dead, figures who emerged from a Near Eastern pagan antiquity and whose founding actions and often violent deaths could be understood to have determined the character and essence of Britain, its countries, regions, cities and laws. As long as the Brutan histories were believed, the English were required to find their origins in Brute and those earliest founders who were, to paraphrase Ebrauk's assertion to Henry VII, primitive of their progeny. But, as the sixteenth century ended and the seventeenth began, for increasing numbers of readers and playgoers the Brutan histories were becoming unbelieved.

3

Reading Brutan Erosion (1604–8)

Thus far, I have examined Brutan drama from the perspective of audience members and readers for whom the Brutan histories represented the lived past. In tracking these histories' slow erosion, however, the focus moves from historical certainty to doubt. I will return to Paul Veyne's 'modalities of wavering belief' (1988: 56), and the notion of a spectrum of historical dissonance oscillating between belief and disbelief. This sense of 'wavering belief' may have further extended and complicated a process that already involved the deep, affective transformation of an individual's sense of their national, civic and thus personal origins. I suggest that readers and spectators' unease would have been projectable onto plays such as *Leir*, *King Lear* and the contemporary Brutan drama *No-body and Some-body* (*c.* 1604; pub. 1606). All three of these playbooks use the genre designation 'true chronicle history', an ironic categorization given the Brutan histories' eroding claim to historicity. It is also one which was applied almost exclusively to Brutan playbooks. These were published as Brute was being appropriated for some of his most spectacular and widely disseminated appearances, all in the name of James VI and I's short-lived dream of British union. This sheer cultural *usefulness*, along with the vertiginous lack of anything with which to replace the Brutan histories, also energized those that resisted their erosion. As noted in the Introduction, Edmund Bolton had expressed concern that their abandonment would leave a 'vast Blanck upon the Times of our Country, from the Creation of the World till the coming of Julius Caesar' (1722: sig. Cc2v–3r). For readers aware of this 'blanck', or even of its possibility, the playbooks explored here may have provoked a sometimes direct, sometimes peripheral, contemplation of this void. 'Who of nothing can something make?' (1606: sig. A2v) asks the prologue in *No-body and Some-body*, a play which forces its putatively historical Brutan monarch Elidure to share the stage with a character called Nobody. '[N]othing can come of nothing', *King Lear* replies (1608: sig. B2r; 1997: 1.1.90).

Intentionally or otherwise, Brutan drama evoked etiological erosion even as that etiology was being deployed to 'reunite' England and Scotland, kingdoms supposedly created by Brute's originary division of Britain. The possible influence of the London edition of James VI and I's book of advice to his son Henry, *Basilikon Doron* (1603), on Anthony Munday's *Triumphs of Re-United Britania* (1605) shows how official appropriation of historiography might influence drama. Further, this was increasingly a public, rather than a historiographical, debate. A sequence of Latin poems by John Ross of the Inner Temple attests to the public nature of the Brutan controversy in the early Jacobean period. *Britannica* (1607) recounts the Brutan histories' core narrative and demonstrates the continued engagement with those histories on the part of London's legal community (Hardin 1992: 235). In an appended 'apology', Ross echoes the official defence of Brutan historicity as proving Britain's originary unity and therefore supporting James's plan for union: 'we are to be transformed from English and Scotsmen and be called Britons once more' (2010). Yet Ross also characterizes the public debate surrounding the Brutan histories as emotive and suffused with doubt:

> For the question of whether Brutus existed or not is on all men's lips. Good God! Nowadays what is not called

into question by these petty little doubts? In meetings, at banquets, in assemblies, even in barbershops men wrangle over this. . . . I do not desire to conjecture what any man might feel or whisper about this thing, since I am quite familiar with the fact that nothing is ever so well-polished, nothing can be so complete, as they say, down to its very fingertips, which other men (and learned ones at that) cannot rip it to shreds. (2010)[1]

I am interested in the 'petty little doubts' identified by Ross, and how these might have worked upon readers and spectators of Brutan drama. Unlike Ross, I will conjecture what some may have been provoked to 'feel or whisper' regarding these doubts, and how *Leir*, *No-body and Some-body* and *King Lear* might have agitated this uncertainty, much as Anne Lake Prescott has described the historiographer John Selden's sceptical 'illustrations' to *Poly-Olbion* (1612) as eroding Michael Drayton's Brutan themes 'like acid eating a book from its edges' (Prescott 1991: 309). Hadfield describes Drayton's engagement with the question of union in *Poly-Olbion* as 'beset by nervous anxiety and division' (2004: 160). Radicalizing and foregrounding this erosion, anxiety and doubt, however, was the public utilization of the Brutan histories in the service of James VI and I's union project, a strategy that appeared to originate with James himself.

The playbooks explored in this chapter were published between 1605 and 1608, when questions of nationhood and 'Britishness' were triggered by James VI and I's recent accession to the English throne. The accession 'gave an additional impetus' to the Brutan histories (Parry 2000: 156). It was argued that James was reuniting Brute's sundered Britain, rather than splicing together two discrete and traditionally hostile nations. Of course, the same self-serving precedent had been used by Edward I to the Pope in 1301, and later by Henry VIII in 1542. James's project 'was so prominent in public discourse' that it served as a particularly potent and complex theme for playmakers (Marcus 1988: 148). Yet, despite a rush of panegyrics and enthusiastic 'British' materials printed in the immediate wake of James's accession, these dutiful and perhaps strategic expressions of unificatory optimism may have been propagandizing a sentiment that was neither deeply nor widely felt. As Jenny Wormald puts it 'the name of Britain might be on at least some men's lips, but the concept of Britain was repugnant to their minds' (1994: 29–30). In fact, James's struggles and debates with his English parliament to create 'Great Britain' are summarized by Conrad Russell as 'one single reiterated point: the House of Commons said "no" . . . With each "no", James retreated to a smaller request, but the "no" remained the same' (2011: 127). I suggest that the faltering progress and ultimate failure of James's union project can be figuratively mapped onto the nature and publication of Brutan playbooks in the period. In particular, the 1603 London edition of *Basilikon Doron* exercised an authorizing effect upon Munday's 1605 Lord Mayor's Show, *The Triumphs of Re-United Britania*, which spectacularly performed the narrative of Brute and his sons before Londoners and London's livery companies in order to configure James as a 'second Brute'.

In the 1603 edition of *Basilikon Doron*, James VI of Scotland advised his young son, Henry, to beware the dangers of dividing the realm between heirs: 'by deuiding your kingdomes, yee shall leaue the seed of diuision and discord among your posteritie; as befell to this Ile, by the diuision and assignement thereof, to the three sonnes of Brutus, Locrine, Albanact, and Camber' (1603: sig. H2r). It seems revealing that James would turn to the Brutan histories when considering both good rulership and the division of Britain. However, the passage relating to Brute and his sons did not appear in the book's original version, which was published in a limited run of seven copies in Edinburgh in 1599 (Shapiro 2015: 39–40). It was inserted later, into the English edition published in London in the wake of Elizabeth I's death in March 1603. This suggests that the text was amended with a specifically English readership in mind, one familiar with and receptive to, or believed to be familiar with and receptive to, the use of

Brutan history as a tool of persuasion. In appropriating Brutan history, *Basilikon Doron* was not only favouring English histories over the Scottish alternative but also negating the influence of James's former tutor, George Buchanan (1506–82), of whom Williamson argues that 'no single intellect from the British Isles had greater impact on the political culture of the late sixteenth century' (2008: 49). Buchanan had argued for a model of constitutional monarchy that allowed for the deposition of bad rulers (Abbott 2004), and this was the argument that he worked to instil in the young James; and he supported this through myriad examples from Scotland's own history. Indeed, Buchanan was as enthusiastic a proponent of Scotland's own received 'ancient' history as John Bale or Richard Harvey were of the Brutan histories, hence Harvey's attack on the long-dead Buchanan in *Philadelphus*. However, accounts of Scottish antiquity shared with the Brutan histories issues of fictiveness and, despite the familiar claim of providing access to remote antiquity and consequential founders, these also had medieval origins.

Scotland's antiquity had been created by John of Fordun in the late fourteenth century as a direct response to Edward I's invocation of the Brutan histories to claim suzerainty over Scotland. According to Fordun, 'the progenitors of the Scottish race were a Greek prince named Gathelus (the Greeks did after all defeat the Trojans!) and the eponymous Scota, daughter of Pharaoh, whom Galethus married *circa* 1500BCE' (Mason 1987: 64). Fordun was followed by Hector Boece's *Scotorum Historiae* (Edinburgh, 1540), which, like Geoffrey's *Historia*, claimed access to previously unknown sources to illuminate the most ancient Scottish history, which Fordun had left 'virtually blank' (Mason 1987: 65). Boece's text subsequently served as the foundation for Buchanan's *Rerum Scoticarum Historia* (Edinburgh, 1582), which featured a sustained and furiously argued attack on the historicity of Brute while simultaneously refusing to accept that 'the first seven centuries of Scottish history as retold by Boece were a fabrication' (Mason 1987: 74). Boece's writings featured a sequence of forty ancient kings deposed by the Scottish people for their various evil actions, conveniently providing Buchanan with the model for the supposed 'Ancient Constitution' of Scotland, by which, '"the people" elected and deposed kings'; this history was used to demonstrate to Elizabeth that the Scottish people were authorized in their 1567 deposition of Mary, Queen of Scots, James's mother (Wormald 1991: 40). The tensions between James, Buchanan and James's exiled mother are usefully summarized by Wormald: 'James was educated – savagely – by the man who was Mary's most outspoken and vicious critic, and whose personal attack on her had been subsumed into a political theory which made James's power ultimately dependent on the will of the community' (1991: 43).

Unsurprisingly, James would eventually repudiate Buchanan's intellectual legacy. In 1584, two years after Buchanan's death, the Scottish Parliament suppressed his *Rerum Scoticarum Historia* and *De Iure Regno apud Scotos* (*c.* 1567; pub. Edinburgh, 1579). This repudiation extended to Buchanan's historiography, as James sought to construct arguments for monarchical absolutism that would have been anathema to his old tutor. To this end, James's *True Lawe of Free Monarchies* (Edinburgh, 1598) 'rewrites Scottish history' by eliminating Boece's forty spurious kings (Wormald 1991: 45). *True Lawe* turns instead to 'the arguably historical figure of Fergus, fifth-century king of the Scots of Dalriada' (Wormald 1991: 44–5). Fergus was said to have settled a barely inhabited Scotland, demonstrating to James's satisfaction that 'Kinges were the authors & makers of the lawes' (1996: 69).

The London edition of *Basilikon Doron* in 1603, then, with its inserted reference to Brute and his sons, rejected or suppressed two Scottish historiographies, Boece's ancient kings and King Fergus, in favour of the Brutan histories that provided justification for British (re)union. In doing so, *Basilikon Doron* prioritized English readers, and English historiography, over their Scottish counterparts. Citing an unpublished study by Peter Blayney, Wormald narrates the 'dramatic' London publication of *Basilikon Doron*. Within four days of Elizabeth's death on 24 March 1603, James's book appeared in the Stationers' Register, and by 13 April it is likely that eight editions were issued, with between 13,000 and 16,000 copies printed overall: one stationer, Edward Allde, was fined for pirating, while the official publisher, John Norton, was fined for overcharging (Wormald 1991: 51).[2] The book was phenomenally successful, suggesting that 'Londoners were busily reading it for clues about the new king' (Goldberg 1983: 55). James Forse has argued that *Basilikon Doron* provides evidence that 'James knew his legendary British history' (2014: 56). However, the insertion of the reference to Brute and his sons might instead suggest collaborative intervention. John Norton was a 'friend to [Robert] Cecil', Elizabeth's secretary of state and a possible recipient of the Edinburgh edition of *Basilikon Doron* that was used as copy for the London editions (Wormald 1991: 51). James's manuscript for *Basilikon Doron* shows that, among its many crossings-out and amendments, there is no mention of Brute or Locrine.[3] Thus the insertion of Brute's narrative may have been at the suggestion, or even the instigation, of Cecil or the text's London stationers, creating perhaps the most widely disseminated episode of Brutan history in early modern print. *Basilikon Doron* was translated into thirty languages (Wormald 1991: 51), the Welsh edition including a preface foregrounding its Brutan context (McManus 2008: 189). It was also adapted to appeal to the perceived historical consciousness of James's new subjects. In the aftermath of the accession, this recourse to apparently outmoded but identifiably English, rather than Scottish, historiography would have a powerful effect on playmakers and stationers – although by the time many of these texts began appearing in print from 1605, James's union project had stalled in Parliament (Hill 2008: 20). In 1604, however, the use of Brutan themes in the service of the new Jacobean regime was visible in the responses of pageant writers. Even here, however, a theme emerges in which the celebratory use of Brutan history in pageant performance is undermined in print by paratextual intervention.

While deference to Brutan truth seems to have often been considered a required ingredient for celebrations of the incoming king, some invoked Brute with apparent reluctance. The entertainments prepared for James's royal entry into London in 1604 were, as Parry notes, 'dense with meaning' and detail 'extravagantly superfluous to the occasion' (1981: 3). Yet neither text foregrounds Brutan themes or iconography, although Brute is indicated as a source of James's legitimacy by Thomas Dekker, who has the allegorical figure Circumspection speak of James wearing a 'triple Diadem, / Weying more than that of thy grand Grandsire Brute' (1604: sig. F1v), and there is a reference to Brute's division of Britain (sig. I1r). Ben Jonson's text is even more circumspect, featuring only a passing reference to 'Brutus plough' (1604: sig. B3r). The printed edition of Jonson's contribution, *B. Ion: His Part of King Iames His Royall and Magnificent Entertainement*, demonstrates a discomfort with Brutan themes that would, on the evidence of the printed dialogue, have been absent from the pageant's performance: 'Rather then the Citie shuld want a Founder, we choose to folowe the receiu'd story of *Brute,* whether fabulous, or true, and not altogether vnwarranted in Poetrie: since it is a fauor of Antiquity to few cities, to let them know their first Authors' (sig. B3r).

If this disclaimer, or justification, for his passing reference to Brute, echoes that of Camden's *Britannia*, it's worth noting that Camden had been Jonson's much-admired tutor at Westminster College (Parry 2000: 157). Jonson's annotation is another demonstration of the intellectual contortions that many found necessary when confronted by an etiology that, while triggering Ross's 'little doubts', was popular, emotive and useful to the Jacobean moment. Yet Jonson appears to recoil. In contrast, Anthony Munday's *The Triumphs of Re-United Britania*, in performance at least, gave the Brutan histories what was perhaps their most spectacular and full-voiced embodiment of the early modern era.

Lord Mayor's Shows celebrated the structures and power of London's authorities. In utilizing the City itself as their arena of performance, they reached huge audiences and could draw upon substantial material resources. These were '*public* events, witnessed by thousands' and 'some of their more spectacular qualities far exceeded those that the playhouses were able to stage' (Hill 2010: 118). In some ways, *The Triumphs of Re-United Britania* was a strange occasion for a rhapsody on James's accession and British union. Putatively a celebration of the investiture of the Merchant Taylor, Sir Leonard Holliday as Lord Mayor of London, it was a civic, rather than a royal event; local, rather than national. James himself was absent, represented in the Show by an empty chair (Hill 2008: 23). As Manley notes, '[t]he history of London street pageantry is practically identical with the history of collaboration and conflict between the twin jurisdictions of the Crown and the City' (2011: 216). What was true in London was true of England at large, and *Triumphs* was in many ways a continuation of the tradition of resurrecting Brutan founders as mediating figures between civic authorities and the monarchy.

Triumphs features an entry led by '*Corineus* and *Goemagot*, appearing in the shape and proportion of huge Giants' (1605: sig. B1r). These were almost certainly the traditional pageant figures so familiar to Londoners, bound with 'chaines of golde' (1605: sig. B1r). They drew behind them a 'Mount triangular', or what appears to have been a pyramid-shaped pageant representing Britain, upon the tiers of which stood children costumed as figures of Brutan etiology. A sense of historiographic integrity, of presenting these figures as emerging from an identifiable past, is evident in Brute's costuming 'in the habite of an aduenturous warlike *Troyan*' (sig. B1v). Brute is performed alongside his three sons, also costumed 'in their antique estates' (sig. B2r), and 'female representations' of their kingdoms, Loegria, Cambria and Albania, as well as children representing Britannia, Troya Nova and the rivers Humber, Savarne and Thamesis (sig. B1v). Brute announces their reanimation and return, that 'after so long slumbring in our toombes / Such multitudes of yeares, rich poesie . . . does reuiue vs to fill vp these roomes' (sig. B3v). As Philip Schwyzer notes, 'there are two separate resurrections heralded here: that of Brutus and his kin, who are awakened from death . . . and that of Britain itself' (2008: 37). If *Locrine* enacts the ways in which the deaths of Brutan founders instil the landscape with their essence, *Triumphs* reverses that play's suicidal infusion through collective rebirth. Britain's founders are resurrected and its topography joyfully doubled and embodied.

Richard Dutton argues that Munday focused on Brutan tropes because their 'allusions and the symbolism were part of the common discourse of the time' (1986: 143). Yet, in its theme and dialogue, the pageant seems highly targeted, perhaps even drawing directly from *Basilikon Doron*. The three kingdoms, as Munday explains in his description of the 'Pageant', take turns recounting the events of Locrine's reign and serve to 'reproue [Brute], for his ouermuch fond loue to his sons, and deuiding' Britain into three (1605: sig. B1v). The princes themselves speak next. Albanact, representing Scotland, serves as an agent introducing James to England: 'I bring that Monarch now into the field, / With peace and plenty in his sacred hand' (sig. B4r). The visual effect of the pyramid-shaped pageant, which was large enough to hold twelve children, must have been impressive, its passengers' voices harmonizing in the service of unity. Yet Hill notes that Savarne and Thamesis's description of James as 'great Britaines King' (sig. B4v), as performed and printed at the end of 1605, might have served less as a compliment and more as a 'reminder that the English parliament were still refusing to countenance the title' (2008: 20). Yet despite, or perhaps because of, this, the pageant is relentless, almost incantatory, proclaiming James a 'second Brute' no less than four times (sig. B1v–B2r; sig. B3v; sig. B4v; sig. C3r).[4] *Triumphs*, perhaps, can make this comparison without risking the insinuation that James will repeat Brute's perceived error of dividing his kingdom precisely because this is the very mistake identified and foregrounded in *Basilikon Doron*: Brute is thus revived not as a warning from the past but as proof that the lesson of history has been, or is about to be, assimilated and learned. In performance, this endorsement and its supporting historiography are presented as triumphant and unequivocal. But, in print, Brutan historicity is compromised from the text's opening sentence.

Anthony Munday 'was a writer whose career regularly demonstrates his willingness to exploit any chance that came his way', and as such he might be expected to 'trade explicitly on . . . the union of nations that the king hoped his reign would bring about' (Hill 2008: 18). This is doubly likely when Munday was writing at the behest of his own livery company, the Merchant Taylors. There appears to be 'a degree of congruence between the number of copies of Shows printed . . . and the number of livery members of the Companies that commissioned them' (Hill 2010: 220), raising the possibility that *Triumphs*, in its printed form, served as either a programme for, or memento of, the performance. If so, this would have localized its distribution to a tightly specific textual community, one that seems to have endorsed and celebrated the Brutan histories: Munday's introduction is a retelling of the Brute story taken 'virtually *verbatim*' from Holinshed (Dutton 1986: 141). Yet from its opening sentence, *Triumphs* in print introduces doubt. Agency for this intervention is given to the Merchant Taylors, to which Munday belonged and from whom he claims it was 'earnestly solicited', to address the 'variable opinions' relating to ancient Britaine: 'Because our present conceit, reacheth vnto the antiquitie of *Brytaine,* which (in many mindes) hath carried as many and variable opinions: I thought it not vnnecessary, (being thereto earnestly solicited) to speake somewhat concerning the estate of this our Countrey' (1605: sig. A2r). The passage's confusing syntax buzzes with dissonance. In acknowledging, indeed opening, with such doubts, the quarto of *Triumphs* presents a far more damaged and wavering vision of Brutan history than the performed version. It might be read that there are 'many and variable opinions' carried in the 'many mindes' of numerous individuals or, both additionally and alternatively, that each of these 'mindes' carries churning within it 'many and variable opinions', that is, multiple and unstable conceptions of the past. If Hill is correct, and copies of Munday's text were

distributed to guild members present at the performance of
Triumphs, this presents a vivid example of the ways in which
the reception of Brutan drama was determined by factors such
as literacy and textual community. Spectators viewing only
the pageant would experience an unequivocal endorsement
of Brutan history and its meaning for, and authorization of,
the Jacobean moment. Those with the social capital to access
the text, however, could not help but encounter its equivocal
prose introduction, opening guild members' minds to doubt
even as the Brutan celebration they had paid for was filling
London's streets with bombastic noise and spectacle in the
name of James's British union. These 'little doubts' and 'variable
opinions' surrounding the Brutan histories may have fed back
into doubts regarding the desirability of union. Doubt in one,
in other words, perhaps agitated doubt in the other. These
concerns also encompass the material presented in *Leir*, *No-
body and Some-body* and *King Lear*. The following sections
explore how a sense of etiological erosion might be triggered
by reading these plays in the early Jacobean context of an
emergent and often resisted 'British' future.

   Leir, *No-body and Some-body* and *King Lear* belonged to
a – probably accidental – micro-genre of Jacobean printed
drama that, while brief and thinly populated, nonetheless had
the potential to bear meaning for early modern readers: the
Brutan 'true chronicle history' play. The phrase appears on the
title pages of five Jacobean playbooks, all of which address
British history. Of these five, four address British antiquity.
These include the plays named earlier and *The Valiant
Welshman* (1615), attributed on its title page to 'R.A.' and
set in the immediately post-Brutan Roman Britain that blurs
with the themes and character types of *Cymbeline*. Tellingly,
in the wake of *Leir*, *No-body and Some-body* and *King Lear*,
'True chronicle historie' also appears on the title page of the
1610 edition of the *Mirror for Magistrates*, which announces
its temporal reach back to 'the first entrance of Brute into
this iland'. This generic designation may have, cumulatively,
worked to bind these plays together in readers' minds. Yet the

focus on historical truth seems, and may have seemed, ironic, a triple tautology, protesting too much, given the widening public doubt in the Brutan histories attested by Munday and Ross. That the term 'true chronicle history' is usually only addressed by critics in relation to *King Lear* overlooks the fact that Shakespeare's play was the fourth playbook in six years to be so defined. In other words, it was a late entry into an established print subgenre. The designation first appears on the title page of the anonymous *The True Chronicle Historie of the Whole Life and Death of Thomas Lord Cromwell*, a Lord Chamberlain's Men play published by William Jones in 1602. There seems little to connect *Cromwell* to *Leir*, the second play to carry the designation, beyond a few similarities of action. *Leir*'s stationer, John Wright, would come to know Jones, since he purchased the rights to the popular *Mucedorus* from Jones's widow in 1618 (McKerrow 1910: 160). Wright seems to have looked to Jones's *Cromwell* when preparing *Leir*, which was his first published playbook (Michie 1991: 5). The trend continued the following year with John Trundle's 1606 playbook *Nobody, and Some-body, With the True Chronicle Historie of Elydure*. *King Lear* followed in 1608, the updated *Mirror for Magistrates* in 1610, with *The Valiant Welshman* a somewhat later entry in 1615. I focus this interconnectedness on the plays in print, rather than more generally, in part because, in every case, the playbook title pages differ from the titles recorded in the Stationers' Register.[5] In each case the genre designation 'true chronicle history' appears to have been chosen by the stationers over the titles inherited from the copy texts they had received, or at least as these are recorded in the Stationers' Register. Coincidental or otherwise, the 'true chronicle history' designation interconnected a series of texts that, in their language, forms and dramaturgy, might seem to manifest the processes through which the Brutan histories were becoming exiled from historicity and 'banished from the library to the chimney corner' (Morse 2013: 123). The first of these Brutan playbooks, *Leir*, erodes its own historicity by dislocating its action from antiquity into the Christian epoch.

Leir

To examine *Leir* within the Jacobean moment is to uproot the play from the conditions of its earliest recorded performance at the Rose in 1594, and to examine it instead as a 1605 Jacobean playbook.[6] To ask why stationers chose to publish Brutan plays at all at this time – beginning with the more-than-decade-old *Leir* – is to pose productive questions about the interests of those stationers' customers. *Leir*, a play about a king's division of Britain and the kingdom's subsequent happy reunion, would have been topical at any time in the first years of James's reign. Zachary Lesser argues that it is possible to move 'from the readings that publishers imagine', when they select which texts to invest in, 'to the meanings that their customers made out of these books' (2004: 17–18). In 1605, the meanings made by purchasers of *Leir* would have been shaped by the relevance of its Brutan subject to the rhetoric of union and, perhaps more directly, to events current in the royal household. This utility also highlighted the play's function as an account of history; a perspective that, perhaps paradoxically, might provoke a sense of historical dissonance.

Lesser suggests that we ask of any early modern playbook 'why does it exist?' (2004: 81). For *Leir*, I ask why John Wright chose this particular old play as his first playbook. Referring to the title page's claim that the play had been 'sundry times lately acted' (1605: sig. A1r), Clegg admits that '[w]e cannot be certain why *Leir* was currently being revived in print and, likely in repertory' (2008: 17). James's struggle with Parliament to bring about the union of England and Scotland seems to have been in a hiatus in 1605, and a Parliament that had 'originally been prorogued to 7 February 1605' was further postponed, possibly to avoid the embarrassment of admitting to the king's financial difficulties (Russell 2011: 43). In October, James abandoned a plan to make union a key focus of the new parliament, due to the recalcitrance of both the Scottish and English parliaments (46). Upon reopening in November, any anticipated order of parliamentary business was, figuratively, blown to pieces by the discovery of the Gunpowder Plot, which became the urgent subject of James's only speech to Parliament that year and, for 1606, Russell notes that 'the entire failure of the Union to appear in the public business . . . is one of the key facts' of that year's Parliament (46). Thus, while union was in the air, as manifested in *Triumphs*, it was not in motion. There is, however, an additional parallel that may connect *Leir* to the Jacobean moment, at least within the field of possible allusions available to its first readers.

In 1605, King James and Queen Anna's daughter, Mary, was born. Mary was not only the first Stuart born in England but also the first English royal birth since 1537. The event triggered widespread celebration, including bonfires lit by London's citizens and bells ringing throughout the day (Brown 1994: 69–70). Mary's birth was a major event both in London and nationally, but has received little attention in the context of the formative years of the Jacobean era, despite being considered significant enough, as Leeds Barroll mentions, to be recorded along with a lengthy account of her baptism in the continuation of Stow's *Annals* (1615: f. 862–4). Public prayers, first for Anna's safe delivery and then in thanks for Mary's birth, were published for reading aloud in churches (Carney 2013: 59). Barroll has stressed the theatrical qualities of the rituals surrounding the birth, from the extraordinary cost of Anna's lying in bed to James's immediate commissioning of the tombs of both Queen Elizabeth and 'his decapitated mother' (2001: 105) after whom the child was named, thus sublimating those monarchs, symbols of a divided past, through the advent of a newborn 'British' royalty. On 5 May, Mary was 'carried down from the queen's apartments' at Greenwich palace, and 'through the hall where the king was' before being taken to the chapel by a crowd of bishops, barons and peers for baptism (Barroll 2001: 106). Three days later, *Leir* was registered for publication.

At the time, this optimistic play about the estrangement and reunion of a pious British king and his beloved youngest daughter – a reunion that brings about the reunification of

Britain – may have seemed serendipitously appropriate. Cordella's exemplary filial virtues are signalled throughout. Before her first entrance the envious Gonorill complains that Cordella is 'so nice and so demure; / So sober, courteous, modest, and precise' (1605: sig. A3r). Cordella's pious humility is demonstrated in her claim to the disguised king of Gallia that '[m]y mind is low ynough to loue a Palmer, / Rather then any King vpon the earth' (sig. C3r). Here, virtue is conventionally, and lightly, expressed. Yet a more powerful demonstration of Cordella's significance appears in Leir's description of a terrifying dream, from which he awakes in the moment before a murderer, employed by Ragan and Gonorill, makes an attempt upon his life:

> Me thought, my daughters, Gonorill & Ragan,
> Stood both before me with such grim aspects,
> Eche brandishing a Faulchion in their hand,
> Ready to lop a lymme off where it fell,
> And in their other hands a naked poynyard,
> Wherwith they stabd me in a hundred places,
> And to their thinking left me there for dead:
> But then my youngest daughter, fayre Cordella,
> Came with a boxe of Balsome in her hand,
> And powred it into my bleeding wounds,
> By whose good meanes I was recouered well,
> In perfit health, as earst I was before.

> (1605: sig. F1v)

Leir's dream, which seems at first to offer a prophetic confirmation of his death, suddenly alters in tone, configuring Cordella as a miraculous and restorative force. Having been stabbed in 'a hundred places' by his two wicked daughters, Leir is revived by Cordella's act of pouring balsam into his wounds; for a reader in 1605, sensitive both to James's struggle for union and to the symbolic power of a new 'British' princess, *Leir* may have seemed particularly apposite and Cordella a key symbol of such renewal. Reunited, Cordella and Leir vie for one another's forgiveness, each repeatedly kneeling before the other. Leir asserts that it is 'my part to kneele, / And aske forgiuenesse for my former faults', and Cordella responds 'O, if you wish I should inioy my breath, / Deare father rise, or I receiue my death' (1605: sig. H4r). This creates a sense not only of filial duty but also of mutual restoration and ascension. Leir must 'rise' that Cordella can live; and Leir's later reply that, in welcoming him back Cordella 'gaue life to me' (1605: sig. H4r), speaks not only of his own life but also of the understanding that a king's life, and afterlife, depend upon the character and vitality of his heirs. Leir and Cordella mutually strengthen and renew one another in ways that may have spoken to readers in the months after Mary's birth when, symbolically at least, a sense of British renewal was embodied in the new princess. If the play's action resonated with events close to its publication, the present rather than the remote past, then its Christian setting also served to distance the narrative from history, estranging these characters from the chronicles' inexorable movement towards Cordella's eventual defeat and suicide. If so, this dislocation also rendered *Leir* untimely, uprooting its characters from the Brutan epoch and dislocating them from the continuum of world history presented in almanacs and chronicles, the continuum that underwrote the Brutan rhetoric of *Triumphs* and James's argument for union.

Genealogies and Brutan timelines were invaluable to James VI and I's self-legitimation and union project. In 1605, the genealogist Thomas Lyte was working on an illustrated table 'comprising nine parchment skins . . . over two metres wide and almost two metres high' that traced the Stuart ancestry from Brute and included a depiction of a temple of Janus said to have been founded by Lear (de Guevara 2013). Lyte's table shows the importance of situating forbears and ancestors securely within chronological space if they were to offer meaning and authority in the present. In contrast to this anchoring of King Lear's narrative within the Brutan–Stuart timeline, *Leir* disrupts Brutan temporality through pervasive Christian references, anachronisms that might be perceived as eroding the title page's claim to represent 'true chronicle history'. For *Leir*'s early Jacobean readers the play's dislocation of its Brutan narrative from the apparatus of world chronology – and thus from the continuity of royal descent – held the potential to trigger those 'petty little doubts' in Brutan historicity. These doubts may have been compounded and personified by the character Skalliger who, in a correlation that has gone almost unnoticed by critics, shares his name with two prominent early modern scholars, Julius Caesar Scaliger and his son Joseph Scaliger – the latter being the era's foremost theorist and collator of world chronology. These associations were available even to non-specialist readers, who could have encountered references to both Scaligers in a wide variety of texts.

Like *Locrine* and *Gorboduc*, *Leir* may digress or adapt, but it ends in secure alignment with the Brutan histories' genealogical continuity. However, the play extracts itself wholesale from wider accounts of the pre-Christian world, a concatenation of international historiographies known as 'universal history', representing the 'scholarly desire to impose some kind of order, some rational time scheme' upon world history (Ferguson 1993: 147). Universal history's macro-narrative accommodated biblical, classical and national narratives, and many historiographic texts provided marginal timelines or commentary that worked to situate a particular timestream within this wider context. For example, Holinshed anchors Lear, along with all Brutan kings, within universal chronology, stating that he ruled 'in the yeare of the world 3105, at what time Ioas reigned in Iuda' (1587: I, *Hist.* 12). In uprooting its narrative from this accepted chronology, *Leir* predisposes readers to contemplate the fragility of Brutan time. Biblical and Christian references infuse *Leir*'s language and temporality with the same insistence as *Locrine*'s relentless classical allusions and references to Locrine and Guendolen's wedding in the 'temple of Concordia' (1595: sig. C2r), or the clown Strumbo's dwelling by the temple of Mercury (sig. D3r), situate it within a pre-Christian, pagan time and landscape.

Of course, there will always be anachronisms, large and small, that are better attributed to playmakers' haste or imperfect knowledge than to authorial strategy, such as Gloucester's use of 'spectacles' in *King Lear* (1608: sig. C1v; 1997: 1.2.36). Stuart Piggott has argued that the 'propensity of early writers (and illustrators) to project the modern into the ancient world without any sense of what came to be known as anachronism, is a commonplace' (1988: 44). This is certainly true, but *Leir* does not so much 'bring the modern into the ancient world' as parachute the ancient and pagan into the Christian world. Christian imagery permeates the play, and Christian thinking drives its characters' beliefs and behaviour.

Leir's good counsellor, Perillus, calls upon 'iust Iehoua, whose almighty power / Doth gouerne all things in this spacious world' (1605: sig. F3v). Biblical references are precise rather than generalized: Leir compares an unexpected banquet to 'the blessed Manna, / That raynd from heauen amongst the Israelites' (sig. H2v–H3r) and, upon being reconciled with Cordella, offers her the same 'blessing, which the God of *Abraham* gaue / Vnto the trybe of *Iuda*' (sig. H4v). These Old Testament references could be argued to still, loosely, situate *Leir* within a pre-Christian, internationalist, Britain. Yet the characters exhibit explicitly Christian behaviour and references. Leir pledges to 'take me to my prayers and my beads', in the care of his daughters, 'the kindest Gyrles in Christen dome' (sig. C1r). The play's engagement with Christianity extends to referencing post-biblical figures such as the patron saints of, respectively, Paris and England, 'Saint *Denis,* and Saint *George*' (sig. I3r). These are invoked by the king of Gallia as he prepares for battle to restore Leir to his throne; they thus represent the two powers united both by Gallia's marriage to Cordella and by their joint support of Leir's cause. The play's references to post-Brutan, and post-biblical, Christianity are not mere decoration, but often offer thematic commentary. Taking in both Catholic doctrine and early modern Protestant caricature, Gonorill calls Cordella a 'Puritan' and threatens to 'make you wish your selfe in Purgatory' (sig. I3v). To present the wicked Goneril as adopting a term of abuse used towards those perceived as radical Protestants transports these Brutan figures into, and defines them via, the sectarian milieux and schisms of post-Reformation England. The more persistently *Leir*'s characters adopt the language of early modern Christianity, the more they dislocate Brutan time from its pre-Christian chronology. For some readers of the 1605 playbook, this dislocation – unremarkable in much early modern literature – has the potential to aggravate those dissonant 'petty little doubts' in Brutan historicity. This potential is amplified by the presence of the villainous character Skalliger.

Lord Skalliger, a character inserted into *Leir*'s Brutan plot by its playmakers, is a meddling, villainous adviser. He is textually prominent, the only character other than Leir to speak and be named on the play's opening page, thus prioritizing his presence and name. Skalliger's first action is to propose the fateful love test, that Leir should reward his daughters '[a]s is their worth, to them that love profess' (1605: sig. A2v), before immediately rushing off to 'bewray your [Leir's] secrecy' to Goneril and Ragan (sig. A3r). Thus Skalliger 'betrays Leir's confidence [and] it is Skalliger, not Leir, who supports giving a larger portion to the daughter who wins the love contest' (Brink 2008: 214). By instigating and manipulating the love test, Skalliger triggers the play's 'historical' events. His influence over the defining events of Leir's reign, then, is considerable. These interventions are almost dramaturgical, as Skalliger directs, even creates, events purporting to be historical. His authorizing agency and manipulation of 'history' become significant when we consider that Skalliger shares his unusual name with two renowned early modern French scholars. Apart from Sidney Lee's edition of the play (1909: xxxiv), critics have rarely noted, and never explored, the relationship between *Leir*, Julius Caesar Scaliger and, especially, his son Joseph Scaliger. Drawing attention to a 'villain' sharing these scholars' name, *Leir* also draws attention to the play's temporal dissonance.

The possible influence of the Scaligers upon *Leir* suggests evidence of an interaction between continental literary and historiographic theories, popular drama and Brutan history. Clare McManus has stressed the importance, when considering 'British' culture, of remembering that 'although it came late to the Renaissance, in its "high" cultural form at least, Britain consciously based its self-expression upon an idea of learning and a value system from beyond its own borders' (2008: 187). *Leir*'s Skalliger could have been interpreted as displaying, and perhaps satirizing, just such an influence. Julius Caesar Scaliger was a theorist of poetics and 'the most notorious of Renaissance categorizers' (Orgel 1979: 113). His *Poetices Libri Septem* (Lyons, 1581) sought to assiduously define and assert rules regarding literary and poetic genre. Scaliger's work was praised in Philip Sidney's *Defense of Poesie* (*c.* 1580; pub. 1595). Stephen Orgel has noted that both writers' resistance to drama derived from the fact that 'neither is capable of the minimally imaginative effort required by plays which ignore the unities of place or time' (1979: 115). *Leir*'s Skalliger may have appeared to some as a playmakers' rebuke against such 'limited' critiques of drama, pertinent to a play that, disregarding 'unities of place and time', leaps nations and dislocates itself from one temporality to another.[7]

It is Scaliger's son, Joseph Justus, however, who had the greater presence in English print by the Jacobean period, and who dedicated his career to perfecting a theory of universal chronology, the very system into which chronicles such as Holinshed's embedded Brutan history and from which *Leir* extracts itself. Scaliger junior addressed the problem of 'how to harmonise Biblical chronology with the chronologies of the other nations of antiquity' with his *De Emendation Temporum* (Paris, 1583) (Burke 1969: 47). *De Emendation* was 'lavishly illustrated with tables', and 'reduced all chronologies to a new one, the Julian' (Burke 1969: 47). Anthony Grafton outlines the significance of Joseph Scaliger's work: '[he] won renown for his reformation of the traditional approach to chronology', by combining and coordinating data from classical and biblical sources in an effort to detect 'gaps in the historical record [and] fill them by astonishing feats of historical detective work'

(2003: 77). His 'achievement inspired widespread excitement' (78), although attempts to unite so many disparate histories in a single timeline meant that his pagan chronologies often predated the creation of the world, which Scaliger defined as 'proleptic time' (Grafton 1975: 172). This caused acute historical dissonance; as Grafton asks, 'In what sense, if any, did he consider these dynasties to be real? What sort of history could be said to have happened before the Creation?' (1975: 173). Similarly, readers of *Leir* might have asked what kind of eighth century BCE British aristocrats might inhabit a Christendom of saints, palmers and puritans.

References to Joseph Scaliger, frequently praiseful, abound in English print. John Eliot's French primer, *Ortho-epia Gallica*, includes a translation of a poem by Bartas praising Scaliger as a polymath who

> Not by one onely Idiome
> his secrets to vnfold,
> But as the learned Scaliger,
> whom men the wonder hold
> . . . .
> O rich and supple spirit that can
> his tongue so quickly change,
> Cameleon-like into what author
> likes him best to range.

(1593: f. 17–18)

This poem was reproduced in a different translation in Robert Allott's poetry anthology *Englands Parnassus*, presenting Scaliger as an exemplary polymath, although its reference to Scaliger as 'wits Chamelion' (1600: f. 495) suggests a quality that, in the negative, could also apply to *Leir*'s Skalliger, who adapts his demeanour and honesty according to his schemes. Perhaps most allusive to *Leir*'s treatment of Scaliger is a reference from the clown Clove in Jonson's *Every Man Out of His Humour*. Clove cites Scaliger as 'the best Nauigator in his time' (1600: sig. H4v), thus suggesting, punningly, a figure adept at temporal orientation. *Leir* uproots itself from the Brutan chronology that was essential to its potential meanings and emphasizes this dislocation by naming the play's villainous instigator after the era's most famous custodian and theorist of universal history.[8] The mischievous manipulation of the play's 'historical' events by this character was not, perhaps, so different from the charges of manipulation and fictionalizing levelled at Geoffrey of Monmouth. Skalliger's final words before disappearing from the play appear to be in direct address:

> And me a villain, that to curry favour
> Have given the daughter counsel 'gainst the father
> But us the world doth this experience give,
> That he that cannot flatter, cannot live.

(1605: sig. C4v)

The appropriation and promotion of Brutan iconography by writers and stationers in support of James's union project could, like Skalliger's cynical invocation of 'experience', be perceived as disingenuous flattery of the monarch driven by self-interest. History, in this light, is a function of just the kind of political contingency that was driving the union project. In its new Jacobean context, the Elizabethan *Leir*'s temporal relocation and insertion of Skalliger combine in ways that might agitate Brutan certainties. If *Leir* enacts the dislocation of Brutan time, however, *No-body and Some-body* represents the Brutan histories' absorption into the semiotics of the play's subplot, which is characterized by the overwhelming repetition of the language of nothingness and non-being.

No-body and Some-body

This anonymous play was published under the full title *No-body, and Some-body, With the True Chronicle Historie of Elydure, Who Was Fortunately Three Seuerall Times Crowned*

King of England. It was probably written and performed around 1603–5 (Wiggins 2015: 5, ref. 1460). It was published for John Trundle, 'to be sold at his shop in Barbican, at the signe of No-body' (1606: sig. A1r). The sublimation of the play's historical story of the Brutan king Elidure to its subplot – the misadventures of the titular Nobody and his nemesis Somebody – thus began at the point of sale, beneath the presumably painted sign under which potential buyers would pass. This sublimation is reasserted before the playbook is even opened, via the title page's striking woodcut illustration of an actor in costume as Nobody, his breeches reaching to his neck, showing him as having no 'body' or physical torso, only a head and limbs, the centre amputated. Finally, within the play itself both the Brutan histories and James VI and I's conceptualization of Britain as 'one body' are undermined by association with *No-body and Some-body*'s negating and satirical dramaturgy and obsessively repetitive language of negation.

In his 1603 proclamation, James VI and I directed his subjects to consider England and Scotland 'presently united, and as one realme and kingdome, and the subjects of both the realms as one people, brethren and members of one body' (1973: 19). Later, in a speech given to Parliament in 1604 and published shortly after, James described himself as 'the head wherein that great body is united' (1994: 135). He claimed too that, not only was he husband to the realm, and that refusal of union would make him a bigamist, but also that 'I being the Head, should have a monstrous and diuided bodie' (136): '[o]ver and over again, the king's propagandists churned out the line that England and Scotland were now "one body". This is what their opponents denied' (Russell 2011: 130). This repetition might usefully be contrasted with *No-body and Some-body*'s opposing and negative terminology. The word 'nobody' is used over 150 times, becoming an incantatory, contaminating feature of the play's semiotic fabric that spills into embodiment in the figure of Nobody. From its opening prologue the play prods at the

impossibility of creation *ex nihilo*, a concept also at the heart
of Brutan anxieties:

> A subiect, of no subiect, we present, for No-body, is
>   Nothing:
> Who of nothing can something make?
> It is a worke beyond the power of wit,
> And yet inuention is ripe:
> A morrall meaning you must then expect, grounded on
>   lesser then a shadowes shadow:
> Promising nothing wher there wants a toong;
> And deeds as few, be done by No-bodie:
> Yet something, out of nothing, we will shew.
>
> (1606: sig. A2v)

The play prologues Nobody in language that pre-empts *King
Lear*'s annihilating 'nothing can come of nothing' (1606: sig.
B2r). Yet it also promises 'something, out of nothing', an
'invention' that turns out to be, with heavy irony, Nobody
himself. The relentless iteration of the word 'body', embedded
within the titular 'Nobody', also takes in Nobody's villainous
opposite, Somebody, creating a polarity and pairing that is as
'monstrous and diuided' as the severed realm of James's pro-
union rhetoric. The punning tension between the antagonists
allows for running social commentary, illustrated by the
response of Somebody's servant to the question of why
Nobody is widely admired:

> Come twentie poore men to his gate at once,
> Nobody giues them mony, meate and drinke,
> If they be naked, clothes, then come poore souldiers,
> Sick, maymd, and shot, from any forraine warres,
> Nobody takes them in, prouides them harbor,
> Maintaines their ruind fortunes at his charge,
> He giues to orphants, and for widdowes builds
> Almes-houses, Spittles, and large Hospitals,

And when it comes in question, who is apt
For such good deedes, tis answerd Nobody.

(1606: sig. B4r)

The joke, of course, is that in reality no one takes responsibility
for charity or caring for the poor, mutilated soldiers, orphans or
widows. Neither, it hardly needs to be added, does Somebody.
The play's prologue might also encompass and absorb
Elidure and the Brutan histories from which he was taken as
'something, out of nothing'. In fact, Elidure was already in
some ways culturally insubstantial, a relative Brutan nobody in
early modern print beyond the standard historiographic texts.

As the title of *No-body and Some-body* states, Elidure
was crowned king three times. His confusing narrative is
summarized in Stow's *Chronicles*: the corrupt King Archigallo
is dethroned by his subjects for having 'deposed the noblemen,
and exalted the vnnoble' and 'extorted from men their goods
to enriche his treasurie' (1580: f. 29). Archigallo is replaced
by his reluctant brother Elidure, 'a vertuous & gentle Prince,
who gouerned his people iustly' (f. 29). However, encountering
the deposed Archigallo while hunting, Elidure forgives his
brother, reconciles him with the nobility and restores him to
the throne. A chastened Archigallo rules wisely for ten years
before dying; Elidure is restored to the throne but his younger
brothers Vigenius and Peredurus rebel, usurp and rule together
until their deaths bring the virtuous Elidure to the crown for
the third time. *No-body and Some-body* squeezes this see-
sawing narrative into a play already boasting a prominent
subplot. Anthony Archdeacon has argued that 'the historical
plot is constantly teetering on the edge of comedy', citing an
episode where 'Vigenius and Peridure literally wrestle for the
crown' (2012: para. 19). Either way, any potential for serious
representation the historical plot may have carried is suffocated
by the subplot. In terms of the subplot's cultural and satirical
context, the play's provenance shows *No-body and Some-body*
emerging from a theatrical milieu of satire directed towards

James VI and I; a context in which Brutan historicity becomes collateral damage.

While James promoted union, his accession created the need for formal divisions in terms of the royal court, and three new courts were created, one for the king and two 'alternative centres of power in the Households of Queen Anne [*sic*] and Prince Henry' (Peck 1991: 14). The division of the court led to the development of separate cultural coteries and institutions reflecting each royal's self-presentation and tastes. These divisions were reflected in the theatrical culture, as 'all three resident theatre companies in London . . . were taken under royal patronage': the Admiral's Men became Prince Henry's Men, Worcester's Men became the Queen's Men and the Chamberlain's Men, famously, became the King's Men (Forse 2014: 66). *No-body and Some-body*, as the title page states, was 'acted by the Queens Maiesties Seruants' (1606: sig. A1r). Clowning seems to have been central to the company's status and the former Chamberlain's man, Will Kemp, was initially the 'undoubted leader of the company' (Griffith 2013: 71–2) before being replaced by the clown Thomas Greene, who became the 'named leader' after Kemp 'left, or died' in 1603 (83). The company's prominent clowns may be one reason for the playbook's prioritizing of its comic subplot.

The figure of Nobody had previously appeared in Jonson's 1603 entertainment for Queen Anna at Althorp, 'attired in a paire of Breeches which were made to come vp to his neck, with his armes out at his pockets, and a Cap drowning his face' (1604: sig. B2v). Taking place during Anna and Prince Henry's progress from Edinburgh to London, the entertainment 'highlights the public importance of the Queen and Prince Henry's arrival in the locality' and the wider importance of their progress in 'anchoring' the new regime (Knowles 2012: 395). The text of the Althorp entertainment was appended to Jonson's 1604 edition of *The Magnificent Entertainment*, producing an earlier Jacobean text in which 'Nobody' and Brutan themes subtly shared space. This coincidence is suggestive in terms of *No-body and Some-body*'s possible connections to Queen Anna's theatrical coterie (Wiggins 2015: 5, ref. 1460). Anna's companies were also associated with staging satirical plays, often at the expense of James and his Scottish nobles (McManus 2008: 194–5), as well as the king's perceived propensity for doling out peerages and wealth to his favourites.

The 'most significant of the anti-Scots theatrical satires, *Eastward Ho!* . . . and John Day's *The Isle of Gulls* (1606) were performed by the Children of the Queen's Revels', another company of which Anna was patron (McManus 2008: 195). Yet unlike these plays, *No-body and Some-body* seems to complexly embody (or rather dis-embody) the cultural moment rather than take a coherent satirical position. It was performed at a time when Scots were suffering assaults in London to the point that they 'kept away from the theatres and all parts of the town except Charing Cross' (Wormald 1994: 35). In *No-body and Some-body*, Nobody, new to London – or Troynovant as the play interchangeably calls the city – is attacked in the street, 'which made me fly / To the Thems side, desired a Waterman, / To row me thence away to Charing-crosse' (1606: sig. F1v). Many of the characters' virtues might as readily be applied to James and his Scots as the wickedness of others. In the play's opening exchange, the virtuous Elidure, yet to become king, speaks of royal primacy as an institution that 'Brookes not taxation' and that 'kings greatest royalties / Are that their subiects must aplaud their deedes, / As well as beare them' (1606: sig. A3v). This might have pleased James, whose *True Lawe of Free Monarchies* consisted in substantial part of multiple ingenious variations of the same sentiment, such as his insistence that the biblical king Nebuchadnezzar, a 'Tyrant, and vsurper of . . . liberties' should not only command the loyalty of his conquered subjects but also that they should 'pray for his prosperitie' (1994: 71). However, Elidure's position, and therefore the *True Lawe*'s, is challenged by the monstrous behaviour of King Archigallo, who is deposed in Buchanan-esque style by his lords, the Duke of Cornwall complaining that he has '[t]he Clergie late despisd, the Nobles scornd, / The Commons trode on, and the Law contemnd' (1606: sig. B2r). Cornwall's final point echoed current concerns, public and parliamentary, regarding James's view that union could be brought about by royal power alone. Yet this power depended upon conceptions of the 'marriage' between the monarch and the one body of the kingdom. As *No-body and Some-body* progresses, Elidure increasingly shares the stage with Nobody, 'a social hero who, rather uncomfortably for everyone, doesn't really exist' (Archdeacon 2012: para. 11). The performed, royal and Brutan, presence is thus drawn within the radius of a clown's costumed embodiment of 'nothing'. By inhabiting the same space as Elidure and his Brutan macro-narrative, Nobody weakens the integrity of both.

No-body and Some-body's personification of nothingness and creation *ex nihilo* were of course echoed in Jacobean debate over the Brutan histories: Elidure, it was argued, was also 'nobody'. He was not a historical king but a product of Geoffrey of Monmouth's twelfth-century fabrications, a parallel strengthened in the play by his generous and blameless character's similarity to Nobody. By the play's conclusion, negation is virulent. Nobody is exonerated by Elidure and the slanderous Somebody is executed, thus becoming a species of 'nobody' himself. This contamination is, for me, encapsulated in the semantic oscillation of the following stage direction: '*A fight betwixt Somebody and Nobody, Nobody escapes*' (1606: sig. D4r). In performance, the character Nobody makes a getaway offstage. On the page, the sense is more complex: the conflict between truth and untruth, being and non-being, between opposing historiographies, between history and satire, creates a vortex of doubt from which nobody and nothing can quite escape.

Nobody's 'escape' and his absorption of the play's Brutan context continued long after *No-body and Some-body*'s publication. The play was performed and heavily adapted by English players in Germany during the early seventeenth century. It was subsequently translated into German, surviving in a manuscript edition dated to 1608, a print version appearing in the multi-play volume, *Engelische Comedien vnd Tragedien*, published in Leipzig in 1620, and eventually manifesting as a scripted puppet show (Schlueter 2016: 235). In each iteration, Elidure and his Brutans are further subsumed. Nobody's plotline expanded from one-third of the play in the English version, to half in the Graz manuscript and to two-thirds in the 1620 volume (Schlueter 2016: 242). Further, the German translation was itself translated into Dutch, going through an impressive eight editions from 1645 to 1649 (Wiggins 2015: 5, ref. 1460). Thus, even as the obscure Elidure may have become one of the Brutan theatrical figures most widely read and performed beyond England, he becomes ever more in abeyance to his play's negating semiotics.

In the long term there would, of course, be very definite outcomes to the debates over the Brutan histories and to James's union project. The short term, however, as John Ross and Anthony Munday observed, was characterized by doubt, dissonance and conflict. Richard F. Hardin frames Ross's work as communicating 'his sense of the entire period from the settlement by Brutus to the exile of Cadwallader as a continuously woven fabric' (1992: 243). Echoing this text/textile metaphor, Escobedo describes the ways in which historiographers attempted to incorporate the Brutan histories into their visions of history: '[t]heir narratives resemble long tapestries that, even as they grow longer, produce their own rips and tears, forcing the weavers to go back and repair them' (2004: 3–4). However, the anxiety underlying this work is identified by Ross, who admits that 'nothing can be so complete, as they say, down to its very fingertips, which other men (and learned ones at that) cannot rip it to shreds' (2010). The following section redirects the examination of negative terms in *No-body and Some-body* towards *King Lear*, arguing that, if the play may be read as sensitive to the Brutan controversy, it might also be imagined as one of the sites wherein the Brutan histories themselves, already unthreaded from chronology in *Leir*, are ripped to shreds.

King Lear

In the version of *King Lear* published among the tragedies included in the 1623 folio of Shakespeare's plays, the Fool ends his topsy-turvy prophecy with a comment that situates him, and therefore the play, within the Brutan continuum: 'This prophecie *Merlin* shall make, for I liue before his time' (1623: f. 197; 1997: 3.3.95–96). However equivocally or satirically, the Fool's comment looks ahead to the post-Christian centuries of Arthur and Merlin (de Grazia 2013: 141). This passing expression of wider chronological context was not included in the play's 1608 quarto, resulting in its frequent reading as a play that transcends history, notably characterized by David Scott Kastan as existing in 'a time that offers neither restoration nor regeneration but only defeat and destruction' (1982: 102). However, just as the play has been shown to engage closely with early Jacobean questions of British unification, I suggest a particular textual quirk elided by subsequent editorial practice may have, like the presence of Skalliger in *Leir*, resonated with historical dissonance for the playbook's first readers in 1608–9.

According to Peter Blayney, few early modern printed playtexts contain as many 'self-evident blunders' as the first quarto of *King Lear* (1982: 184). For editors, one of the least apparently troubling of these 'blunders' occurs during Lear's recognition of his own rising madness: 'O how this mother swels vp toward my hart / *Historica passio* downe thou climing sorrow' (1608: sig. E4r; 1997: 2.2.247). The term '*Historica passio*' is almost universally emended in modern editions to '*Hysterica passio*'.[9] However, early modern stationers allowed the original reading to stand until F4 in 1685 (Halpern 1991: 215). This suggests that Q1's '*Historica*' was, or could be, received not as a misprint but as invoking some sense of historicity.[10] This association was perhaps strengthened for readers, even if only subliminally, by the phrase's appearance in Q1 only three lines below the running title, '*The Historie of King Lear*'. I suggest that *Historica passio* may be read as a coinage that, even if unfamiliar, could cause the reader to reflect upon its possible meanings, provoking reflection on the play's representations of 'true chronicle history', inviting a reading of its 'division of the kingdoms' not only as a historical or topical reference but also as resonant of a terminal division between Brutan and lived history. Richard Halpern, the only critic I have identified to accept and address the original reading, imagines *Historica passio* as 'the bearing or enduring or manifestation of historical force through one's person and one's body', produced by the tensions of representation between dramatic character and the 'historical actants – collective or impersonal' those characters represent (1991: 217). Halpern is discussing forces of historical change relevant to his reading of the play as exploring 'tension between feudal and proto-capitalist cultures' (216). But the physicality of his formulation is evocative and useful to the present reading, in which *King Lear* is read in the context of the Brutan histories' erosion. *Historica passio* thus becomes a term suggesting embodied historiographic crisis: a once-historical figure's agonistic experience of the process by which he becomes a fictional non-being.

King Lear was published in 1608, contemporaneous with Parliament's final rejection of James's union proposals, 'perhaps the most humiliating rebuff suffered by a Stuart king from the House of Commons' before the 1640s (Russell 2011: 62). James's vision of a 'reunited' Britain had proved no match for the resistance of both James's Scottish and English subjects who were, ironically, united in their opposition to union: '[p]olemicists demanded Union in the name of Henry VII, Henry VIII, in the name of Aeneas, Christ and the pagan gods, but the Commons saw the projected Union simply as the policy of a Scotsman called James' (Axton 1977: 135). The pro-unionists' arsenal of archetypes and dubious historical precedent naturally included the Brutan histories in which, late in the debate, even James may have conceded doubt; his 1607 speech makes reference to the historical precedence of English laws, but only 'if many famous histories be to be believed' (1994: 171). These famous histories were of course, for many, *not* to be believed. As noted, readings of *King Lear* as a 'union text' are well served. Analyses broadly pivot upon the question of whether *King Lear* presents Lear as James's disastrous antithesis, thereby supporting the union project, or as an analogue critiquing his perceived absolutism. Both readings are possible, of course, and Annabel Patterson highlights the play's 'flexible hermeneutics' (1989: 107). However, few have examined the play as a putatively historical narrative, the possible meanings of its location in British antiquity, or the ways it might resonate with the Brutan controversy. Reading closely between the presentation of the Brutan histories in *Triumphs* and *King Lear*, Richard Dutton notes that, in *Triumphs*, 'Brute rejoices in the power of poetry that has revived the characters of ancient legends, allowing them to witness the final resolution of the discord which their own actions had created' (1986: 142). *King Lear*, however, not only cancels the Brutan line through the childless deaths of Regan and Cornwall but also enacts 'violence' upon the Brutan histories 'as a whole' (146); that is, to their structural and historiographic integrity.[11] To read *King Lear* in 1608 was to encounter all aspects of this negative conjuration in the aftermath of failed union and, as has been less often observed, royal bereavement. Finally, *King Lear*'s language of negation, its insistence that 'nothing can come of nothing', had the potential to work upon a reader's perception of Brutan historicity.

While in conception and performance *King Lear* may have included James's union project among its authorizing effects, as a 1608 playbook it may have read like an autopsy for that same project. Further, as previously noted, James and Anna's daughter Mary had been born in May 1605. Mary died on 16 September 1607 (Weir 1996: 251). Another daughter, Sophia, had both been born and died in June that year (Carney 2013: Appendix 1, 8). A sense of tragically lost British futurity may have been mirrored in the play's savage depiction of filial death and parental grief, epitomized in Lear's mental collapse as he cradles Cordelia's body: 'why should a dog, a horse, a rat of life and thou no breath at all, O thou wilt come no more,

neuer, neuer, neuer' (1608: sig. L4r; 1997: 5.3.307).[12] Two
months after Mary's death, on 26 November, *King Lear* was
logged with the Stationer's Register (*DEEP* 2007: ref. 517).
This sense of belatedness might also infect the play's perceived
status as history. To situate *King Lear* in Brutan time is not,
however, to mitigate its annihilating energies, but to extend
those energies' effects to Brutan historicity, and therefore to
the play's macro-narrative. Philip Schwyzer argues that the
play's temporal closed system derives from a rejection of 'the
nostalgic spirit of nationalism', resulting in a narrative that is
'thorough in its dismantling of the figurative technologies of
the union campaign', cancelling the means 'by which the past
can reach forward and touch the present' (2008: 45, 42). Yet,
etiological erosion goes further than this; the Brutan past is not
only severed from the present but also erased in, and *as*, the
past. The division of the play's characters from their audience
and putative descendants might be conceived not as the vast
but navigable temporal division between the once-living and
their ancestors, but the void between lived reality and fiction,
closing the channel between past and present that is opened in
the 1486 Brutan pageants and in *Gorboduc*. In short, for some
of its first readers *King Lear* may have appeared disturbingly
aware of its collapsing historiographic macrostructure. Reading
King Lear in this context invites the strange question of how
it might feel physically to suffer the kind of historiographic
rejection the Brutan histories were undergoing, a *Historica
passio* – Halpern's 'manifestation of historical force through
one's person and one's body' – and how that suffering might
be expressed.

In this reading, Lear embodies what Ross characterizes
as the unhappy loss of Brutan history, as if the histories
themselves could physically and emotionally experience
their own implosion into the 'vast blanke' of which Edmund
Bolton had warned. Ross frames the Brutan histories' critics as
thankless, warning that '[i]f they ungratefully reject it . . . they
unhappily lose it' (2010); Lear also fixates on gratitude and
loss, complaining that his daughters' ingratitude has 'wrencht

my frame of nature from the fixt place' (1608: sig. D2r; 1997: 1.4.260). He defiantly pledges to reclaim the status of king that he has surrendered, and to 'resume the shape which thou dost think I have cast off forever' (sig. D2v; 1.4.301). Here, Lear's words also resonate with those fighting to sustain the Brutan histories within the 'fixt place' of English time and universal history from which they were being 'wrencht' and in which they had only ever been a forged entry. In his madness, Lear, too, denies forgery, crying 'they cannot touch me for coyning. I am the king himself' (sig. I3v; 4.6.83–4). In evoking a monarch's authority to licence the creation of money, he also invites the double sense that the 'king himself' is counterfeit. The *Historica passio*, however, overpowers these objections.

At York in 1486, in *Gorboduc*, in Elizabeth I's entry to Norwich and in *Triumphs* in 1605, Brutan figures and narratives were used in performances before, or invoking, the monarch, as a means of navigating questions of local or national transformation. These figures often spoke a language of temporal resilience and as entities that had endured across millennia. To place Lear within this tradition for a moment, if not as a pageant figure then as a Brutan ruler performed before an English monarch, this transtemporal privilege and authority collapses:

> Doth any here know mee? why this is not *Lear*, doth *Lear* walke thus? speake thus? where are his eyes, either his notion, weaknes, or his discernings are lethergie, sleeping, or wakeing; ha! sure tis not so, who is it that can tell me who I am? *Lears* shadow. (1608: sig. D1v; 1997: 1.4.216–21)

In the Norwich entry, King Gurgunt has the temporal resilience 'in presence to appeare' before the monarch after '[t]wo thousand yeares welnye in silence lurking still' (1578: sig. B3r) so that he might assert his Brutan lineage and that of his descendants, just as Ebrauk had declared himself the source of Henry VII's 'progenie' at York. Lear, in contrast, has only questions, and anxiously calls for the renewed remembrance of an identity that appears to be slipping from him. Similarly, Brute's announcement in *Triumphs* that 'after so long slumbring in our toombes / Such multitudes of yeares, rich poesie . . . does reuiue vs' (1605: sig. B3r) repeats Gurgunt's formula of a vital awakening. Lear, experiencing *Historica passio*, cannot discern between 'sleeping, or wakeing'. The historiographic force that had enabled Gurgunt's 'presence' and Brute's revivification is terminally weakened. Lear cannot define himself and, less than an embodied Brutan founder or inhabitant of lived history he has become '*Lears* shadow' or, to cite *No-body and Some-body*, a 'shadowes shadow', a secondary effect of something that is itself without substance, the nothing that comes of nothing. Lear's authority thus collapses into an impotent stammer: 'I will haue such reuenges on you both, / That all the world shall, I will doe such things, / What they are yet I know not, but they shalbe / The terrors of the earth, you thinke ile weepe' (1608: sig. F2v–F3r; 1997: 2.2.469–71). Without historical authority Lear becomes incoherent, intermingling Jacobean and Brutan questions of power. He complains that '[t]hey told me I was every thing, tis a lye' (1608: sig. I3v; 1997: 4.6.103–4). Brute as rejected Brutan founder and James, rejected British unifier and notional occupant of *Triumphs*'s empty chair, might have sympathized.

It is not only Lear but his fellow Brutans and their containing narrative that are subject to erosion. Attacking Cordelia, the woman who in the Brutan histories was to become his royal successor, Lear berates her 'little seeming substance' (sig. B3v; 1.1.199), claiming that 'we have no such daughter' (sig. B4v; 1.1.264–5), configuring her first as flimsily transparent, then in some way non-existent. Even Albany, representative of James's Scotland and the only Brutan to survive, exclaims that he too is 'almost ready to dissolue' (sig. L2v; 5.3.202). When the potential for futurity is restored at the play's conclusion, this is achieved through the Brutan histories' displacement by a synthesis of characters drawn from a subplot lifted from Philip Sidney's *Arcadia* and a more securely historical Anglo-Saxon dynasty. *King Lear*'s Gloucester subplot is adapted from the

Arcadia's 'story of the Paphlagonian King and his two sons' (Dutton 1986: 147). Dutton also notes that Shakespeare's choice of the name of Gloucester's son Edgar gestures towards an Anglo-Saxon king with a claim to being 'the first historical (as distinct from mythological) King of Britain' (1986: 148). This realignment may also have resonated with Richard Verstegan's contemporaneous *Restitution of Decayed Intelligence* (1605), which argued that the Saxons, rather than the ancient Brutans, were 'the racial and cultural source of modern England' (Escobdeo 2008: 75). Yet, just as in *Leir* the presence of Skalliger might trigger readerly preoccupations with the Brutan histories' chronological and historiographic security, it is the *Arcadia*-derived subplot that can be perceived as driving *King Lear*'s annihilating digressions from Brutan continuity. The *Arcadia* received its first seventeenth-century edition in 1605 and served as a source for several contemporary plays.[13] Shakespeare's use of Sidney's romance was, in literary terms, topical.

As has been noted, *King Lear* cancels historical continuity through the killing of Cordelia before she can become queen and through the deaths of Cornwall and Regan as the parents of a future king, Cunedagus. Lear's death, too, represents a slippage from the Brutan histories. He dies without being restored to the throne, his and Cordelia's invasion of Britain having been defeated in direct contradiction of tradition. All of these events – the defeat of Lear and Cordelia, Cordelia's execution, even the poisoning of Regan by her sister – are caused by the intervention of a non-Brutan character, Edmund, based on the *Arcadia*'s Plexirtus, the illegitimate 'hard-harted vngratefulnes of a sonne' of the king of Paphlagonia (1593: f. 69v). In *King Lear*, an illegitimate villain derails an illegitimate history. It is Edmund who leads the army that defeats Lear and Cordelia's invasion, his victory emblematized through his entrance 'with Lear and Cordelia prisoners' following the battle and it is Edmund who orders Cordelia's execution (1608: sig. K4r; 1997: 5.3.27–38); it is Edmund whose dual seduction triggers the rivalry between Goneril and Regan that leads to the sisters' deaths – as he admits, 'one the other poysoned for my sake, / And after slue her selfe' (sig. L3r; 5.3.238–9).[14] His function within his subplot gradually insinuates its nihilistic presence into *King Lear*'s wider structure, his ambition and actions redirecting and wrecking the Brutan histories' flow and continuum until their representatives are reduced to a pile of corpses: 'The bodies of Gonorill and Regan are brought in' (sig. L3r; 5.3.229); 'Enter Lear with Cordelia in his armes' (sig. L3v; 5.3.254). If, at the play's end, not only Cordelia but also everything around her will 'come no more' (sig. L4r; 5.3.306), this is largely Edmund's doing. Thus, the cancellation of Lear and his daughters' futurity is brought about by a character representing fictionality, a force more powerful than the Brutan histories and, indeed, the force from which they had emerged via Geoffrey of Monmouth's ingenious and imagined *liber vetustissimus*. At Lear's death, the non-Brutan Kent, as if speaking to those readers still shoring up their Brutan faith, counsels Edgar to allow Lear to die, to 'let him passe', marvelling that 'the wonder is, he hath endured so long' (sig. L4r; 5.3.312–15). Exasperated sceptics, for whom Lear and the Brutan histories were manifest fictions, might have agreed.

After almost five centuries of cultural utility, King Lear's heightened visibility and historiographic resonance in drama and public life coincided with the moment at which the historicity underwriting that very utility was being rejected. I have argued that, in *Leir*, the presence of Skalliger may have foregrounded the play's temporal dislocation and that, in *Nobody and Some-body*, Elidure and his Brutans are absorbed by Nobody's negating proximity and the play's satirical function. In *King Lear*'s first quarto, the accelerating erosion of this same historicity runs parallel to the aftermath of James's failed reunion project, his own *Historica passio*. With the Brutan histories' authority eroded, the division of the kingdoms was an originary state, not a royal decree. No king, Lear or James, could damage or repair a union that had never been.

Although I have focused here on the years 1603–8, I am not arguing that this period saw the final erosion of the

Brutan histories, only that these years provide a useful focus for exploring historical dissonance. When visiting York in 1617, James was greeted with a long oration by the Recorder of York, Sir Richard Hutton, in which the city was described as 'builded by Ebrauk, the fowerth king after Brute' (*REED* 1979: 1, 552; l. 31). Over 130 years after Henry VII's visit, then, York still engaged with monarchy via its Brutan heritage. And, as noted at the beginning of this chapter, the erstwhile *Mirror for Magistrates*, a source for so much Brutan drama, was republished in 1610, its first edition since 1587. The new title page described the work, in the precise terminology of a Jacobean Brutan playbook, as 'a true chronicle historie of the vntimely falles of such vnfortunate princes and men of note, as haue happened since the first entrance of Brute into this iland' (1610: sig. A1r). By adopting the term 'true chronicle historie', and highlighting Brute as the inaugural figure of British history, the 1610 *Mirror* appears to respond to *Leir*, *No-body and Some-body* and *King Lear* as a useful model for re-marketing this Elizabethan material in a new era.[15]

Yet, in another mode, *King Lear* may provide a more long-term, and barely visible, example of Brutan drama feeding out into the wider culture and reshaping conceptions of Brutan history. Sometime between the first staging of *King Lear* and 1620, a ballad deriving from Shakespeare's play appeared.[16] Printed as the first entry in *The Golden Garland of Princely Pleasures*, a ballad collection similar to Deloney's *Garland of Good Will*, 'A Lamentable Song of the Death of King Leare and his three Davghters', leads a sequence of ten ballads loosely based on English monarchical history, followed by one deriving from *Titus Andronicus*. *Golden Garland* places Lear within a context of popular history that, it seems, continued to embrace Brutan material. Indeed, the critic Wilfred Perrett noted in 1904 that he, as well as 'thousands of children', had grown up with the ballad (qtd in Wells 2000: 277). This raises the possibility that between the 1620s and early twentieth century the ballad of Lear, with Shakespeare's savagely terminal ending, was the most well-known version of the story.

Unlike Deloney's earlier ballad of Guendolen and Estrild, the Lear ballad assigns direct speech to many of its characters. One effect of this might have been that, through the model of performed history proposed in the Introduction, the most frequent, and often communal, performance of Lear's story would have been by the consumers of ballads, by 'professional distributors in marketplaces and at public executions; by people at work, particularly where their labour had a rhythmic aspect (milk maids and weavers were well known for their singing); [and] by individuals and groups' (Marsh 2019: 127–8). An important implication of this popular context is that Cordelia and her sisters may have been the only Brutan figures to have been publicly performed by women in the early modern period. Nonetheless, the playbooks of 'true chronicle history' provide the last evidence of a sustained output of Brutan drama in the early modern period, in terms of theatrical repertory and print. As far as can be told from the extant evidence, drama of the 1620s and 1630s saw only sporadic engagement with Brutan themes. However, as the next chapter will argue, these texts are notable for their dramaturgical diversity and the ways in which they seem to reconfigure Brutan time as a mythic and, eventually, post-mythic phenomenon.

4

The Diminution of
Brutan Time (1610–37)

Brutan time did not survive as history. Nor, however, did it
survive as myth. Rather, the stories, rulers and prophets of
pre-Roman Britain eventually disappeared almost completely
from cultural use. This final chapter asks a perhaps esoteric,
admittedly slippery, question: What did Brutan myth become
once its time had passed, and what did this passing mean
for the spectators and readers of Brutan drama? If there are
articulable answers to be found, I suggest that some of them
can be apprehended in the final extant Brutan drama to be
staged in London before the Restoration: *Cymbeline*.

Despite, or perhaps because of, the re-energizing of Brutan
tropes as part of the English cultural response to James VI
and I's British union project, the early Jacobean era saw new
historiographic texts working harder than ever to jettison the
Brutan histories. These texts were characterized by greater
recourse to the Roman sources that contradicted and threatened
Brutan tradition. *Cymbeline* (*c.* 1610; pub. 1623), set during
the early years of Roman British interaction, occupies a liminal
historiographic space shared by Brutan and Roman time and
as such may have evoked not merely a sense of etiological
erosion but the post-erosion state this chapter addresses. In
this play, belief gives way to a perception of the iconography
of Brutan time becoming overburdened and oversaturated,

then diminishing and ultimately dispersing. A detailed study
of dispersal within *Cymbeline* and the 1623 Shakespeare folio
(F1) as a whole is followed by three short case studies offering
snapshots of Brutan dramatic texts and performances from the
1630s. Collectively, these suggest ways in which the vanishing
of Brutan historicity continued to be felt and processed in
modes that take us back to the beginning of this study. Yet these
dramas simultaneously show Brutan figures presented in new
forms that estrange them from their historiographic origins and
suggest possible – yet ultimately unfulfilled – Brutan futures.
The Oxford University play *Fuimus Troes* (*c.* 1611–33; pub.
1633) returns to the academic drama that produced the first
Brutan play, *Gorboduc*. Aurelian Townshend's court masque
Albions Trivmph (1632) shows the masque's key performer,
Charles I, absorbing the Brutan figure Albanact into his own
iconography and embodied presence, symbolically ending the
tradition, traceable to the 1486 post-Bosworth pageants, of
using Brutan figures to confront the English monarchy. Finally,
John Milton's *A Masque Presented at Ludlow Castle* (1634;
pub. 1637) suggests a possible Brutan afterlife, when Locrine's
daughter Sabren emerges from the Severn waters in which she
drowned as the powerful and liberating water nymph Sabrina.

Cymbeline – that irreducible hybrid of folk, Roman, Brutan
and self-reflexively Shakespearean materials – provides a suitably
encompassing and unstable lens through which to contemplate
the end of Brutan time. First, through its performance *c.* 1610–
11, its Brutan iconography served King James's self-image
and foreign policy, even as this iconography was complicated
by contemporaneous performances of Thomas Heywood's
sequence of mythic *Age* plays and *Cymbeline*'s tendency to
overload even its most passing symbols and references with
extraneous meaning. Second, by analysing *Cymbeline* in print
we encounter Brutan time's transition from being perceived as
history, via early modern myth, into a post-mythic space that
eludes conventional definition but not, perhaps, description.
While the play's semiotic complexity can be seen as a barrier to
interpretation and a field into which Brutan iconography seems

to become undifferentiated from other contexts, certain textual details in *Cymbeline* afford insights into its Brutan resonance. This chapter focuses on a single instance in F1 of Guiderius's pseudonym 'Polidore' being rendered as 'Paladour' (1623: f. 382; 2017: 3.3.86) and a reference by Imogen to the 'diminution of space' (f. 371; 1.3.18–19). The first example, I suggest, unravels one of *Cymbeline*'s key icons – Jupiter astride an eagle – thereby weakening the play's apparent prophetic force. In the second case, Imogen's speech in which she imagines her husband Posthumus's departure in exile from Britain (f. 371: 1.3.17–37) is explored for the way in which it draws together Brute's wife Innogen and her near-namesake Imogen from their respective positions at the opposing polarities of Brutan time, thereby collapsing the fictional and historiographic space between them. All of this potential for temporal instability, however, perhaps originates in the strangely insubstantial chronicle figure of Cymbeline himself.

King Cymbeline existed at a confluence of Brutan, sacred and Roman time. Unlike the earlier king Cassibelan, whose military exploits against the Romans were recounted in some detail by Julius Caesar and re-imagined in similar and oppositional detail by Geoffrey of Monmouth, very little information about Cymbeline or his Roman parallel, Cunobelinus, was recorded or fictionalized. The information that was provided, however, would have been significant for early modern readers: 'Kymbalyn . . . was a good man and well gouerned the lande in moche . . . sperite and pees all his lifes tyme and in his tyme was borne Ihus crist our sauyour' (Caxton 1480: sig. B6v). Hardyng records that Cymbeline was the king 'In whose tyme was both peace and all concorde / Through all y^t worlde, and borne was christ oure lorde' (1543: f. 38v). Stow is similarly brief, although revisions to subsequent editions of his work reveal the tensions between Roman and Brutan accounts. In his *Summarie*, Stow records that 'Cymbalinus' had ruled '[w]hen Cesar Augustus the second emperour by the wyll of God hadde stablyshed moste sure peace thorough the worlde', and when 'oure Redemer Iesu Christe, very God and man, vpon whom peace wayted, was borne' (1565: sig. C4r). For *The Chronicles of England*, Stow altered the British king's name to the Roman equivalent, 'Cvnobelinus' (1580: sig. C2r). Holinshed, as Ros King notes, was characteristically both inclusive and disorientating, offering 'Cymbeline, Cynobelinus and Kymbaline', only to 'rather [give] up on the name for Cymbeline's eldest son', referred to as 'Guiderius or Guinderius (whether you will)' (1587: III, *Hist.* 36; qtd in King 2005: 72). All these texts associate the reign with 'peace', a central concern of *Cymbeline* and James VI and I. John Clapham presented Cunobelin, crediting him with a civilizing influence on the British who, without their Brutan inheritance, were reconfigured as the woad-daubed primitives of Caesar's *Commentaries*. According to Clapham, Cunobelin

> began first to reclaime the Britans from their rude behavior: and to make his estate more respected, he afterwards caused his owne Image to be stamped on his Coine after the maner of the Romans . . . . During the time of his government, the divine mysterie of humane redemption was accomplished by the birth of our Saviour Christ. (1602: f. 21–2)

For Clapham, despite the shift to Roman historiography, the reign of Cymbeline-Cunobelin remains defined by its synchronous relationship to the Incarnation, the event by which the redemption of humanity is accomplished and the pagan epoch concluded. By either Roman or Brutan account, Cymbeline is the ruler who connects British time to the biblical infinite.

Cymbeline, then, is a figure who, uniquely among those Brutan rulers represented in early modern drama, comes with almost no narrative of his own but serves instead as a function allowing ancient Britain to participate in the state of world peace that early modern theology believed was brought about by the Emperor Augustus's consolidation of his empire. This was known as the *pax Romana*, or *pax Augustus*, and was a prerequisite for the Incarnation (Geller 1980: 243). The consequences for *Cymbeline* of this interweaving of Brutan, Roman and biblical historiographies are complex. While much critical energy has been exerted on attempting to sift, resolve or prioritize the play's many discrete yet interacting contexts, the following analysis attempts to embrace the play's hermeneutic excesses as bearing meaning in their own right and as creating an unusually free textual space in which the vanishing of Brutan time can be explored.

Cymbeline and Jupiter, *c.* 1610–12

Valerie Wayne, in a characterization representative of much *Cymbeline* criticism, describes the play as 'malleable and complex, yet difficult to make sense of in its collocation of times and cultures' (2017: 2). D. E. Landry, approaching the play as an example of 'dreams as history', notes that critics have struggled 'to interpret the play in any unified way' or to 'assign it any structure' (1982: 68). One reason for this may be the play's setting during a historical reign for which the chronicle sources offered no narrative. To fill this void, *Cymbeline* draws on disparate, seemingly unrelated, occasionally historical and manifestly fictional sources, a concatenation characterized as 'heterogeneous, being partly based on the written records of British chroniclers but also . . . a number of popular myths and national legends, and folk-lore motifs' (Gibbons 1993: 22). The tale of a wager and a jealous husband taken from Boccaccio's *Decameron* provides the central plot of Princess Imogen's escape from attempted murder at the command of her exiled husband Posthumus, who has been gulled into believing that he has lost a bet regarding the inviolability of her chastity to the scheming Roman, Iachimo. A subplot, wherein the royal party of Cymbeline, his queen and her brutish son Cloten negotiate with Augustus's Rome in a dispute over unpaid tribute, provides a fictional prelude to a Roman invasion assigned in the chronicles to the reigns of Cymbeline's sons, Arviragus and Guiderius.[1] In the play, these sons are portrayed as unknowing kidnap victims raised since infancy in a British wilderness associated with Wales. The Incarnation goes unmentioned. *Cymbeline* concludes in a long scene containing multiple narrative resolutions, unmaskings and revelations. Forgiveness and peace are finally asserted by Cymbeline's declaration that 'Pardon's the word to all' (1623: f. 398; 2017: 5.5.421). However, one central concern of *Cymbeline* criticism since the 1960s has been to investigate in what ways, in or around 1610, this play incorporating such disparate materials might reflect its moment and have worked upon its audiences.[2]

In 1961, Emrys Jones observed that '[f]ew of the critics who have written about *Cymbeline* seem to have thought about the impression it made on audiences when . . . it was a new play' (1961: 87). This oversight has since been comprehensively addressed, critics often adding much nuance to, but not significantly departing from, Jones's core observation that the play 'centres on the character and foreign policy' of James VI and I (1961: 89). Jones argued further that the play's implicit setting at the moment of the Incarnation echoes that moment's 'attempted re-creation at the very time of the play's performance', in order to speak to the interests of the peace-oriented James, or 'Jacobus Pacificus' (1961: 96).[3] Frances Yates fused these approaches, arguing that *Cymbeline* was drawing upon 'the idea of Empire through which the Roman Empire was sanctified and Christianized because Christ chose to be born during the reign of Augustus Caesar' (1975: 42).[4]

The term 'Jacobus Pacificus' is invoked in David Bergeron's study of *Cymbeline*'s Roman affiliations, connecting the notion of *pax Augustus* to King James's irenic foreign policy, as demonstrated by his personal motto 'Beati Pacifici' (1980: 33).[5] W. B. Patterson tells us that James saw a pan-European 'resolution of differences between Protestants and Roman Catholics' as essential to the establishment of a 'stable community of nations' (2011: 342). This schema can easily be mapped onto the play's concluding peace between Rome and Britain, although this peace is achieved through Cymbeline's beneficence, his army having thwarted the Romans' invasion.

James's association with Augustus as a peacemaker extended to the wider notion of *translatio imperii*, the medieval and early modern model of history that saw a divinely sanctioned empire moving gradually westward from Rome. English proponents of this theory unsurprisingly saw the emergent British Empire as the latest manifestation, even a culmination, of this trend, a view that seems to be supported by *Cymbeline*'s closing prophetic image of a 'Romaine Eagle / From South to West, on wing soaring aloft', and foretelling the concluding peace between 'Th' Imperiall Caesar' and 'Radiant Cymbeline' (1623: f. 399; 2017: 5.5.469–74). Patricia Parker describes this as a passing of Roman virtue from Rome to a Britain symbolized by 'Posthumus and Imogen and by the king's recovered heirs' (1989: 205). The eagle is a powerful and recurring image in *Cymbeline*: Imogen defends her marriage to the lower-born Posthumus by declaring 'I chose an Eagle' (f. 370; 2017: 1.1.140); the Roman Soothsayer dreams of 'Ioues Bird, the Roman Eagle wing'd / From the spungy South, to this part of the West' (f. 390; 4.2.347–48), and thus predicts Roman victory over Britain, an interpretation he must later re-spin in the aftermath of Roman defeat. Famously, this association with Rome and Jupiter is materialized in *Cymbeline* by the god's spectacular descent riding an eagle and delivering the cryptic, irenic prophecy that is interpreted as having foretold the play's resolving peace (f. 394; 5.4.63–83).

Cymbeline's presentation of the virtues associated with eagles, James and *translatio imperii* has been characterized as occurring within a fully Romanized antiquity. That is, the British towards whom the 'Roman Eagle' is soaring are, as Escobedo terms it, 'already Romanized, worshipping Jupiter and the other gods of their enemies' (2008: 70). Paul Innes describes this association as ahistorical, arguing that the play goes to 'great lengths to Romanise Cymbeline's Britain by means of Jovian terminology' (2007: 12). In this, the play would seem to gesture more towards the Cunobelinus of Roman accounts than the Brutan Cymbeline. According to the Brutan histories, however, Jupiter was worshipped in Britain long before even the *foundation* of Rome. His cult arrived at Albion with Brute who, after all, had been pointed the way by the goddess Diana. Jupiter is invoked by Estrild in *Locrine* who cries out for aid in her suicide: 'Strengthen these hands O mightie Iupiter / That I may end my wofull miserie' (1595: sig. K2v). King Lear, too, invokes Jupiter moments before invoking *Historica passio* (1608: sig. E3v; 1997: 2.2.211). Jupiter then, from a certain perspective, was a Brutan god before he became a Roman one.

For *Cymbeline*'s first audience in 1610–11, therefore, Roman-Brutan Jupiter could have been perceived as emerging from a more ancient and far less civilized pagan antiquity. In fact, this was precisely the kind of Jupiter presented throughout Thomas Heywood's ambitious sequence of five plays on the classical gods and heroes: *The Golden Age, The Silver Age, The Brazen Age* and the two parts of *The Iron Age*, which appear to have been written between 1609 and 1612. The first play, and probably its sequels too, were performed at the Red Bull playhouse, placing the sequence in competitive repertory with *Cymbeline* at the Globe and Blackfriars. Heywood's plays are described succinctly by David Mann as an 'episodic admixture of bloodshed, amours and algolagnia' (2013: 185). *Cymbeline*'s dignified pre-Christian deus ex machina would therefore have been closely associated with a parallel stage Jupiter, whose lustful and violent actions arguably complicate the symbolic exemplarity critics have perceived in *Cymbeline*'s eagle-rider. *The Golden Age*, having presented a euhemerized version of the lives of Saturn and his son Jupiter, concludes with a spectacular event that must have been central to the play's commercial appeal, appearing as it does on the title page as 'the deifying of the Heathen Gods' (1611: sig. A1r). At the play's conclusion, Jupiter and his brothers Pluto and Neptune draw lots for rulership of heaven, earth and hell. Jupiter draws heaven and is presented with 'his Eagle, Crowne and Scepter, and his thunder-bolt', after which he 'ascends vpon the Eagle' (1611: sig. K2v). This is an almost precise mirror image of Jupiter's appearance in *Cymbeline* 'in Thunder and Lightning, sitting vppon an Eagle' after which he 'throwes a Thunder-bolt'

(1623: f. 394; 2017: 5.4.62). *The Golden Age*'s contemporary association with *Cymbeline*'s famous moment has been noted (Wayne 2017: 46–8). But it hasn't, I think, been fully explored. *Cymbeline*'s Jupiter has been read as symbolizing 'a dying god' presiding over the 'coming of a new era' (Marshall 1991: 25). In other words, he represents either or both – the Christian epoch replacing the pagan or a Jacobean *translatio imperii* from Catholic Rome, casting *The Golden Age* and *Cymbeline* as polarities: the beginning and end of pagan time. Like *Cymbeline*, though in passing, the *Age* plays incorporate Brutan time into their construction of universal history. In *2 The Iron Age*, Hector addresses Aeneas regarding his future:

> Hence Aeneas post from Troy,
> Reare that abroad the gods at home destroy.
> . . . .
> Citties more rich then this the Grecian spoyle,
> In after times shall thy successors build,
> Where Hectors name shall liue eternally.
> One Romulus, another Bruite shall reare,
> These shall nor Honours, nor iust Rectors want,
> Lumbardies roome, great Britaines Troy-nouant.
>
> (1632: sig. E2v)

Here, Rome and Troynovant are explicitly configured as sharing a single origin: Romulus and 'Bruite' raising cities 'more rich' than Troy. Heywood's *Age* plays may, for a London playgoer conversant with Brutan tradition, have contributed to a sprawling cross-repertory account of classical, and indeed Brutan, time that seemed to conclude with *Cymbeline* and Jupiter's descent.

Heywood's Jupiter, however, is childish, transgressive and violent, jarringly different from the remote and patriarchal deity critics have discerned in *Cymbeline*. In *The Golden Age* Jupiter rapes Callisto and Danae and, in *The Silver Age*, uses deception to seduce first Alcmena in the shape of her husband Amphitryo, then Semele, resulting in her annihilation after

she is tricked by Juno into demanding that Jupiter appear
before her in his true, divine form. His marriage to his sister,
Juno, is by contrast a comparatively genteel event. The tone
of these extended episodes is – disturbingly for the twenty-
first-century reader – often comic and always bombastic.
Jupiter takes on multiple disguises, including cross-dressing
as one of the goddess Diana's followers, and indulges in comic
play with mistaken identities. *The Silver Age* was performed
at court before Prince Henry and Queen Anna in January
1612 (Wiggins 2015: 6, ref. 1645). Wiggins speculates that on
this occasion *The Golden Age* and *The Silver Age* may have
been performed in repertory with *Cymbeline* (ref. 1637).[6]
For this court audience, and for wider audiences aware of
both *Cymbeline* and the *Age* plays running in the London
repertory, this would have presented a strange continuity
in which the reckless and amoral prince-turned-god of
Heywood's sequence appeared at the end of pagan time
in *Cymbeline* as the iconographic cipher for King James's
foreign policy, herald of *translatio imperii* and harbinger of
a Brutan-inflected *pax Romana*. In its original performance,
Cymbeline's Jupiter-eagle – which critics have associated with
dynamic assertions of English virtue, nascent imperialism and
the Incarnation – may have been equally suggestive of pre-
Brutan antiquity, and thus of Britain's putative roots in an
indecorous, even brutal, classical paganism. If *Cymbeline*, in
performance around 1610, both channels and complicates
the Brutan histories' symbolic potential, its presence and
placement in the 1623 First Folio suggests ways in which
those histories are finally, figuratively, dissolved and dispersed
into post-mythic nothingness.

Reading *Cymbeline*, 1623

In *The Historie of Great Britaine* (1611), John Speed presents
an exhaustive survey of previous writers' attitudes towards

Brutan historicity before reiterating and ultimately endorsing the most damaging argument against them: that their fictiveness 'appeareth by the silence of the Romane writers therein, who name neither Brute nor his father in the genealogie of the Latine Kings' (1611: f. 164). Strengthening his theme, Speed characterized pre-Roman Britain as a time 'of obscurity, through whose mists no Egles eies could pierce' (1611: f. 170). The totality of this 'obscurity' was formalized by Speed's decision to sever Brutan time from historicity altogether and 'begin the succession of Great Britains Monarchs, at the entrance and person of Iulius Caesar' (1611: f. 170). Caesar's *Commentaries on the Gallic War* (*c.* 52 BCE) provided the first externally verifiable account of ancient Britain, namely his conflicts with British forces led by the general Cassivellanus. The British, as described by Caesar, were not the Trojan-descended dignitaries of the Brutan histories but people who 'clothe themselves in animal skins . . . paint themselves with woad' (1996: 5.14). Other early seventeenth-century historiographic texts also followed this drift. As shown in Chapter 1, Samuel Daniel's *The First Part of the Historie of England* named Brute only once, noting that 'the first certaine notice we haue' was from Julius Caesar and that 'with what credit, the accoumpt of aboue a thousand years from Brute to Casseuellaunus, in a line of absolute Kings, can bee cleared, I do not see' (1612: f. 7). The years surrounding the Roman invasions of Britain, therefore, mark the outer limits of the Brutan histories and set the boundary between 'history' and 'myth', or 'legend'. These latter terms, as shown in the Introduction, do not tell the whole story.

So far, I have tracked Brutan performance through what Jonathan Gil Harris terms, in relation to temporal shifts more generally, the 'transitional phase' in which 'that which is historical becomes . . . myth' (2009: 11). However, John Clapham's 1602 *The Historie of Great Britannie* demonstrates one way in which use of the term 'myth' suppresses a crucial phase of the Brutan histories' journey and, certainly, their ultimate destination. Pre-empting Daniel and Speed, Clapham begins his account of British history with Caesar's invasions. He also includes a disavowal of Brutan history that is familiar in its apology to tradition and the reconfiguring of Brutan history as essentially fictive:

> As for the stories of Brute, from his first arriuall heere, vntil the comming of the Romans, diuerse Writers holde it suspected, reputing it (for good causes) rather a Poeticall Fiction, then a true History . . . . Howbeit, seeing it hath beene for so long time generally receiued, I will not presume, (knowing the power of prescription in matters of lesse continuance) absolutely to contradict it: though for mine owne opinion I suppose it to be a matter of more antiquitie, then veritie. (1602: sig. A4r)

Clapham speaks of Brute as an honourable – that is, nationally ennobling – 'Poeticall Fiction', a term that often shows writers grappling with questions raised by material that would now be called myth. Just as modern readers might recognize qualitative differences between very old and more recent and verifiable historiographic texts, so Clapham identifies a distinction between 'antiquitie' and 'veritie', suggesting that the Brutan histories, bending more to the former, are compromised in the latter category: verifiable truth. This, however, is not the issue. In the subsequent 1606 edition of Clapham's *Historia*, the preface was removed altogether. Brutan history is not engaged with, acknowledged or apologized for. It is amputated. It is at this moment that, I suggest, the terms 'myth', as defined by Barthes, and 'poesie historical' find their limitations as they relate to etiological erosion.

If poesie historical might be equated with Barthes's conception of myth, as something acted, spoken and received, then the Brutan histories were becoming unspoken. Brutan time thus moves into a post-mythic space that, while elusive to definition as a fixed state, might be described as a transformative process analogous with early modern theories of matter and eternity.

Where the language and conceptual apparatus of early modern historiography falters, we can look to texts such as Helkiah Crooke's *Mikrokosmographia* (1615), the 'largest and fullest anatomical work produced in England up to its day' (O'Malley 1968: 11; qtd in Birkin 2004). In its attempts to describe and conceptualize human anatomy, *Mikrokosmographia* frequently makes recourse to philosophical and spiritual material. Arguing that 'perpetuitie and immutability' were the best proof of divinity, Crooke conjures a model of temporalities that proves useful in thinking about mythic time and its afterlives. While perpetuity is not inherent in 'all the parts of time Past, Present, and to Come', it can be found in the present, which, as a sequence of endless points, creates 'a kinde of eternity' similar to a 'clew of yarne, such as the Poets faigned the Destinies to spin', and which may be extended endlessly (1615: f. 198). For Crooke, matter itself is therefore eternal, as proved by the world's inexhaustibility. It is also clear to any observer, however, that individual objects, people and things are not permanent. Crooke thus perceives that while the object or 'particular thing' may end, its material does not, but rather is eroded and transformed into something new:

> The dissolution of created things is but a resolution of one thing into another; hence comes the perpetuity of all things though subiect to alteration, a perpetuity I say, not of the same particular thing distinguished by one and the same forme, but of the Elementary parts whereof it was compounded. (1615: f. 198)

In *Cymbeline*, as it appears in F1, we can trace the dispersal, or 'dissolution', that follows the erosion of Brutan time as a fiction, or 'created thing'. The 'Elementary parts whereof it was compounded' – names, narrative tropes, symbols, places, temporalities – escape into *Cymbeline*, both infusing the play's exegetical potentials with Brutan and 'British' resonance and disappearing into the flux of the play's oversaturated semiotic field. While Brutan texts would continue to be republished and produced – *Fuimus Troes* in all likelihood attempted its own Brutan-Roman fusion several years later at Oxford – *Cymbeline* encapsulates figuratively a moment at which Brutan time's mythic function within early modern society is eroded and dispersed into new forms.

I suggest that the dispersal of Brutan time's mythic function is detectable in the tension between *Cymbeline*'s apparent presentation of a series of complex allegories and symbols to be decoded, and those same symbols' numerous and often mutually eroding interconnections. For example, in one of the play's most tonally confounding moments, Imogen wakes from apparent death and mistakes the headless corpse of Cloten, her would-be husband and would-be rapist, for that of her beloved husband Posthumus. The tableau is the result of Cloten dressing himself in Posthumus's clothes in order to inflect his intended violence on Imogen with blunt irony. Heather James describes this moment as a 'semiotic matrix which confuses differences among sources, characters and historical moments and generates more meanings than it can authorize and contain' (1997: 156). Yet James also insists that the image 'makes sense only in terms of the *translatio imperii*' (1997: 156).[7] Here, the specifics of a particular reading are of less significance than the way in which James's interpretative tension demonstrates that the urge to codify *Cymbeline* is always compromised by the play's overwhelming multiplicity.[8]

Russ McDonald identifies similar overabundance, compression and complexity operating at a syntactical level in the plays regarded as Shakespeare's later works:

Lengthy, convoluted verse sentences may be strung together, or may be interspersed with brief ones, or may be broken up with exclamations, short and long, that may not be sentences at all . . . any generalisation must be modified immediately with a list of exceptions, but these are often so prominent and widespread as to demand a contradictory generalisation. (2006: 135)

The same might be said of attempts to fix, or interpret, *Cymbeline*. McDonald further notes of Shakespeare's late plays that they appear to contain 'patterns and fractals' at every level (2006: 29), creating a 'synecdochic style, a set of codes' that repeat and act upon meanings perceptible at the level of language, character and plot (37). To characterize the play's effects thus, is not anachronistic. Its elusiveness in the face of interpretation is recognized in marginalia found in a copy of F1, where a seventeenth-century reader notes above *Cymbeline*'s closing scene of multiple revelations and unmaskings, 'Infinit questions of the circumstance of strange chances'.[9] This response may relate to the play's credulity-stretching resolutions. But it also evokes the dizzying polytemporal and metatextual contexts activated by the competing genres of its plots and iconography and embodied in its characters' many names and aliases. Tracey Miller-Tomlinson, writing on the play's temporalities, describes these as 'time-travelling names' (2017: 231). They allow the world of the play to snake out into Virgilian, Brutan, Roman, Jacobean and Christian-eschatological temporalities. Two of these names – Imogen, and the name under which the kidnapped Guiderius is raised, Polidore or 'Paladour' (1623: f. 382; 2017: 3.3.86) – will serve as case studies for the diminution of Brutan time.

The following section removes *Cymbeline* from the immediate political and cultural context of its first performance and examines the play in print, just over a decade later, when it appeared as F1's concluding statement. Even in its original performance context, *Cymbeline* has been characterized as presenting an ancient Britain 'where anything could happen' (Schwyzer 2004: 17), allowing 'all possibilities free play' (Miller-Tomlinson 2017: 225). As the final play in F1, *Cymbeline*'s openness to semiotic oversaturation is intensified, in part by that volume's preceding material. The play's infinite questions and strange chances are the portal through which the Brutan histories can be explored in their final transition from historiographic tradition, via myth, into a category of text that is material yet obsolete, extant yet silent.

Cymbeline was one of eighteen previously unpublished plays appearing in the 1623 folio *Mr William Shakespeare's Comedies, Histories, & Tragedies*. More specifically, it was positioned as the final play in the sequence of tragedies, and thus the final play in the volume. *Cymbeline*'s peculiar position among F1's tragedies (which, given its multiple happy conclusions, has long puzzled critics) may be of less significance than its position in relation to F1 as a whole. It is, or could be, perceived as fulfilling the role of a 'last' play and, as such, one in which the multifarious themes, genres, character types and temporalities of the preceding thirty-five plays could be reflected and, in ways that are not easy to quantify or categorize, both resolved and dissolved. Among its many swirling contexts, the sequencing of plays invites the reader to reflect upon the outer boundaries of Brutan time as the setting for the end of, among other things, F1 itself. I suggest that this sense of multiple endings, of retrospection and resolution, creates a readerly encounter with *Cymbeline* in which the play's already acute preoccupation with finality is heightened and extended even further. The Brutan histories provide the frame for F1 *Cymbeline*'s sense of finality and yet, paradoxically, they can also be seen to vanish within the very context they establish.

If the playbooks of 'true chronicle history' examined in Chapter 3 were relatively ephemeral texts in a print market of competing plays and other books in a similar price range, F1 stood largely alone in a field 'usually reserved for works of conspicuous seriousness: Bibles and works of theology, law, topography, heraldry, genealogy and history' (Smith 2016a: 66). Although Ben Jonson's *Workes* of 1616 had included his plays alongside his poetry and other work, F1 was 'the first English book which consisted entirely of a large collection of scripts commercially performed outdoors' (Taylor 2006: 64).[10] In terms of textual community, 'the price of the folio would have restricted some readers from even setting their eyes' on the book (Lyons 2016: 14). The price was determined in part by the book's size, weight and the considerable logistics of acquiring the rights to the plays' manuscripts and composing these for print, alongside the substantial cost of paper, a commercial risk meaning that, regardless of its content, 'the physical format of the book itself [asserted] its cultural legitimacy' (Taylor 2006: 64). This sense of 'legitimacy' perhaps invited attentiveness to textual details and scholarly allusions at a time when the historiographic legitimacy of Brutan history was in decline. The purchaser of F1 would have seen in its catalogue list of plays a sequence of dramatic texts copious and inclusive enough to shuffle figures of Scottish, English and Roman history randomly among its variously sourced fictions, while gesturing towards a sense of sequential logic and cohesion via its generic categories and the histories' chronological arrangement. The conclusion of this sequence, like any last thing implying a summation of what has come before it, was 'Cymbeline King of Britaine'. The running titles name the play 'The Tragedie of Cymbeline', and this classification has caused much critical consternation, Crumley complaining that F1 'misclassifies Cymbeline with vigor' (2001: 297). However, in a study of Cymbeline as F1's final play, Wayne argues that the play 'was a good candidate to conclude the book' specifically because it 'includes multiple modes and genres', citing Jonathan Bate's observation that its 'stylistic experimentation almost serves as an ironic epilogue to the Folio's tripartite division' (2007: 2240). Taken together, these readings of Cymbeline's placement may have both a resolving and a dissolving effect upon readers' perceptions of the preceding material. On the one hand, its generic and allusive capaciousness appears to offer an oblique summary and resolution of what has come before.[11] On the other hand, Bate's characterization of the play as an 'ironic epilogue' creates in F1 an object that, in its final pages, both re-collects and dissolves the foregoing material into a narrative steeped in Brutan, Roman and eschatological themes and imagery. For F1's first readers, the 'end' of Shakespeare's works takes place at the 'end' of pagan and Brutan time.

Approaching the plays in F1 as a sequence rather than as individual works may alter readers' reception of these in terms of temporality, as well as genre and theme. For example, Emma Smith observes of the histories that, while in quarto each play may stand alone as a self-contained narrative, in F1 each play's ending 'seems provisional . . . the end of a chapter rather than anything more conclusive' as a turn of the page reactivates the violent, relentless sequence of English civil wars (2016a: 28–9). However, while few have argued for an intended structure for either the sequence of comedies or tragedies, Smith argues that for those reading the plays in sequence 'there might be some shaping of their response to later plays in the light of reading earlier ones' (29). Smith's focus on the physical practice of reading has important implications when considering the effects of *Cymbeline*'s apparent absorption and synthesis of so much that precedes it.

In her discussion of F1, Smith cites Wolfgang Iser's *The Act of Reading: A Theory of Aesthetic Response* (2016b: 166). Iser examines what he calls the reader's 'wandering viewpoint', a cognitive quirk meaning that the whole of a text 'can never be perceived at any one time' and that to read requires both 'retention' and 'protention', encountering individual sentences or syntactic units that require the reader to both look ahead and retain that which has been read and is already passing out of immediate perception (1978: 110–12). From this perspective, *Cymbeline* invites 'retention' on a vast scale, the weight of F1's preceding plays pressing on the final 'chapter' in the sequence, and a foreshortening of the capacity for 'protention': the book itself is running out of time, there is less to foresee and this is felt in the reader's physical sense of the object exhausting its pages: another way in which *Cymbeline* provokes a sense of looking back, of endings and resolutions. Russ McDonald notes that the play's 'festival of discoveries and recognitions is as long and complex as it is so as to afford the audience a release commensurate with the foregoing confusion and frustration' (2006: 179). To this can be added the cumulative effects of the discoveries, recognitions, confusions and frustrations of F1 as a whole. In fact, a localized sense of *Cymbeline* as belonging to some kind of sequence might have been triggered by the preceding play, *Antony and Cleopatra*, which recounts events of world history immediately prior to *Cymbeline*'s historical frame. The play's Octavius is mocked by Antony as a 'young Roman Boy' (1995: 4.12.48). Yet he will become the Emperor Augustus, the offstage power in whose name the Roman army invades and who was said to have provided Cymbeline with wardship in Rome as a child. *Antony and Cleopatra* also subtly foresees the Incarnation, *Cymbeline*'s great unspoken context, in Caesar's declaration that 'The time of universal peace is near' (1995: 4.6.5). This association is embedded in an ekphrastic account of Imogen's bedchamber, where Iachimo describes a number of objects, including a tapestry depicting Cleopatra (1623; f. 379; 2017: 2.4.69–70).[12] However, even as *Cymbeline* invites a strong sense of finality and resolution, it further complicates this by looking out beyond its own ending through its emphasis on the power of prophecy.

Imogen appears in *Cymbeline*'s closing scene disguised as a page, Fidele. The lost princes, Guiderius and Arviragus, recognize her as the boy they befriended and whom they believed to be dead. They cry out but Belarius quietens them: 'Peace, peace, see further' (f. 396; 2017: 5.5.124). His meaning is that they should observe what happens next. Yet this passing phrase also indicates the play's irenic conclusion: its final word, and thus F1's final word, is 'peace' (f. 399; 5.5.484). It also, in Belarius's instruction to 'see further', invokes the play's unconstrained temporal perspectives. Dissolved as an account of the lived past, the Brutan histories become untethered from universal chronology, affording them far greater plasticity. They can ravel backwards, or perhaps inwards, to their own origins or, as here, expand into prophetic futures. In *Cymbeline*, the impulse to see further is enacted through the dreams of the Roman Soothsayer and delivered in textual form to Posthumus by Jupiter. These moments operate as the final node of a sequence running throughout F1 that establishes a sense of prophetic momentum that may have been experienced as reaching an apotheosis, or at least an ending, in *Cymbeline*. Kastan, discussing the Shakespearean 'romances' in general, describes this as directing the reader 'beyond the tragic, demanding that we see beyond time's annihilating effects, beyond suffering and loss to forgiveness and reconciliation' (1982: 128). This is certainly the register of *Cymbeline*'s final scenes. A sense of prophetic accumulation would have been perceptible to readers with little or no passing knowledge of the intricacies of Brutan history but also, for those with specialized knowledge, additional associations may have revealed destabilizing fissures undermining the play's Brutan iconography. These fissures are visible through close examination of Cymbeline's lost son, Guiderius, or, rather, through his pseudonym 'Paladour'.

Soothsayers, oracles, supernatural farsightedness and characters who can see beyond their time appear throughout F1 and perhaps serve to create a sense of blurring at each of the book's generic borders. The sequences of comedies, histories and tragedies each conclude with a play ending or hinging on prophecy: *The Winter's Tale*, *Henry VIII* and *Cymbeline*. *Troilus and Cressida* feature the prophetic and unheeded Trojan Cassandra, a putative Brutan forebear. A Soothsayer warns Caesar of the Ides of March, and the 'weyward sisters' draw Macbeth into regicide with equivocal prophesies but conclude with their vision of a line of kings reaching from the murdered Banquo to James himself. *King Lear*'s Fool, in the passage not present in the 1608 Quarto, offers his topsy-turvy prophecy-of-a-prophecy that, centuries later, 'Merlin shall make, for I live before his time' (1623: f. 197; 1997: 3.3.95–96). Here, the Fool breaks open *King Lear*'s temporality, both anchoring it in Brutan historicity – the centuries before Merlin – and expanding its reach into prophetic time, aligning it with *Cymbeline* in ways unavailable to readers of Q1 *King Lear*.[13] Many of these, the Oracle in *The Winter's Tale*, Cassandra and the Soothsayers of *Julius Caesar* and *Antony and Cleopatra*, are ignored, with tragic results for those to whom they have offered their farsightedness. *Cymbeline*'s prophecies, as noted, have been framed as endorsing James VI & I's irenic foreign policy and the notion of a Rome-to-Britain *translatio imperii*.

Yet the use of an eagle as one of *Cymbeline*'s central motifs of prophecy and imperial futurity may also have, subtly, opened F1's concluding British peace to a set of associations that were rooted in, and erosive of, both Brutan iconography and prophecy's fundamental value as a polemical and theatrical device.

Following Cymbeline as king of Britain in the Brutan histories was Guiderius, his eldest son, and it was Guiderius's wars with the Romans that Shakespeare appropriated for *Cymbeline*'s Roman invasion (Floyd-Wilson 2002: 101). It is Guiderius who encounters and summarily beheads the rampaging Cloten and this, combined with their cave-dwelling, 'primitive' lifestyle, has led critics to associate Guiderius and his brother with the alternative model of ancient Britain suggested by Roman histories, and to which writers such as John Speed had turned. The associations are, as everywhere in *Cymbeline*, as multifariously allusive as the pseudonyms Belarius gives the two princes as a means of obscuring their identities, usually presented in modern editions of the play as 'Polydore' and 'Cadwal'. Howard Felperin observed that these names were suggestive of the *Historia*'s final king, Cadwallader, and of Polydore Vergil, the 'historian who chronicled those shadowy kings, however sceptically' (1972: 193–4). However, as Curran notes, these names 'suggest not the sixteenth-century political relevance' of Brutan history, 'but rather the means by which the Galfridian tradition was exploded' (1997: 287). Miller-Tomlinson sees in this an instance of the play's metatextual self-awareness, that '[i]n an attack on the illusion of objective distance assumed in conventional historiography – an illusion perpetuated in Polydore Vergil's attack on Geoffrey – Polydore is reduced to a character in the history he writes' (1997: 231).[14] Vergil, of course, was the author who enabled early modern Brutan scepticism, and Cadwallader, the *Historia*'s final king, might also be seen as alluding to the end of Brutan time.

There is, however, a further possible reading of Guiderius's alias, one made available by the play's appearance in print and, like *King Lear*'s *Historica passio*, subsequently submerged by editorial practice. Guiderius's pseudonym is standardized in modern editions of *Cymbeline* to 'Polydore'. However, in its first use in F1, spoken by Belarius, the name is spelled 'Paladour' (1623: f. 382; 2017: 3.3.86), before settling on 'Polidore' (never, significantly, 'Polydore'). This one-off variant was retained up to and including the 1685 fourth folio, then altered by Rowe to 'Polydor' (Wayne 2017: 249). The use of a single spelling variant may seem an insubstantial basis for an alternative reading but its perceptibility is attested by *Cymbeline*'s Restoration adaptation *The Injur'd Princess* (1682). Here, Thomas d'Urfrey changed the name of the character based on Guiderius to 'Paladour' throughout the text, demonstrating early modern readers' sensitivity to even minor variants in spelling and naming.[15] Examination of the name's usage in early modern print opens up Brutan associations that have striking implications for *Cymbeline*.

In the Brutan histories, Paladour was not a person but a place: a site of historiographic and etymological instability, expressed in terms of prophecy and eagles – prophesying eagles, in fact – imagery central to *Cymbeline*'s theme of futurity. According to the *Historia*, King Rud Huddibras, the grandfather of Lear, had founded 'the town of Mons Paladur', subsequently known as Shaftesbury. Geoffrey states that '[w]hile the city-wall was being constructed there, an eagle spoke; and if I thought that its prophecies were true, I would not hesitate to set them down here with the rest' (2007: 36). The phenomenon of a speaking eagle passes unquestioned, yet its pronouncements are dismissed. From its earliest appearance, then, 'Paladour' is inseparable from aquiline prophetic untrustworthiness. Over the course of the Brutan histories' medieval transmission, however, the eagle of Mons Paladur undergoes a metamorphosis. Grafton's chronicle takes a euhemerizing approach to this apparent myth and argues that, when speaking of an eagle, Geoffrey's chronicler antecedents were in fact describing a human prophet named Aquila – Latin for eagle – and that this became misunderstood in subsequent iterations with the result that 'many report how an Egle should then speake' (1569: f. 45). The eagle becomes a human prophet, a figure described in Holinshed as residing in 'mount Paladour' and named 'Aquila a prophet of the British nation' (1577: I, *Hist.Eng.* 19). Even Speed appears to have acknowledged Aquila's prophecies as foretelling James's reign (Brinkley 1932: 8–9). Drayton's *Englands Heroicall Epistles* notes that 'Cair-Septon in mount Palador' was 'now called Shaftsbury, at whose building it was sayd an Eagle prophecied (or rather one named Aquilla) . . . of the recouery of the Ile by the Brittains bringing backe with them the bones of Cadwallader from Rome' (1593: sig. G2v). Thus, for readers of F1, 'Paladour' might evoke the prophetic eagle that Geoffrey of Monmouth both invented and claimed to doubt along with subsequent debate around the euhermized Aquila's prophecies. The name thus binds together two of *Cymbeline*'s key symbols, the descending Jupiter-eagle and, as Cymbeline's heir and future king of Britain, Guiderius, arguably compromising their value as exemplary symbols of both Brutan antiquity and Britain's glorious futurity. Additionally, as well as associating Guiderius with a particularly unstable moment of Brutan history, the episode of the prophesying eagle also connects *Cymbeline* to early modern arguments for the 'satanic' nature of prophecy itself.

The eagle-prophet of Paladour was the subject of a vicious attack on the very concept and practice of prophecy in David Powel's 1584 edition of Humphrey Lhoyd's English translation of the fourteenth-century *Historie of Cambria, now called Wales*. Here, prophecies are characterized as satanic 'toies and fables' by which 'the simple and ignorant haue bin in all ages deluded and brought to great errors and blindnes by the practise of sathan, with these fained reuelations, false prophesies and superstitious dreames of hypocrites and lewd persons' (1584: sig. C3r). At the very best, according to Powel, those who endorse or believe prophecy are 'simple and ignorant'. *The History of Cambria* attacks prophecy itself as not only foolish and vain but as a product of satanic influence as proven by historical evidence, 'as is manifest in our histories' (1584:

sig. C3r). Powel's attack appears in a book on the ancient history of Wales, the country Arviragus and Guiderius inhabit, arguably strengthening its potential to draw associations with and complicate *Cymbeline*.

Cymbeline anchors its temporal farsightedness in its apparently optimistic series of reunions and prophecies, central to which is the interconnected imagery of eagle, prophecy and royal heirs. For readers familiar with Brutan origins and etymology, however, the Jupiter-eagle, the future king of Britain Paladour-Guiderius and the play's tone of prophetic optimism, might be compromised by their association with Mons Paladour, a case study in superstition, unreliable Brutan historiographic transmission and the 'dreams of lewd persons'. This association disrupts the possible meanings of the play's conclusion, whether in terms of Jacobean peacemaking or the new British era that Guiderius is required to inaugurate. John Speed had characterized pre-Roman Britain as a time 'of obscurity, through whose mists no Egles eies could pierce' (1611: f. 170). The implication of Paladour-Guiderius's semiotic network is that, partitioned from us by obscurity and mist, the eagle was not an eagle at all and that, whether eagle or man, as a prophet it should not be trusted to 'pierce' futurity. And those who do believe, according to Powel, are 'simple and ignorant'. This far less edifying reading of *Cymbeline*'s iconography coincides with the erosion of Brutan time itself through the efforts of Speed, Daniel, Clapham and others. Similarly, Imogen, in the language she uses and the scenarios she constructs, embodies a model of Brutan time that expands backwards towards its fictive inception and, finally, collapses into itself. Her name, after all, is a homonym for 'imagine'.

Imagining Imogen Imagining Innogen

Imogen, as an emblem of Brutan origins, is elusive. Like Lear, she can be seen as embodying the experience of evaporating myth, as *Historica passio*: 'I am nothing', she announces, in a moment of despair, echoing *King Lear*'s nihilism, 'or if not, / Nothing to be were better' (1623: f. 390; 2017: 4.2.365–66). Her name, while directly invoking Innogen – wife of Brute and mother of Locrine, Albanact and Camber – also seems to invoke notions of fictiveness. The name Imogen is widely agreed to arise from a compositor's error for 'Innogen'.[16] But John Pitcher, reflecting on the uses of naming in *Cymbeline*, argues that this name 'gives every indication of having been anglicized from the Italian noun for "likeness" or "image"', citing John Florio's 1611 definition of an 'Imagine' as 'an Image, a similitude in forme, a figure. Also a colour for any thing. Also an imagination, a thought or opinion of any thing. Also remembrance or apprehension of a thing' (1611: 234).[17] Regardless of whether the spelling is accidental or intentional, a reader of F1 may have drawn associations between 'Imogen' and the punning inference suggested by Florio's 'Imagine': an entity embodying imagination and memory, as well as similitude in form, thought and opinion. All of which serves to erode and diminish Innogen as a historical figure by evoking through her near namesake many of the charges levelled at Brutan historicity. Heightening this, Imogen is also specifically associated with the element of air. A remorseful Iachimo declares that, having wronged Imogen, 'The Princesse of this Country', the 'ayre on't / Reuengingly enfeebles me' (1623: f. 392; 2017: 5.2.3–4), as if the British air and Imogen are interconnected. In a second attempt to interpret the prophecy left by Jupiter for Posthumus, the soothsayer Philarmonus parses the text's reference to the 'tender Ayre' which Posthumus must embrace as one of several conditions necessary for the restoration of peace to Britain. He does this by defining the tender air as representing Imogen in Latin as '*Mollis Aer*', which the soothsayer translates via '*Mulier*' (woman) to 'this most constant Wife' (f. 399; 5.5.446–8), configuring Imogen as merely a similitude in form of Innogen, a founder, or un-founder, at the end of Brutan time. She is thus aligned with the dispersing element of air, as *Locrine*'s Brutan founders give their names to massy landscape and rivers. Yet if these

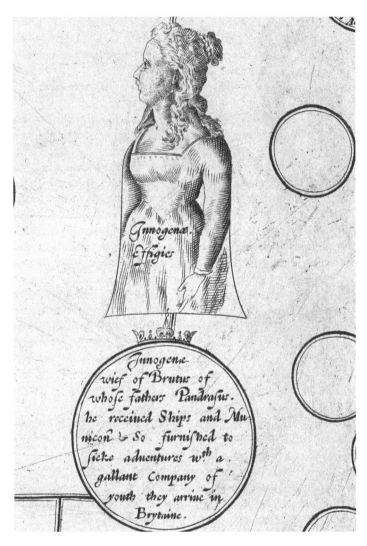

FIGURE 3 Innogen, wife of Brute. From Henry Slatyer's genealogical table *Genethliacon* (1630; f. 7). © The British Library Board (G.1190).

founders served to demark boundaries and material space, Imogen's presence and language serve to ravel in and eliminate boundaries and difference.

Cradling the headless body of Cloten, whose corpse she believes to be Posthumus's, and thinking the servant Pisanio has contrived this killing with forged letters, Imogen cries out that 'to write, and read, / be henceforth treacherous' (1623; f. 390; 2017: 4.2.315–16). Here, she expresses the way in which *Cymbeline*'s semiotic oversaturation creates a kind of hermeneutic snowblindness, where previously separate categories and temporalities flow together, where language, reading and writing, cannot be trusted. Impatient to leave for Milford, she declares her confusion in terms that collapse the distinctions between one place and another, between the present and the future, restating the temporal collapse hidden in Aquila's transformations: 'I see before me (Man) nor heere, not heere; / Nor what ensues but haue a Fog in them / That I cannot looke through' (1623: f. 381; 2017: 3.2.78–9). Either the present moment or the present place cannot be perceived, and the future is a fog. Expressing difference through a single word is a habit of Imogen's and one which contributes to a sense of distinction collapsing into sameness simultaneous with an emphasis on the heightened consequences of those differences. For example, she speaks of a journey's duration between 'houre, and houre' (f. 381; 3.2.68), and later of weeping 'twixt clock and clock' (f. 382; 3.4.42). This habit also inflects Imogen's response to Arviragus who, believing her a boy and not knowing himself to be her brother, describes her as a figurative brother: 'So man and man should be, / But Clay and Clay, differs in dignitie, / Whose dust is both alike' (f. 387; 4.2.3–5). The linguistic phenomenon of dissolving polarizing entities into one another is repeated at the level of *Cymbeline*'s games with time, source and history, and is manifested most acutely in a short exchange which, despite its passingness, draws the temporal poles of Brutan time to a single point, with Imogen at its vanishing centre.

Imogen asks Pisanio how long he watched from shore as his master Posthumus sailed away into exile. She castigates Pisanio for not watching longer and claims that, had she been at the waterside, she would have watched until Posthumus seemed to disappear:

Imo.
Thou should'st haue made him
As little as a Crow, or lesse, ere left
To after-eye him.

Pisa.
Madam, so I did.

Imo.
I would haue broke mine eye-strings;
Crack'd them, but to looke vpon him, till the diminution
Of space, had pointed him sharpe as my Needle:
Nay, followed him, till he had melted from
The smalnesse of a Gnat, to ayre: and then
Haue turn'd mine eye, and wept.

(1623: f. 371; 2017: 1.3.14–22)

In this description Posthumus shifts from the appearance of a needle to that of a near-dimensionless gnat and finally into Imogen's element of air, in a process she names the 'diminution / Of space', a unique phrase in early modern print that might be read as describing the trick of perspective through which Posthumus appears to dissolve. Yet the phrase has paradoxical qualities. The space between Posthumus and the watcher on the shore is not in fact diminishing; it is widening as the ship travels farther away. Additionally, the notion that the diminution of space is working upon Posthumus alone, shrinking him, is insufficient. The phrase suggests a more encompassing process of spatial contraction; not localized but enveloping *Cymbeline*'s wider space. This meaning is invited by Thomas Blundeville's *The Art of Logic*, which defines diminution among types of motion, as 'a decreasing or diminishing of quantitie in the whole, as a body that consumeth or pineth by disease or otherwise' (1599: sig. H2r), giving the diminution of space a sense of moving from the state of being something to being consumed by sickness to less than it was. The sickness, for *Cymbeline*, might be imagined as Lear's *Historica passio*. The word 'space' also carries a temporal meaning and is used frequently in the early modern period, as it is now, to indicate a 'space of time'. Thomas Wilson's *Christian Dictionary* defines time as '[s]ome certain space, as houre, day, weeke, yeare, &c.' (1622: f. 490).[18]

The word 'diminution' appears only once elsewhere in F1, in *Antony and Cleopatra*, another example of the play's subtle interleaving with *Cymbeline*. Antony, failing in battle, is described as having a 'diminution' in his brain that 'restores his heart' but damages his reason (1995: 4.1.203). Otherwise, it is a word almost entirely absent from early modern print drama but which appears frequently in religious and philosophical works in ways that often engage with perceptions of temporality.[19] Luis de Granada's *Spirituall and Heauenlie Exercises* invokes Seneca to illustrate time's mutability in terms that pre-empt the tensions Crooke identifies between permanence and dissolution: 'All things passe away, sayth Seneca, and are in continuall diminution & augmentation . . . . Nothing remayneth steadie of all those thinges we see: behold they are changed, whilst I speake, and I also am changed' (1598: f. 118). William Jewell's *The Golden Cabinet of True Treasure* also speaks of time, as 'beeing eyther past or to come', so that 'this moment, this pointe of time, deserueth rather to bee called a little little nothing', that, once lost, contributes to the 'great diminution of our days' (1612: sig. E8v). Brutan history, in Imogen's quayside vision, is implicated in these conceptions of temporal mutability and vanishing into a 'little little nothing'. This can be compared with the multiple temporalities of Othello's handkerchief as envisaged by Harris, an heirloom that is 'not a linear geometric sequence but a dynamic topology, in which supposedly secure points become mobile vectors in seismic shifts that superimpose past and present' (2009: 186). In *Cymbeline*, the handkerchief of Brutan time not only folds in on itself but disappears altogether, first blurring into the 'Gloue, or Hat, or Handkerchife' (1623: f. 371; 2017: 1.3.11) that Pisanio sees Posthumus waving from the deck of his departing ship, an object the indeterminacy of which increases as it vanishes. The diminution of space enfolds the diminution of time, spoken of in a moment when Imogen and Posthumus, two figures identified with both the prehistory and foundation of Brutan time, are imagined as drifting apart from one another. Their drifting apart also invokes the *Aeneid* and Geoffrey of Monmouth's *Historia* and collapses the space between the two.[20]

Imogen, as noted, *almost* shares her name with Innogen, the wife of Brute and thus co-founder of the Brutan dynasty. Posthumus, more complexly, has been associated with Brute and Brute's putative grandfather, Aeneas. He is compared by Imogen to 'false Aeneas' later in the play.[21] The image of a woman watching her lover depart by ship invokes the moment in the *Aeneid* at which Dido of Carthage is abandoned by Aeneas and awakes to see his fleet sailing away, leaving 'nothing left behynde at shore' (1573: sig. L2r).[22] This creates an associative synecdoche in which a fictional moment situated at the very end of Brutan time – Posthumus's departure for Rome during the reign of Cymbeline – is overlaid with an evocation of Brutan prehistory; that is, those events that enabled and predated the beginning of the *Historia*, both in terms of Geoffrey of Monmouth's vision of Brutan history's Trojan origins and in one of the texts he turned to when creating that history, the *Aeneid*. Yet the image has further parallels.

In a passage that appears to be absent from subsequent iterations of the Brutan histories, Geoffrey's *Historia* also provides a striking model for *Cymbeline*'s quayside episode. In the *Historia*, Innogen sails away from her homeland, Greece, having been awarded to Brute following his defeat of her father Pandrasus: 'She lamented at leaving behind her parents and country, and kept her gaze fixed on the coastline until it faded from view' (2007: 18).[23] Innogen's marriage and her departure with Brute are the events necessary for the foundation of Britain and the establishment of the Brutan bloodline. Conversely, Imogen's marriage with Posthumus takes place at the opposite end of Brutan time, where the *Historia* begins to interact uneasily with Roman histories. The *Historia* places Innogen on deck, looking back to shore. In *Cymbeline*, Imogen imagines herself on the shore watching her husband depart, echoing her forbears' epochal voyage. A reader familiar with the *Historia* might detect in this moment not only a diminution of the space between these two distant poles of Brutan time but also the mirror image of one in the other, a paradox of increased closeness and amplified difference analogous with Imogen's habit of contrasting 'clock and clock' and 'hour and hour'. As Innogen watches the shore, Imogen watches *from* the shore; Innogen is severed from her homeland by her father's command and her new husband's departure, while Imogen, kept ashore by her father's command, watches as her husband is severed from their shared homeland. The distant figure Imogen imagines waving from the ship could almost be her antecedent, Innogen. Indeed, Imogen's linguistic associations intensify the moment: the vision of Posthumus sailing away until he is 'melted . . . to ayre' (1623: f. 371; 2017: 1.3.20–1) draws centrifugally upon parallel episodes from the *Aeneid* and the *Historia*. But the single moment into which they are compressed is never lived but only imagined by Imogen.[24]

In this scene, *Cymbeline* enacts one of Harris's 'seismic shifts that superimpose past and present' (2009: 186). It draws together the poles of Brutan time, its fictive root and sources and in doing this, allusively, extinguishes the centuries that separate them. As Cymbeline exclaims, attempting to articulate the effect of the play's concluding revelations upon its participants, 'the counter-change is severally in all' (f. 398; 5.5.395–6): Posthumus-Aeneas-Brute disappears to nothing and this diminution of space, the counter-change, takes Brutan time with it. Throughout the play, Imogen appears singularly susceptible to, or emblematic of, such temporal retraction and disturbance. Having escaped house-arrest, as she thinks, to reunite with Posthumus at Milford Haven, Imogen speaks of her absence from Cymbeline's court as 'the gap / That we shall make in Time' (f. 381; 3.2.62–3) – a phrase evocative of temporal as well as spatial absence and emptiness. From the beginning of this study, a recurring theme in the survival of Brutan history has been the underlying fear of, and resistance to, the gap its absence would make in historical time, Edmund Bolton's 'vast Blanck upon the Times of our Country'. Before awakening from apparent death, Imogen speaks in her sleep, bewildered in a dream that, despite having travelled 'all night', Milford is 'sixe mile yet' away (f. 390; 4.2.292). Carr describes this moment as a 'nightmare in which [Imogen] can never walk far enough to reach Milford Haven' (1978: 325). That is, Imogen dreams herself as trapped in a kind of spatial and temporal bubble. But perhaps this space is simply the gap in time, once filled by Geoffrey of Monmouth, that has become a blank once more.

Imogen, in the sense explored here, embodies Cymbeline's diminutions, of the blank spaces between fiction and history, and of the gaps in time dividing its multiple temporalities. She is emblematic of something airy and imagined, something like the Brutan histories. She functions as a synecdoche for Cymbeline's free temporal space, its games with time, fiction and historiography, and in this way she completes the cultural work of dispersing the eroded Brutan histories into the play's, and F1's, surrounding and competing semiotic fields. Having recovered from her time-warping dream of travelling to Milford Haven, Imogen reflects that although she knows it is not true, the dream continues to inhabit her emotions and senses: '[t]he Dreame's here still: even when I wake it is / Without me, as within me: not imagin'd, felt' (f. 390; 4.2.305–6). Moving beyond what is imagined into what is 'felt', Imogen describes the disorientating experience of retaining bodily and affectively a habit of belief that has in all other respects been eroded and revealed as insubstantial. As such, it might serve as a fitting way to imagine the phenomenological experience of longing, confusion, nostalgia and loss perhaps felt by those early modern readers and playgoers who were finally accepting that the strange millennium of Britain's pagan antiquity had always been, as Richard Harvey had accidentally intuited, 'books of nothing' (1593: sig. H3r). For some of these individuals, I suggest, reading F1 *Cymbeline* might have felt like waking from a dream.

All canons are temporary, however. In 1664, the third Shakespeare folio saw the addition of seven plays that had been in one way or another associated with Shakespeare via tradition or title page attribution in quarto. The final play in this new sequence, and therefore the concluding play of the folio, was *Locrine*. Thus, the kaleidoscopic resolution of Brutan time outlined earlier became muted within the wider textual scheme as *Cymbeline* becomes prologue to *Pericles*. Instead, F3 ends with massacre and self-drowning instead of reunion and peace and with the beginning, not the end, of Brutan time. It is resonant that, in 1664, when seeking a concluding logic for the expanded volume, the stationers chose a Brutan play.

In other ways, too, F1 *Cymbeline* cannot represent the final Brutan text or performance. As noted in the Introduction, a cluster of new and reprinted historiographic texts, chronologies and plays appeared in the years around 1630–7, the early years of Charles I's 'personal rule'. William Slatyer's pictographic genealogy *Genethliacon* (1630) opens with illustrations of Brute and Innogen and was dedicated to King Charles. John Taylor's 1630 edition of *A Memorial of all the English Monarchs* includes the addition of Taylor's declaration that 'I follow the common opinion . . . there was a BRVTE' (1630: sig. B1r). Both argue that Brutan belief persisted, or was perceived as persisting, by these authors and their stationers hoping for royal favour or success in print – an achievement for which Taylor had a notable talent. No single text or conclusive piece of evidence indicates why these years should see what appears to be a Brutan revival, including a 1634 staging of *Cymbeline* before Charles I. *Fuimus Troes*, the final Brutan play to appear in print, appeared in 1633, the year following the 1632 royal masque *Albions Trivmph*, but was probably first performed many years before. John Milton's *A Masque Presented at Ludlow Castle* was performed in 1634 and published anonymously in 1637. Each of these texts figuratively suggests etiological erosion in very different ways. *Fuimus Troes* quixotically asserts Brutan historicity, while *Albions Trivmph* reactivates the propagandistic interaction of Brutan figures and monarchs evidenced throughout this book. However, as will be shown, in *Albions Trivmph*, performed at the outset of the 'personal rule', the monarch himself 'becomes' the Brutan figure Albanactus. This moment of semiotic absorption is contrasted with *A Masque* which, in reviving the drowned Sabren as the benevolent water goddess Sabrina, enacts in a single figure the imagery of erosion and 'mythic' transformation explored in *Cymbeline*.

Fuimus Troes

Fuimus Troes is the final extant Brutan play of the pre-Restoration era. It is thus curious, and a little ironic, that it is also the only early modern drama to explicitly cite and, seemingly, endorse Geoffrey of Monmouth. Performed for and by students at Oxford's Magdalen College, *Fuimus Troes* attempts to harmonize Roman and Brutan accounts of Julius Caesar's invasion of Britain in a way that subtly authorizes Brutan historicity. Even its title is taken from the *Aeneid* ('we were Trojans') and draws the play's Roman and British forces into a shared ancestry.

Caesar's *Commentaries* described the Romans' clashes with indigenous British tribes in the south-east of Britain. As noted, their leader, Cassibelan, was the first figure of British antiquity to be accepted as historical by those writers, such as Speed and Daniel, who dismissed the Brutan histories (1611: f. 170). The Brutan histories, however, also featured Cassibelan's clashes with the Romans as a central narrative (2007: 68–80). There were many differences between the two accounts, one difference in particular demonstrating their fundamental incompatibility. As Holinshed put it, 'according to that which Cesar himselfe and other autenticke authors have written', Britain was made 'tributarie to the Romans by the conduct of the same Cesar'; however, 'our histores farre differ from this, affirming that Cesar comming the second time, was by the Britaines with valiancie and martiall prowesse beaten and repelled, as he was at the first' (1587: III, *Hist.* 30). According to Caesar, the British had been overpowered and compelled to pay tribute to Rome (1996: 5.22). According to the Brutan tradition, it was Caesar who had been 'beaten and repelled'. The British, then, were either a people entirely absent from the historiography of antiquity who emerged into recorded time only to suffer military defeat by their conqueror-chronicler or scions of Trojan founders and conquerors who gloriously fought off their continental invading cousins. Of core significance to this second conception of the British past was the notion of Britain and Rome's shared Trojan origins. It is unsurprising that so many English favoured the latter, a preference perhaps legible in the compressed and eccentric title under which the play appears on its title page, set out in what Lisa Hopkins describes as 'its own bizarre typography' (2002: 38): *Fvimvs Troes Æneid 2. The True Troianes* (1633: sig. A2r). Like 'true chronicle history', protesting too much perhaps, this triplicate title asserts Britain's Trojan origins, posits the play as a kind of sequel to Virgil's original and foregrounds historiographic tensions by referring to '*True Troianes*'. The term could refer to the play's Britons, its Romans or both. Both claimed Trojan origins via historiographies that were, as many early seventeenth-century writers insisted, fundamentally incompatible. *Fuimus Troes* attempts to reconcile these two positions.

Fuimus Troes was published in 1633, and attributed to Jasper Fisher by Anthony Wood, the seventeenth-century historian of Oxford (Butler 2007). The date of the play's original performance has been harder to establish.[25] Wiggins examines Oxford's records for unnamed plays performed during Fisher's residence at Magdalen (2016: 7, ref. 1890). Finding a single instance of a suitable play, logged in 1619 according to an appropriate genre – 'tragedy' – Wiggins proposes this as potentially being *Fuimus Troes*. The play was, according to its title page, '[p]ublikely represented by the Gentlemen Students of Magdalen Colledge in Oxford' (1633: sig. A2r). The play was performed within a tradition of academic performances that 'were written for and seen by a select audience', participation in which was seen as 'contributing to the training of orators destined for the law courts and the pulpit' (Astington 2009: 19). The pedagogical and intellectual aspirations of the form should, however, be considered against much evidence that audiences were 'frequently unruly', with students passing out, even being stabbed or trampled, despite the oversight of armed guards, or 'whifflers' (Elliott 1997: 69). University drama is, after all, the genre that produced the less-than-pedagogical lampoon of arch-Brutan Richard Harvey, 'Duns Furens'. There is also a sense of possible insularity: many extant university plays reveal the attitudes 'of an elite in-group, sceptical if not downright scornful of those outside it' (Astington 2009: 22). This could suggest that *Fuimus Troes* reveals the historiographic bias and interests of a very specific textual community. However, Andrew Gurr quotes the prologue to Thomas Tomkis's *Albumazar*, staged before King James at Trinity College in 1615, to note that it was performed in English 'for the sake of the ladies in the audience', while an earlier play, *Club Law* (*c.* 1599–1600), was 'allegedly written in English so that the uneducated citizens of the town would understand it' (2009: 46). *Fuimus Troes* is in English and, while the playbook's paratext includes un-glossed quotes in Latin, the play uses almost none and, in one case, when the character Eulinus quotes Ovid in Latin, this is followed immediately by its English translation, as if to accommodate non-Latin speakers: 'For well my Poet saies, *Militat omnis Amans,* Each Louer is a Souldier' (1633: sig. C1v).[26] Nor should it be imagined that, in being 'academic', *Fuimus Troes* is untheatrical. It opens with a Seneca-like dialogue between Mercury and the ghosts of the Brutan Brennus and his Roman enemy Camillus, whom

Mercury has recalled from the underworld (sig. A3r); frequent musical interludes are performed by a historiographically appropriate 'Chorus of fiue Bardes laureate' and a harpist (sig. A2v). These provide regular breaks in the action, while the inclusion of a clown-like cowardly soldier, the gluttonous Rollano, 'a Belgicke', seems again to recall an earlier theatrical era and, specifically, *Locrine*'s Strumbo.

Strikingly, the British general Cassibelan's defiance of the Romans' demand for tribute is performed via a ritual wherein the British generals kiss his sword (1633: sig. C1v). This action seems to be associated with the ancient world and the Near East. Locrine kisses his sword before his suicide in *Locrine* (1595: sig. K2r). In Thomas Goffe's *The Courageous Turk, or Amurath the First* (pub. 1632), the Turkish character Aladin calls upon his followers to show their loyalty against the protagonist Amurath by kneeling and kissing his sword (sig. F2v). Goffe's play was performed at Christ Church, Oxford, in 1619, the same year proposed by Wiggins for *Fuimus Troes*. In Oxford this would have dimly recreated, in repertory terms, the Turkish-Brutan hybridity examined in Chapter 2.[27] However, many of these dramaturgical strategies also seem to support a particular version of history, detectable not only in the dialogue's dense classical and Brutan allusions but also in the play's staging. Academic didacticism is evident in the precision of the play's costumes, rituals and stage directions, which suggest an attempt at historical reconstruction and substantial material preparations for, and material investment in, the production.

Caesar's army enters bearing an '*Ensigne*, A two-neck'd Eagle displayed sable' (1633: sig. A4v), while the British druids enter in 'hats like Pyramids' and carrying 'branches of Mistletoe' (sig. C3r). The British priests perform a ritual before a temple of Diana, 'thou first guide of Brutus to this Ile' (sig. D2r), below which a 'Shrine opens' (sig. D1v). In terms of stage ritual and spectacle, the play prioritizes and specifies the performance of ancient Britain. A closer examination of the text reveals the play's obsessive historiographic detail and a subtle, if persistent, engagement with Brutan conceptions of pre-Roman history.

Fuimus Troes is the only extant early modern drama to engage explicitly with the Brutan controversy. It does this via strategies that are far more dependent upon sophisticated historiographic knowledge than the Brutan drama examined thus far, particularly in terms of the playbook's paratextual apparatus. Butler observes that, alongside its two historical military rivals, the play's 'two main sources', Caesar's *Commentaries* and Geoffrey's *Historia*, might be 'regarded as the real protagonist and antagonist among the *Dramatis Personae*' (2007). This tension is diagrammatically inscribed in the play's dramatis personae list, which groups its characters according to the sources from which they derive – principally Caesar's *Commentaries* and, specifically, the fourth book of Geoffrey of Monmouth's *Historia*.

Butler observes that by listing the character of Cassibelan twice, first as Caesar's Cassibellaunus, then as the *Historia*'s Cassibelane, the text seems to 'assert an equivalence between Caesar and Geoffrey's texts as "history"' while presenting the two groups of characters as representative of these competing historiographies (2007). The playbook's historiographical inclusiveness, however, bends and warps its characters. To accommodate the two histories' differences, the British traitor Androgeus appears 'onstage with his Caesarian double, Mandubratius' (Butler 2007). Assimilating accounts in this way materializes through performance the notion that apparent incompatibilities might be harmonized as alternative perspectives on the same remote past. Yet this could also appear as simply peopling the past with as many additional bodies as are required to preserve Brutan historicity. From this perspective, *Fuimus Troes* physically enacts the synchronizing impulse of Scaliger's 'proleptic time' approach to universal history, which resorted to situating inconveniently dated chronicle events prior to the Creation. One possible effect of this is to strengthen Brutan historicity rather than balance it with the Roman account. Brutan time is also supported by the use, throughout, and by both Roman and British characters, of the name 'Cassibelane'. When *Fuimus Troes* is forced to choose between versions, it chooses the Brutan. The suggestion that the Brutan is favoured over the Roman is intensified by the play's frequent references to both well-known and marginal figures of Brutan antiquity.

Of all the plays examined in this book, *Fuimus Troes* offers perhaps a deeper, or at least more detailed, engagement with its Brutan sources than *Gorboduc* and *Locrine*. Associations of landscape and founder are invoked: Locrine and Estrild's drowned daughter Sabren, or Sabrine, endures as the personification of the river Severn, described as 'that boyling streame, / Where Sabrine louely Damsell lost her breath' (1633: sig. D1v). Guendolen appears in one of the play's several songs as 'The Amazon of her daies' (sig. H2v), while the play's chorus refers to the obscure king Morindus, notable only for having been eaten by a sea-monster (sig. H2v). One of the play's two female figures, neither of whom appears onstage, is named 'only once . . . and thus seems to be introduced into the narrative expressly for the purpose of having her name mentioned' (Hopkins 2002: 45). The character's name is Cordella (sig. B4r). These references are bound into the play's cosmology, contributing to its sense of the past's active engagement with the present and beyond into the afterlife. Towards the play's end, a raging Cassibelan foresees the end of British rule as a vast cremation: 'Let Britaines climactericall yeere now runne, / The Series breake of seuentie Kings: Nay let / One vrne conclude our ashes and the worlds' (sig. H3v). The invocation of Britain's seventy rulers asserts the vast reach of Brutan time, indicating the scale of the tragedy Cassibelan believes he faces. The druid Lantonus reflects upon an ancient prophecy, that '[t]he gods foretold these mischiefes long agoe, / In Eldells raigne, The Earth and Sky were fild / With prodigies, strange Sights, and hellish shapes . . . / And bloody droppes speckled the grasse' (sig. C3v). The reference to Eldell, another obscure king known only for this rain of blood falling during his reign, demonstrates that the play's ancient Britons are both familiar with and thus generated by, this history. Equally, Lantonus's belief that these prodigies of antiquity have foretold the events of the present further endorses that antiquity's metaphysical reality. The dying hero Nennius, brother of Lud, aspires to a specifically Brutan afterlife:

> I long euen to behold those glorious Cloysters,
> Where Brutus, great Dunwallo, and his sonnes,
> Thrice noble Spirits walke.
> Thou mighty Enginer of this wondrous Globe,
> Protect this Ile, confound all forraine plots:
> Graunt Thames and Tyber neuer ioyne thair chanells.

> (1633: sig. E4v)

Nennius's hope to walk with his ancestors invokes a cluster of kings and plays: Brute, the founder of Britain, Mulmutius Dunwallo, the lawmaker, and Mulmutius's own sons, Brennus and Belinus, all subjects of several lost and extant Brutan plays. Brennus himself appears as a ghost, returned from the 'glorious Cloysters', at the play's opening. Nennius's wish that 'Thames and Tyber' might never flow together, as the play's competing sources are being forced to do, is, in this sense, undercut as the character of Caesar himself, the author of the *Commentaries* that seemed to refute Brutan historicity, is audaciously enlisted in the Brutan cause, lamenting that he must 'draw my sword against the stocke / Of thrice-renowned Troy' (sig. C4v). A conversation between Caesar and Hulacus, a captured British priest, ends with a further prophecy that extends the metaphysical agency of Brutan time, configuring it as the underlying cause of Caesar's eventual death: 'A Brutus strong / Repayes in Fine: / Thy brutish wrong / To Brutus line' (sig. H3v). Caesar's assassination by Brutus, the play predicts, will be a murderously actualized pun, the nature of his death determined by the name of the man whose descendants he has wronged. *Fuimus Troes* represents the synthesis of Brutan and Roman accounts with the effect of asserting Brutan historicity from its ground zero position at the 'climactericall yeere' of Brutan time. At the metaphysical level of prophecy, the etymology of Britain's founder determines the manner of death for Caesar, the Roman whose written works had become for many historiographers the ultimate rebuke to Brute's existence in historical time. Conversely, the court masque *Albions Trivmph* appears to ravel up Brutan iconography into the person of the monarch himself, thereby uprooting it from the broader source of its resonance and meaning.

Albions Triumph

Charles I's personal rule was not, in itself, exceptional. His father, James, had failed to call Parliament between 1611 and 1621 (Butler 1984: 13; Hirst 1986: 160). However, many critics agree that, unlike James, Charles during this time 'constructed his own imagined world' (Brown 2008: 25). This was achieved through the introduction of new court protocols, rituals and hierarchies that triggered a 'process of isolating the social magic of the Crown within a tightly controlled court culture' (Whitted 2009: 4). Charles's protocols expressed a 'concern for order and majesty', and new orders of 1629 and 1631 focused specifically on behaviour in the vicinity of royal palaces and enforced the maintenance of hierarchies 'both in private and in public' (Hirst 1986: 162). This inwardness was, to an extent, an illusion. Food riots reached a 100-year peak in Kent in 1630–1 (Hirst 1986: 169). Further, the crown's self-image of divinely sanctioned aloofness was compromised by its dependence on funds 'derived from monopolies' (Whitted 2009: 2). This was a series of 'fiscal devices which estranged those on whose support [Charles] was most dependent' (Butler 1984: 16). Nevertheless, during the personal rule, 'an emphasis upon the [royal] prerogative replaced the rhetoric and traditions of communion between the king and his subjects' (Sharpe 1987: 298). The royal person also seems to have absorbed and superseded much of the iconography that had once represented dialogue between institutions, as well as the past and present. Despite the familiar temptation to read Charles's reign as containing the seeds of unavoidable collapse into civil war, in the 1630s he may have seemed destined for 'absolute monarchy on the continental model' (Butler 1984: 14). He ruled, after all, at a time of uninterrupted peace. And this is how it may have appeared to the audiences of court masques and command performances given by the King's Men and others.

The records of Charles's Master of the Revels, Henry Herbert, show how closely Charles worked to construct and manage his entertainments, interceding on issues of censorship with Davenant's *The Witts* (pub. 1636) and enjoying a play, Shirley's *The Gamester*, written 'out of a plot of the king's' given to Shirley, and which Charles claimed to Herbert was 'the best play he had seen for seven years' (1996: 187). The Christmas season during which these actions took place, 1633–4, also featured a performance of *Cymbeline* on 1 January that was 'Well likte by the kinge' (Herbert 1996: 185).[28] This performance can perhaps be contextualized a part of the season's wider design. The records suggest a degree of repertory planning along thematic lines. A revival of *The Taming of the Shrew* was followed by Fletcher's sequel to that play, *The Tamer Tam'd*, in November (Herbert 1996: 185). One performance could reflect a wider scheme, referencing or following from others. A performance of Fletcher's *The Faithfull Shepherdess* followed *Cymbeline* on 6 January 1633–4 and, as Herbert records, utilized scenery from a masque performed for the queen the previous year (1996: 185). For this performance, *The Faithfull Shepherdess* opened with a prologue written for, and spoken to, Charles and Henrietta Maria, declaring them '[w]elcom as Peace t'unwalled Citties, when / Famine and Sword leave them more graves then men' (1656: sig. A4v).[29] This exhortation to peace would seem to follow from *Cymbeline*'s irenic design and concluding 'peace', further suggesting, with a performance of the similarly themed *The Winter's Tale* on 16 January, that this theme was sustained throughout the season. This preoccupation peaked on 3 February with James Shirley's Inns of Court masque *The Triumph of Peace* (pub. 1633). *Triumph* dominated the London streets, concluding with a masque in Whitehall designed to pacify Charles following a controversy over the lawyer William Prynne's recent antitheatrical tract *Histriomastix*, which had been perceived as attacking Henrietta Maria's participation in court performances. The figure of Irene, or Peace, sings aloud the rhetorical question if this 'glorious night, / Wherein two skies are to be seene, / One starry, but an aged sphere another here, / Created new and brighter from the Eyes of King and Queene?' (1633: sig. C2v). Themes of ancient British etiology emerge in the season's closing masque, Thomas Carew's *Coelum Britannicum* (pub. 1634), which presents a dance of ancient British worthies, 'of these famous Isles, / That long have slept, in fresh and lively shapes', which the presenter Mercury describes explicitly as being both 'rude / And old Abiders here, and in them view / The point from which your full perfections grew' (1634: sig. E1r). A dance is then given by a company of 'Picts, the naturall Inhabitants of this Isle' (sig. E1v), presenting British antiquity as both primal and non-Brutan. These themes, of peace, ancient Britain and a semiotic inwardness centring upon the gathering of virtue and meaning exclusively to the royal person, are a persistent presence throughout the 1633–4 Christmas season, a context in which the choice of *Cymbeline* is entirely explicable. The same year, the artist Peter Paul Rubens was busily working on designs for the Banqueting Hall ceiling, the allegorical designs of which centred on the apotheosis of James VI and I, who ascends to heaven astride an eagle (Strong 1980: 52).[30] These irenic themes were established and encapsulated some time before, however, via Charles's personation of the quasi-Brutan figure Albanactus, in Aurelian Townshend and Inigo Jones's masque, *Albions Trivmph*, performed at Whitehall on Twelfth Night 1631–2.

Albions Trivmph establishes themes of platonic love and a classicized aesthetic that would permeate the personal rule's cultural expression. It featured the king and queen and celebrated their union as a mystical expression of a divine cosmic order. Townshend's introduction to the print edition outlines in detail the setting and the characters to be played by the royal couple. The setting is '*ALBIPOLIS* the chiefe City of *ALBION*' (1632: sig. A2r), represented by a backdrop showing a 'Roman atrium' (1632: sig. A3r). The tug of war between Roman and Brutan accounts of history seems here both concluded and irrelevant. The characters are, as seen with the etymology of Brutan origins, explicated by the resonance of their names:

> The Triumpher, *ALBANACTVS,* And *ALBA* this Ilands Goddesse. Names not improper, eyther for the Place, or for the Persons: *ALBION* being (as it once was) taken for *England; ALBANACTVS,* for the King, *Quasi in Albania natus: Borne in Scotland.* And *ALBA,* for the Queene whose native Beauties have a great affinity with all Purity and Whitenesse. (1632: sig. A2r)

The figure of Albanactus, while taking his name from the son of Brute and martial hero of *Locrine*, is dissociated from that narrative, which goes unmentioned and, instead, serves the purpose of representing Charles's Scottish origins, thereby perhaps conflating England and Scotland in one body, that of Charles as 'the ideal Platonic ruler before the temple of Jove' (Strong 1980: 23). This version of Albanact is not present, as he was in *Triumphs of Re-United Britainia*, to advocate for the intercession of the past with the present in the cause of national union or royal glory. He has founded nothing. He exists only, and has meaning only, according to the moment and terms in which the king personates him. Indeed, the names of triumpher, country, city and queen, are locked within a closed, self-authorizing etymological circuit. In the masque, the god Mercury descends and foretells Albanactus's coming. He will be '[m]ighty, as the Man design'd / To weare those Bayes; Heroicke, as his mind; / Iust, as his actions; Glorious, as his Reigne. / And like his Vertues, Infinite in Treyne' (1632: sig. A4v). He is described by the character Publius, who represents the common people of Albipolis, as 'ALBANACTVS CAESAR' (1632: sig. B2r). This title conjoins the Brutan name with the 'imperial dignities that were so often associated with James' (Parry 1981: 190). Yet both titles are severed from the figures they evoke, the source of meaning reversed: the presence and body of the king provides the only necessary context. Albanactus finally appears before a scene of a temple of Jupiter, costumed 'like a Romane Emperour' (1632: sig. B1v). He is exhorted by the figures of Cupid and Diana to surrender and love Alba as this will 'make our *CAESAR* greater yet' (sig. B4v). Struck by Cupid's arrows, Albanactus is described as '*yeilding to the Gods*'; he '*mooves downe the steps in a stately pace to Musick made by the Chorus of Sacrificers*' (sig. C1r). Charles descends from his throne on stage. All is performed in silence, in the convention of court masques (McManus 2002: 7). He dances, then takes his place besides Alba, the queen, concluding his performance.

Stephen Orgel has noted that the masque is 'a world of absolutes, in which all action is inherent in the nature of the individual figures' (1967: 197). *Albions Trivmph* represses the historiography upon which it draws in favour of Charles as the absolute and individual figure through which meaning is determined. Charles's silence is entirely conventional to the royal masque genre; yet just as the conventions of the Elizabethan playhouse enacted a particular effect upon *Locrine*'s vision of Brutan history, here Charles's silence as Albanactus might be seen to present an image of completed etiological erosion. We have seen how, in the English pageants and royal entries of the fifteenth and sixteenth centuries, performers' bodies served as uncanny conduits through which Brutan founders might both reassert the spirit of a place and intercede on behalf of the present; how in *Gorboduc* Brutan drama was inaugurated so that events of British antiquity might be used to influence Elizabeth I's political choices; how for James VI and I's union project Brutan iconography was deployed in strategies, ultimately futile, of persuasion, even as the historiography buckled and collapsed into *Historica passio*. Throughout the early modern era, Brutan rulers were materialized to confront, in one way or another, their putative royal descendants. In *Albions Trivmph*, conversely, the Brutan figure's energies are siphoned from their animating contexts, silencing the dialogue between the past and the present: Albanactus is not himself powerful, but only as 'mighty', 'heroic' and 'just' as Charles is already. He brings no pre-existing qualities or characteristics, no originary essence, to bestow upon the monarch. It is a closed circuit, and the performer's body summons only Charles as the idea of absolute, divinely endorsed monarchy. The semiotics of the 'imagined world' of Charles I's personal rule absorb the fictive Brutan origins they have invoked. Albanactus breaks away from the landmass of Brutan history and is absorbed by the performing monarch. In Milton's *A Masque Presented at Ludlow Castle*, however, the Brutan figure of Sabren escapes human temporality altogether. Reconfigured as Sabrina, nymph of the River Severn, she fulfils the logic of founder, place and essence proposed in Chapter 2 in a manner that releases her from the confines of historicity.

A Masque Presented at Ludlow Castle (*Comus*)

If *Locrine* showed the innocent Sabren's suicide, leaping into the waters of the river that will memorialize her under the name Severn, then John Milton's *A Masque*, performed approximately forty years later, sees Sabren re-emerge from those waters, having undergone a transformation into the 'goddesse of the river' (1637: f. 29). *A Masque* was written for John, Earl of Bridgewater, Lord President of Wales. It was performed on 29 September 1634 at Ludlow Castle by a company including three of Bridgewater's children, Alice (aged fifteen), John (eleven) and Thomas (nine), their music master Henry Lawes and unnamed others. The masque tells of three children lost in the Welsh forests. There are suggestive contextual links to *Cymbeline*'s 1634 court performance in the masque's two brothers and a sister 'lost' in the Welsh wilderness and menaced by a primitive and sexually predatory enemy (Cloten/Comus). John and Thomas had performed at court in *Coelum Britannicum* in February 1634, only a few months before *A Masque* (Lewalski 1998: 304), raising the possibility that they, or at least their father, could have been among *Cymbeline*'s spectators. Topographically, *A Masque* brings the performance of Brutan history tantalizingly close to its putative origins in the *liber vetustissimus* from which Geoffrey of Monmouth claimed to have translated his *Historia*, and which he claimed was written in Welsh, or the 'British tongue' (2007: 4). Yet, just as that book was almost certainly Geoffrey's enabling fiction, so *A Masque* reveals the unsustainability of Brutan time's 'mythic' afterlife.

Alice's character, named only as 'The Lady', becomes separated from her brothers and is menaced by Comus, the barbarous hybrid child of Bacchus and the sorceress Circe. Comus magically traps the Lady in a chair in order to beguile her of her virginity. Aided by a benevolent Attendant Spirit, the brothers scare away Comus but cannot free the Lady from the 'stonie fetters fixt, and motionless' in which she is trapped, until the Spirit summons 'Sabrina faire' from '[v]nder the glassie, coole, translucent wave', that she might '[l]isten and save' the Lady (1637: f. 29). Sabrina releases the Lady by sprinkling drops 'from my fountaine pure' upon the 'marble venom'd seate' (f. 31). Kat Lecky has argued that Sabrina 'naturalizes the Lady into the Welsh body politic' (2014: 133): that is, the performance has an immediate function of resituating Alice Bridgewater within the border country she now occupies while avoiding her absorption into its more threatening wildness. This sustains the purity necessitated by her role as her father's marriageable offspring.

However, there is also a historiographic context. While Sabrina speaks nothing of her origins, the Spirit recounts her role as told through the fate of Sabren in *Locrine*, echoing, deliberately or otherwise, that play's depiction of her death as suicide. As Schwyzer has noted, so that she can function as a figure protective of chastity, 'Milton's greatest innovation is the complete elision of Sabrina's bastardy', her origin as Locrine and Estrild's illegitimate child (1997: 37). Erin Murphy has explored Sabrina's relationship with Brutan historiography, describing her as a figure 'disconnected from mortal time and history' that cannot quite be squared with the Spirit's 'genealogical impulses' to tell Sabrina's history (2011: 101). Sabrina 'no longer functions as a lineal connection to the past' (2011: 102). Yet, as was seen in figures such as Brennus at Bristol, or Ebrauk at York in 1486, a sense of presentness needn't mean severance from history as it does in *Albions Trivmph*. However, there is clearly something different in the way Sabrina does not simply emerge from history. She has instead, as the Spirit explains, been transformed. Pursued by Gwendolen and having leapt into the river, the mortal Sabrina came to the attention of the 'water Nymphs that in the bottome playd' and who thus

> Held up their pearled wrists and tooke her in,
> Bearing her straite to aged Nereus hall
> Who piteous of her woes reatd [*sic*] her lanke head,
> And gave her to his daughters to imbathe
> In nectar'd lavers strewd with asphodil,
> And through the porch, and inlet of each sense
> Dropt in ambrosial oyles till she reviv'd,
> And underwent a quicke, immortall change
> Made goddesse of the river.

> (1637: f. 29)

At the hands of the river nymphs, Sabrina undergoes a 'quicke, immortal change' that mirrors and accelerates the history-to-poetry transformations proposed by early modern theorists such as Puttenham. In *A Masque* this cultural and literary process is recreated as a physical metamorphosis enacted through the medium of water, just as in *Cymbeline* Imogen's embodiment of etiological erosion might have been perceived as occurring through the element of air. However, as Schwyzer notes, this sense of mythic deepening is misleading: 'the goddess Sabrina appears to have had no place in regional lore' (1997: 21). The 'silver lake' of which Sabrina is goddess is in fact shallow and localized to a particular, elite textual community rather than the folkloric networks of myth: very different to the popular tradition that sustained Sabren as a figure of lived history from the twelfth to the seventeenth centuries. Instead, we return to post-mythic Brutan history as explored in *Cymbeline*. As suggested earlier, the ascent of Jupiter in *Cymbeline* may be seen as signalling the end of pagan time at the moment of the Incarnation. Similarly, the stage direction 'Sabrina descends and the Ladie rises out of her seate' (1637: f. 32) might be seen, figuratively, as a moment at which Brutan time, its brief function as myth over almost before it has begun, sinks into immateriality and forgetfulness.

Philip Schwyzer has suggested that, in *A Masque*, 'Milton wrested Locrine's daughter into a new form ... a second, literary immortality while her baser predecessors, so many luckless Habrens, Sabrens, and Sabrines, have been drowned anew in antiquarian obscurity' (1997: 23). Schwyzer's observation touches on something at the core of this study. Brutan time was finally eroded as history; it outlived its propagandistic usefulness and its traceability to a single author and text foreclosed its status as myth. I would suggest, qualifying Schwyzer's observation a little, that the literary life of Brutan history has also retreated into the relative obscurity of academic and cultural–historical interest. If the Brutan histories have a wider cultural life at all in the twenty-first century, it is in drama, kept above water by the sustained commercial primacy of the 'Shakespeare' industry. Although in this book I have worked to bring together as full an account as I can of early modern Brutan drama, it would be disingenuous to claim that the road did not lead back somewhere to my affective response as a reader and spectator of *Cymbeline* and, particularly, of *King Lear*. It is perhaps ironic that the dramatic texts created in response to the Brutan histories' extraordinary medieval and early modern resonance are now a principal cause of why we return to those histories. If Brutan time died as history, and then as myth, sometime in the seventeenth century, it survives today not as poesie historical but in the form through which it has been explored here: as play.

Conclusions

Sometime after the republication of John Taylor's *A Memoriall of all the English Monarchs*, a copy was purchased by the Staffordshire book-collector Frances Wolfreston (1607–77), whose library has been said to represent 'the leisure reading of a literate lady in her country house' (Morgan 1989: 200). As noted, the 1630 edition of *A Memoriall* summarized the lives of 'English' rulers from Brute to Charles I, adding at the outset the strident marginal note 'I follow the common opinion . . . there was a BRVTE' (1630: sig. B1r). Wolfreston's collection, and her occasional marginalia, offers a glimpse of the ways in which drama, popular print and historiography intersected for early modern readers and complicated the reading of British origins via engagement with the Brutan histories. Without the foregoing work on these intersections, certain elements of Wolfreston's reading, and the textual community she created for her household through her choice of books, would be less apparent.

Wolfreston owned several plays, including Heywood's *2 Iron Age*, in which she inscribed the observation that she found it 'trower then the old history bouk' (transcribed in Gerritsen 1964: 273). Here, we have evidence of an early modern reader comparing drama and an 'old history bouk' for the historical verity of Trojan antiquity and finding the drama 'truer'. *2 Iron Age*, as observed in the previous chapter, includes the prophecy that the fleeing Aeneas's descendant Brute 'shall reare . . . great Britaines Troy-nouant' (1632: sig. E2v). Wolfreston, then, is favouring the historicity of a play that endorses Britain's Trojan origins. These comments have prompted Claire Kenward to ask '[w]hat is the old history book which Wolfreston . . . had in mind in her reading of Heywood's play?' (2017: 99). The question is, to an extent, unanswerable, although Woolf has observed that among her 'personal library of verse, drama, and moral theological writings' Wolfreston also owned 'a significant number of histories', including Camden's *Britannia* (1997: 642).[1] As noted, Camden's 1586 work, published in English translation in 1610 and in several further seventeenth-century editions, has been cited as the death-knell of Brutan time. Here, it sits on the shelves alongside popular drama and Taylor's pro-Brutan chronology. Certainly an 'old history bouk' by Wolfreston's time, *Britannia* could perhaps be the work she refutes, in tune with Taylor and Heywood.

I have argued that the Brutan histories carried a powerful affective resonance for English readers and playgoers, a means of self-understanding via Rothstein's concept that 'origin defines essence'. Whether in performance or on the page Brutan figures provided etiological models upon which personal and familial identities might be inscribed, as shown by the many manuscript Prose *Bruts* in which medieval and early modern readers added their own genealogies to household copies (Radulescu 2006: 192). Wolfreston's collection included an analogous example of this type of textual inheritance; a copy of Chaucer's works containing marginalia by many earlier readers identified as 'Wolfrestons's female ancestors', providing 'an example of how several successive generations of early modern female readers negotiated their engagement with a literary text within a domestic context' (Wiggins 2010: 77). For Wolfreston, or someone within the household textual community, this identification was also expressed through Brutan personification. *A Memoriall* includes thumbnail woodcut portraits of each monarch (see Chapter 1). In Wolfreston's copy, someone has sketched two cursory faces (1630: sig. A4r). These are noted by Paul Morgan as 'crowned heads' (1989: 219). What is not noted, however, is that a more finished sketch, appearing a few pages later in *A Memoriall* (sig. B2r), is not simply a 'crowned head' but a copy of the thumbnail portrait representing 'Queen *Cordeilla*' on the opposing page (sig. B1v). It is striking that an early modern woman reader presented with portraits of British and English rulers, from Brute to Charles I, should choose not only a Brutan figure but one of only two Brutan women rulers to reproduce in portrait. Here, I suggest, is evidence of the kind of personal, personified interaction I have been arguing for, and this marginal drawing may be seen as a species of self-recognition achieved through the lens of Brutan history.

Wolfreston appears to have owned more works by Taylor than any other writer, and thus her note in *2 Iron Age*, combined with the marginal portrait of Cordeilla, suggests some sympathy for Brutan history. However, when a copy of the 1655 quarto of *King Lear* was added to the collection, it brought with it that text's disruptive *Historica passio*, its violent negation of Brutan time through the ahistorical deaths of its protagonists, namely Cordelia. By the mid-seventeenth century, *Britannia* may have sat alongside Heywood's Trojan plays and Taylor's Brutan chronology in Wolfreston's collection. Both texts demonstrate particular personal engagement via their annotation; *King Lear* introduced further disruption via the very medium through which Wolfreston appears to have processed a sense of historical truth: drama. Brutan etiology, the means of its erosion and the dramatic texts that both ignored and had the potential to agitate that sense of erosion, are all present in Wolfreston's reading. Her marginalia attest to the intertextual and affective ways in which the vanishing of Brutan history might be experienced on a personal level, and that Brutan figures – here, Cordeilla – might provide a locus for the understanding of origins and, in the form of *Historica passio*, the diminution of those origins through performed history and its textual records. In these ways, Wolfreston's collection encapsulates the centuries of theatrical and historiographic intertextuality explored throughout this study.

The motivation for this project was a relatively simple one: to investigate early modern drama that represented or reproduced narratives and characters drawn from pre-Roman British history, and to explore the ways in which these dramas may have both represented and complicated the model of British origins established by Geoffrey of Monmouth's *Historia*. To accurately assess this corpus, rigorous research was required in three main areas. First, a broad cultural survey, incorporating both close-reading and broader keyword-driven searches on databases, such as *Early English Books Online*, in order to identify and compile those texts from the 1480s to the 1630s that addressed the Brutan histories. These, principally, were chronicle, other historiographic and literary texts. But also important for establishing cultural context were the more passing references to Brutan figures found in other forms – legal and religious treatises, almanacs, travel narratives, books of exempla, where the very passingness of Brutan material testified to its cultural ubiquity. This done, the dramaturgical context of each event, performance and playbook needed to be established: an understanding of not only, for example, the specific qualities and contexts of Inns of Court drama but also how this differed from playhouse or court performance, or how dramaturgical forms changed over time: a civic pageant in 1486 York is not the same as a London Lord Mayor's Show in 1605. Each drama then needed to be compared with non-Brutan texts within its own milieu. *Locrine*'s Brutan idiosyncrasies cannot be identified without comparing the play to those with which it shares dramaturgical DNA, such as *Tamburlaine*, *Selimus*, *The Wounds of Civil War* and others. The corpus of Brutan drama included not only a wide range of texts but also a wide range of evidence: playbooks, eyewitness accounts in manuscript and print, 'lost' plays with no surviving text but much information of how they were placed within company repertory, evidence of readerly response and playbooks requiring careful consideration of the conditions of their publication, intended readership and possible reception. To accommodate these forms of evidence required the synthesis of multiple methodologies: book and print studies, repertory studies, recent work on lost plays and the use of 'unediting' – attentiveness to original spelling and typography – as a means of constructing as broad and comprehensive a model as possible of the conditions in which Brutan drama was presented to its audiences and readers.

This has resulted, I hope, in a book that is original in several ways. Primarily, it is the first book-length study of the Brutan histories in early modern drama. Further, in addressing a unique problem in early modern historiography, it has also proposed an original approach: the reception of Brutan drama has, throughout, been considered as a belief, or a concept, *in motion*. It is the focus on doubt, the instability of belief, its fitful changingness, affective dimension and the possible provocation of those wavering beliefs and their eventual loss by theatrical performance and texts, that sets this study apart from other work on drama representing a particular historical subject or epoch. Further complicating this, I have resisted methodologies that allow the attitudes of a literary and cultural elite to stand in for a discussion of wider early modern English culture, as is the risk with work limited to the close analysis of intellectual expression in literary texts. Instead, my – sometimes necessarily speculative – consideration of popular and non-elite culture, as part of the broader network of textual communities examined throughout demonstrates how much is missed in our potential for a broader understanding if, for example, we write about how *King Lear* lived in early modern performance culture without attending to the play's transmutation into a popular ballad, ahistorical ending and all. My proposition that the conventional term 'Galfridian' does not accurately reflect the transmission and perception of the narratives that Geoffrey of Monmouth originated, and that we might instead term the pre-Roman portion of these narratives 'Brutan histories' offers a key intervention and argues that sometimes it is necessary to decentre the author from questions of cultural transmission.

Elsewhere, my use of the 'unediting' approach pioneered by Marcus, de Grazia, Stallybrass and others has resulted in significant new readings of both *King Lear* and *Cymbeline*. I hope others will work to reinvigorate this important methodology, which has been rendered so much more accessible in the age of digital facsimiles and transcriptions. If my work has the potential for wider significance, it may perhaps be found in the insistence that historical consciousness, and thus the reception of drama purporting to represent the lived past, should not be assessed based on our modern understanding of historical fact or standards of proof. Instead, starting from an acceptance of the affective, shifting, partisan and desire-based conditions in which historical truth was conceived, sustained or rejected, theatrical reception should be approached as fragmentary, even kaleidoscopic. The ways in which this complicates, or initially renders unworkable, conventional methods of categorizing modes of reception or even the plays themselves is, I suggest, productive rather than destructive. I suggest that this approach – embracing the indeterminate, working to track ideas and beliefs in motion rather than as fixed positions – might be usefully applied to other aspects of early modern drama. For example, how did textual community and radical uncertainty shape the reception of the era's often overlooked biblical drama?

These are, I hope, my broad contributions. But there are also conclusions. What I have not found, or argued for, is an identifiable 'canon' of Brutan performance. As demonstrated, the surviving evidence suggests that each piece can be set within wider dramaturgical, literary and cultural trends lying beyond an isolated interest in, or approach to, the Brutan histories. For example, the inclusion of a number of Brutan dramas in Henslowe's *Diary* between 1592 and 1600 can be situated within a London-wide commercial repertory that drew upon 'historical' source material of all kinds, from classical myth, the Old Testament, Middle Eastern histories and English history from the post-Roman period to the Tudor era. The slight rise in Brutan drama published in the early years of James VI and I's reign is, as has long been recognized, a response to the propagandistic utilization of Brutan and Arthurian iconography in the service of the project to unite England and Scotland. Brutan drama was not a genre and, as noted throughout, the texts that survive reflect the dramaturgy of the places and times in which they were produced: *Gorboduc* is manifestly a product of the Seneca-influenced Inns of Court milieu; *Leir* reflects closely what is known of the practice and repertory of the Queen's Men and early 1590s playhouse practice and its publication in 1605 accords with the interest in Brutan subject matter at that time.

Yet to suggest that each example of performed Brutan history appears to fit closely within its cultural context does not preclude the possibility that Brutan subject matter might provoke distinct effects. As I have argued, the particular effects of Brutan drama might be found in its interaction with the wider historiographic collapse of the Brutan histories as an accepted account of British origins. This more than 400-year-old tradition, which claimed to stand for a tradition of millennia, was deeply embedded within all social strata of English society as an affective, intellectual and cultural habit of thought. The distinct effects of Brutan drama, I suggest, are to be found in the moments when it intersects with the varying, fluctuating, disorientating and often deeply felt modalities of belief in the Brutan histories. Thus *Locrine* – despite, or even because of, its condition as a generic response to the popular Near Eastern dramas of its time, notably *Tamburlaine* – can speak to its English audience of their collective origins in ways that no other Tamburlainian drama could. Similarly, *The Triumphs of Re-United Britania*, in reviving *Locrine*'s gloomy suicides to celebrate James's vision of union, may be seen as standing apart from other examples of Jacobean civic pageantry for those audience members and readers for whom the Brutan histories had resonance.

Much scholarship has explored and demonstrated the complexities and emotive nature of the early modern historiographic debates regarding Brutan historicity. Yet, as Nashe's account of audience responses to Talbot in *1 Henry VI* shows, performed history could provide a uniquely affective experience of connection with the past. The embodied presences of Albanact or Lud thus had enormous potential for audiences to commune with their ancestral origins. Conversely, the artificiality of certain dramas and events might also have the potential to undermine or complicate these origins. Examples of this might include *Leir*'s temporal and theological displacement, or *No-body and Some-body* forcing its Brutan king Elidure to share the stage with a character whose name and costume asserted a contagious sense of non-being. Brutan drama was unique to its era not because it demonstrates consistent or distinct qualities of dramaturgy, plotting or theme, although it certainly has these – such as a preoccupation with the division of kingdoms and warring siblings. The particularities of its subject matter related to its capacity to represent and define models of pagan, pre-Roman British origins; and it was unique to its era because it was watched and read by a culture undergoing a complex and extended process of etiological realignment. Its distinctiveness lies in the intersection of these two factors. The relative invisibility of this distinctiveness to many modern readers demonstrates usefully how completely the Brutan histories were eroded as a living cultural force.

One insistently recurring motif, however, is that of the monarch confronted with an embodied Brutan founder. These encounters often occur at key moments of political instability or transformation in ways that might indicate both shifting attitudes to Brutan history and a variety of ways in which monarch and particular institutions might interact. As noted at the end of Chapter 4, there is a great difference in the implied relationship between Henry VII and Brennus encountering one another publicly at the gates of Bristol and Charles I during his personal rule absorbing the semiotic remnants of the Brutan founder Albanact before a private elite audience. Between these two points, however, nuances of relationship are discernible. While the Inner Temple works to school Elizabeth I on the importance of succession through *Gorboduc*'s appropriation of Brutan narratives, the King's Men endorse James's vision of the necessity of British union while knocking out the keystones of their chosen vehicle, the historical account of Lear. If there is a thematic drift across the monarchical-Brutan encounters recorded between 1486 and 1634, it may be that the Brutan is gradually absorbed into the concerns and iconography of the crown, thereby weakening its mediating function. This process, perhaps, might be interpreted as a symptom of etiological erosion.

Excepting perhaps the dissonance that exists between orthodox religious accounts of the past and the historiography that contradicts them, we are unlikely to see a repeat of the full-scale historiographic eradication of entire epochs that took place in the early modern era. The Brutan dramas written, performed and printed at this time stand testament to both a culture's deep-seated need to embody and encounter its origins and the disorientating energies released when those origins begin to erode.

NOTES

Introduction

1 The adoption of members of the Trojan diaspora to establish origins was not unusual for Europe's 'newly emergent nations' seeking 'classical glory' (Weijer 2016: 45).

2 For this account Fox cites BL, Additional MS, 15917; f.5.

3 Euhemerism was central to early modern engagement with the remote past. See Veyne (1988: *passim*); Ferguson (1993: *passim*); and van Es (2002: 112–38).

4 In addressing the staging of a particular period of distant or fictional history, the present work adopts a similar approach to Hopkins's *From the Romans to the Normans on the English Renaissance Stage* (2017), and Elisabeth Michelsson's *Appropriating King Arthur: The Arthurian Legend in English Drama and Entertainments 1485–1625* (1999).

5 The phrase 'Brutan Histories' is drawn from early modern print. In *Philadelphus*, Richard Harvey complains of foreign writers, or 'outlandish intruders', attempting to 'vsurpe the censure of the Brutan Histories' (1593: sig. C3r). In Chapter 1, Harvey will provide the opening case study in Brutan historical dissonance.

6 The term *ex nihilo* has been applied to Geoffrey's creation of the *Historia* by several critics, including Pace (2012: 54) and Davies (1996: 4).

7 A 1587 Latin edition of the *Historia* published by Jerome Commelin in Heidelberg became the standard edition in England (Escobedo 2008: 63).

8 More recently, the term has been adopted for the title of John Curran's 2002 work, *Roman Invasions: The British History, Protestant Anti-Romanism, and the Historical Imagination in England, 1530–1660.*

9   Scottish antiquity was provided by Hector Boece in his
    Scotorum Historiae (Edinburgh, 1540) which, like Geoffrey's
    Historia, claimed access to previously unknown sources (Mason
    1987: 65).

10 The term 'textual communities' is cited by Amy Noelle Vines:
    Vines attributes the term to Brian Stock (1983), who 'presents a
    model of the text's role as a force which offers organisation and
    cohesiveness to a group of people' thus providing 'a useful tool
    in examining patterns in medieval readership' (2006: 71).

11 Throughout *Roman Invasions,* John Curran argues that English
    competition with Rome was the driving motivation for the
    Historia and its early modern proponents.

12 Quoted in MacDougall (1982: 23).

Chapter 1

1   Two of the principal studies in this area are Thomas Kendrick's
    British Antiquity (1950) and Arthur B. Ferguson's *Utter
    Antiquity* (1993).

2   There may be some disingenuousness here. Marlowe and Nashe
    had themselves engaged with Trojan afterlives in *Dido, Queen
    of Carthage* (perf. *c.* 1586–91; pub. 1594), which Andrew
    Duxfield (2016: 13) and Andrew Griffin have argued should be
    considered as implicitly placing Dido's narrative within a Brutan,
    and therefore English and imperial, macro-narrative (2019:
    91–116).

3   Holinshed's *Chronicles*, published in 1577 and in a much-
    expanded 1587 edition, poses several referencing issues, as
    Tim Smith-Laing has outlined. Its sections, though bound into
    large volumes, are separately and inconsistently paginated.
    For example, in the 1577 edition the description of Britain is
    paginated only on the recto of each folio, with the verso taking
    the same number while, in the history of Britain, folios are
    paginated 'in the standard fashion' (Smith-Laing 2012: xx).
    Thus, when referencing Holinshed, I adopt the system developed
    for the *Oxford Handbook to Holinshed's Chronicles* (Smith-
    Laing 2012: xix–xxi).

4 In 1301, Edward I wrote a letter to the Pope defending his right
   to Scotland via reference to Brutan history (MacColl 2006: 257).
   The textual foundation of these uses of the *Historia*, centring on
   the precedence of Brute's son Locrine over the younger Albanact,
   inheritor of northern Britain, is examined by Roger A. Mason
   (1987).

5 London, BL, MS Harley 24, f. 1r. qtd in Drukker (2006: 97).

6 Ferguson (1993: especially 84–105).

7 John Price's *Historiae Britannicae Defensio* (1536) also provided
   a defence of the Brutan histories in a Welsh context.

8 Harvey's *Philadelphus* is an exception, engaging with Buchanan's
   Rerum Scoticarum Historia in great detail.

9 The collators have been described as 'freelance antiquarians,
   lesser clergymen, members of Parliament with legal training,
   minor poets, publishers, and booksellers' (Patterson 1994: vii).

10 Holinshed's 'Epistle' is not included in the *Oxford Handbook*'s
   referencing guidelines. In this instance I adopt the original
   volume's pagination.

11 This process of collapse and fragmentation is proposed in Woolf
   (1988).

12 Albina is a powerful and pivotal figure in medieval and
   early modern accounts of pre-Brutan Britain, although like
   Samothes she appears to have been more securely discredited,
   and much earlier, than Brute. While she makes no direct
   appearance in early modern drama, her elision as a resonant
   figure of female British etiology and the effects of this elision
   on drama are addressed by Jodi Mikalachki (1995). Albina's
   more general adventures in early modern culture have recently
   been given extended consideration by Philip Robinson-Self
   (2018).

13 *Britannia* was translated into English in 1610 by Philemon
   Holland.

14 Spenser proclaims of Camden that 'though time all monuments
   obscure, / Yet thy iust labours ever shall endure' (1591: sig. B3r).

15 The engagement of 'Briton Moniments' with the Brutan histories
   is characterized as 'conventional' by both Mills (1978: 98) and
   van Es (2002: 23).

16 Manley and MacLean, describing the narrative for the lost play 'mandevell', note that the plot is developed in an episode from *Albions England* in a style that 'makes it read almost like a play transcribed' and 'may be a redaction' of the lost play (2014: 134, 135).

17 This has recently been addressed by Philip Robinson-Self, who examines *Albions England* in terms of its engagement with the figure of Brute (2018: 50–61).

18 These include Henry Lyte's pro-Brute *Light of Britayne* (1588), and Thomas Fenne's *Fennes Fruites* (1590), which argues against the Brutan inheritance in terms of the Trojans' moral undesirability as forebears; Buchanan had wondered why the English should choose as their imaginary ancestors those 'of whom all their posterity might justly be ashamed' (2009: para. 8).

19 It should be noted that there are enormous difficulties in ascertaining literacy levels in the early modern period. Hackel reports that '[c]ontemporaneous assessments place literacy rates anywhere between 1 per cent and 60 per cent of the population . . . and surviving records offer clues deeply at odds with one another' (1999: 140).

20 Mason notes that the *Scotichronicon*'s compiler, John of Fordun, referred to the English as 'the British people', and claimed that 'Britain' referred only to the territory subsequently named England (1987: 63).

21 Buc's reference to a 'fewd' is allegorical. No version of the Brutan histories records a conflict between Locrine and Albanact.

22 Tessa Watt notes that single-sheet printed images were at the top end of the price range for cheap print (1991: 142).

23 James and Walker record recollections of the performance from the private papers of Robert Beale, who explicitly associates specific episodes from the performance with political positions regarding Elizabeth's succession.

24 Robert Dudley, the Earl of Leicester, was believed to have sponsored the entertainments of which *Gorboduc* was a part to promote his own matrimonial ambitions towards Elizabeth I. See Doran (1995) and Vanhoutte (2000).

25 For a full account of the differences between the two editions, see Cauthen (1962).

26 If David Kathman's dating of *2 Seven Deadly Sins* to 1597–8 (2004) is correct, the Rose's 'Ferex & Porex' would have appeared two years or so after the Chamberlain's Men had performed their own truncated account of the lives of Gorboduc, Videna and their warring offspring.

27 'Ferrex and Porrex' (*Lost Plays Database*).

Chapter 2

1 The use of hoops perhaps suggests the construction of a hollow body occupied by a performer and thus light enough to be carried through the streets. Mobility may also be suggested by a payment to two men for 'keeping of the giants in the king's coming' (*REED* 2015: 3, 1122); that is, these men may have been operating, or playing, the constructed giants during the pageant.

2 Machyn's knowledge of these figures' names may argue that these were spoken aloud or in some other way indicated during the event, or that their identity in civic pageantry was familiar to Londoners; however, Mortimer has shown that Machyn had antiquarian interests and may have known Richard Grafton (2002: 996), therefore his knowledge of the giants' names may also indicate his association with a particular textual community.

3 This payment for 'brute grenshillde' means that it cannot be determined whether the cumulative evidence relates to one or two plays. If 'Conqueste' was episodic, then a scene or two relating to Greenshield may well have appeared in a chronological sequence between Corineus's wrestling match and Bladud's discovery of the hot springs. Alternatively, Henslowe might be referring to two separate Brutan plays, a possibility which would further extend the known corpus of Brutan drama.

4 The attribution has caused much speculation regarding Shakespeare's possible involvement as reviser or editor; the various theories are summarized by Will Sharpe (2013: 657–63).

5 The Buc notes were long believed to be a forgery by J. P. Collier. However, recent work on Collier has determined the inscription to be authentic (Freeman and Freeman 2004: 2: A26.1).

6 The play's inclusion of a duke, Debon, to rule Devon is taken from *The Faerie Queene* (1590: II.X; f. 328).

7 Albanact and Corineus both return onstage following their deaths, as ghosts calling for revenge (sig. G1r; I4r).

8 Echoing the Humber of the *Historia*, Muly Mahamet in *The Battell of Alcazar*, having also scavenged in the wilderness, is thrown from his horse and drowns in a river offstage (1594: sig. G1r–v), another way in which *Locrine*'s characters might be aligned with stage figures of the contemporary Near East.

9 Jane Lytton Gooch, noting that *Selimus* – which can be securely attributed to the Queen's Men – was also published by Creede, favours the Queen's Men for *Locrine* (1981: 32). Roslyn Knutson also hesitatingly attributes the play to the Queen's Men (2010: 103).

10 See Schwyzer (1997: 26).

11 Steggle notes that the word 'London' is never used in *The Faerie Queene* (2000: 35).

12 The other being 'William the Conkerer'.

13 In contrast, *George a Grene* made only twenty shillings on 15 January but returned on 22 January (Foakes 2002: 20).

14 These include William Perkins's *Two treatises·I. Of the Nature and Practise of Repentance. II. Of the combat of the flesh and spirit* (Cambridge, 1593).

15 Both proclamations were produced as single unpaginated sheets and attributed '*By the Queene*'.

Chapter 3

1 Ross's mention of barbershops is intriguing; Fox notes that these 'acted both as centres of news and gossip and as places where newsletters and pamphlets might be seen' and read aloud for the benefit of non-readers (2000: 39).

2 This was a huge print run in comparison with those given to playbooks and other non-official printed books, which were restricted by guild regulations to a 'maximum press run of 1,250 to 1,500 copies for most editions' (Farmer and Lesser 2005: 17–18).

3 Royal MS 18 B XV (fol. 23v, ll. 12–14).

4 Even here, however, there may be tension. Lisa Hopkins has suggested that this term 'is used so insistently . . . that one might begin to wonder about possible irony' (2017: 7).

5 *Leir* was registered, though apparently not published, in 1594, as 'The moste famous Chronicle historye of Leire kinge of England' and then in 1605 as 'A booke called the Tragecall historie of Kinge Leir' (*DEEP* 2007: ref. 390); *Cromwell* was registered in 1602 as 'A booke called the lyfe & Deathe of the Lord Cromwell' (ref. 332); *No-body and Some-body* was registered as 'A booke called no bodie and som*m*e bodie &c*es*' (ref. 425); in 1607 *King Lear* was registered as 'A booke called. Mr Willi*a*m Shakespeare his historye of Kynge Lear' (ref. 517); and *The Valiant Welshman* was entered in the Stationers' Register as 'a play called the valiant welshman' (ref. 619).

6 As this is principally a study of early modern reception, I will not be addressing the question of *Leir*'s relationship with *King Lear* in terms of its possible influence on Shakespeare. Readers interested in this subject can look to Foakes (1998), Knowles (2002), Brink (2008) and Forse (2014).

7 Scaliger senior was certainly on dramatists' radars; in *Wits Miserie*, Thomas Lodge interrupts a bawdy tale, sarcastically claiming himself 'afraid that Iulius Scaliger should haue cause to checke mée of [for] teaching sinne' (1596: f. 39); similarly, George Chapman attacked Scaliger as 'soule-blind' for his 'impalsied diminution of Homer' (1598: sig. A3v), although the contingency of this judgement is demonstrated by its appearance in Chapman's own Homeric effort, *Achilles Shield*.

8 Treating Scaliger as an embodiment of a historiographic force allows him to be added to an intriguing pattern, identified by Hopkins, of plays on ancient Britain featuring characters named after historians; both *The Misfortunes of Arthur* and *The Welsh Embassador* (*c.* 1623) have characters named Gildas, after the author of the sixth-century *De Excidio et Conquestu Britanniae*;

Fuimus Troes and John Fletcher's *Bonduca* each have a Nennius, after the ninth-century reputed author of the *Historia Brittonum* – although *Fuimus Troes* is also taking this name from a character named by Geoffrey of Monmouth, perhaps in his own not-so-subtle gesture to fictionality (2017: 17).

9 'Hysterica passio' was the term for a medical cause of apparent demonic possession which, as Kaara Peterson (2006: 2) has noted, has long been established as deriving from one of *King Lear*'s sources, Samuel Harsnett's *Declaration of Egregious Popish Impostures* (1603: f. 25).

10 F3's amendment to 'Hystorica' (Halio 2005: 67), adjusting the spelling but retaining the likely meaning, perhaps strengthens the argument that the phrase was at one moment at least understood as deriving from the etymology of narrative and historiography.

11 Regan and Cornwall were the parents of Cunedagus, the king succeeding Cordelia and putative ancestor of James. Their deaths, more than those of Lear and Cordelia, damage the play's usefulness as a potential pro-union text (Schwyzer 2008: 40–1).

12 Although these lines were later realigned into verse, they are set as prose in Q1.

13 These include John Day's *The Isle of Gulls* (1606); John Fletcher's *The Faithful Shepherdess* (perf. 1608; pub. 1610) and Francis Beaumont and John Fletcher's *Cupid's Revenge* (perf. 1608; pub. 1615).

14 Even the Duke of Cornwall's death at the hands of a servant is a result of his interference with Gloucester, another Sidnean figure.

15 The use of the term also seems responsive to *Cromwell*; the volume included a new poem on Cromwell's life by Michael Drayton.

16 The 1620 edition is the earliest extant, but the title page refers to it as 'the third time imprinted'. The existence of a 'thirteenth' edition from 1690 attests to the volume's exceptional popularity.

Chapter 4

1 Emrys Jones notes that in Holinshed it is Guiderius who refuses to pay tribute to Augustus, not Cymbeline, and that Shakespeare

transfers the events of Guiderius's reign to that of his father (1961: 88).

2 The approximate date is most recently argued by Wayne (2017: 30).

3 Critics who have explored in *Cymbeline* in theological contexts include Moffet (1962), Geller (1980) and Marshall (1991).

4 Willy Maley also reconfigured Moffet's terminology towards reading *Cymbeline* as a proto-text of the Union debate and nascent British imperialism, 'a nativity play' that 'deals not with the birth of Christ, but with the birth of Britain' (1999: 148).

5 The frontispiece to James's *Workes* (1616) shows him 'enthroned with a cloth embroidered with the words *Beati Pacifici*' (Wickham 1980: 94).

6 Wiggins examines the possibility of 'creative synergy' between Heywood and Shakespeare's companies regarding these and other plays. Noting that the king's and queen's companies appear to have been working together for the January 1612 court performance, Wiggins proposes that the programme included *Cymbeline*, thereby also accounting for the presence of Jupiter's eagle in both plays, 'without having to hypothesize that 1610–11 was a boom time in the London trade for scenic eagle manufacture' (2015: 6, ref. 1637).

7 Lisa Hopkins also explores *Cymbeline* in relation to the *translatio imperii* (2010).

8 Other critics who have engaged with the challenges raised by *Cymbeline*'s multiplicities are Jodi Mikalachki (1995) and Maurice Hunt (2002).

9 Meisei First Folio; Image 906. This copy of F1 is kept at Meisei University. The annotations are accessible as both transcriptions and facsimiles via a dedicated website. The annotator was named William Johnstone (Smith 2016c: 129).

10 Blayney also notes that the Jonson folio would have cost 'considerably less' than F1, perhaps configuring the latter text as being of greater cultural, in addition to literal, value (1996: xxviii).

11 Wayne notes that 'taken together . . . critics associate *Cymbeline* with twenty-two other plays that Shakespeare wrote or cowrote along with his two narrative poems' (2015: 406).

12 J. K. Barrett has explored the complex temporal relationships between the description of Cleopatra in her barge in *Antony & Cleopatra*, and Iachimo's description of the tapestry depicting her in the barge in *Cymbeline* (2016: 177–208).

13 Brinkley notes that Merlin's prophecies, excerpted from Geoffrey's *Historia*, were popular throughout the medieval and early modern periods, to the point of being prohibited by the Council of Trent (1932: 8).

14 This possible placement of a once-living writer within a text he would have resisted also echoes my own reading of 'Skalliger' in *Leir* (see Chapter 3).

15 George Steevens noted this peculiarity and suggested that 'there are some who may ask whether it is not more likely that the printer should have blundered in the other places, than that he should have hit upon such an uncommon name as "Paladour" in this first instance. *Paladour* was the ancient name for Shaftesbury' (qtd in Furness 1913: 3).

16 A recent summary of the debate regarding whether 'Imogen' is Shakespeare's intended deviation from the source or the result of a compositorial minim error can be found in Wayne (2017: 391–8).

17 The definition appears in Florio's *Queen Anna's New World of Words, or Dictionarie of the Italian and English Tongues*. Florio defines the Italian 'paladore' as 'a fanner, or winnower of corne' (1611: 350).

18 *The Christian Dictionary* was in preparation at William Jaggard's print shop and was one of several books contributing a 'space of time' to the delay of F1's completion (Rasmussen 2016: 20).

19 The dramatic usage appears in *Sir Gyles Goosecapp*, in a passage that appears to satirize pious speech but which also indicates the universal effect of diminution that resonates in Imogen's usage: '[T]he world, / Or that small point of it, where virtue liues / Will suffer Diminution' (1606: sig. I2r).

20 The *Historia*'s deep dependence upon the *Aeneid* was fully staged by Nahum Tate, who decided to alter a play he had written on Dido and Aeneas to a play about Brute (*Brutus of*

Alba) simply by changing the character's names (Adolph 2017: 119–20).

21 Patricia Parker, in particular, has examined Posthumus's Virgilian associations, noting that 'Aeneas's father is named Sicilius Leonatus, the same as Posthumus's' (1989: 195). Heather James suggests that 'Shakespeare formally identifies Posthumus with Virgil's hero at the moment that Aeneas abandons Dido' (1997: 162–3).

22 This quotation is taken from Thomas Phaër's translation of the *Aeneid*, first published in 1573 but reprinted many times into the seventeenth century.

23 Although the *Historia* was not translated into English, or even printed in England in its original Latin, until the eighteenth century, a 1587 Latin edition published by Jerome Commelin in Heidelberg became the standard edition in England (Escobedo 2008: 63).

24 The overlaying of *Aeneid*, *Historia* and Imogen's own moment might have evoked the instability of the *Aeneid* itself. As Richard Verstegan complained, Virgil 'had much fained and fabuled in his tales of *Eneas*', and that 'Queen *Dido* did never see *Eneas* in her life' (1605: sig. M3v).

25 Chris Butler cites Curran (2002: 261), who in turn cites Brinkley (1932: 92); Hopkins (2002: 38) and the editors of *REED* (2004: 2, 810) admit no more secure dating than 1611–33.

26 *Fuimus Troes* is extremely careful in its historiography and chronology. The difficulty for early modern playmakers in keeping control of a play's chronology can be observed in a small slip here, perceptible to only the play's most pedantic spectators and readers: Ovid was not born until several years after Caesar's invasion of Britain.

27 *The Courageous Turk,* and a second play by Goffe, *The Raging Turk, or Bajazet the Second* (*c.* 1618; pub. 1631), also include Turkish characters and dynasties that correlate with plays synchronous with *Locrine*, such as *Tamburlaine*.

28 *The Witts* contains an intriguing reference to 'the archer Cymbeline' (1636: sig. B4r). This is unique in early modern plays other than *Cymbeline* itself and, given that *The Witts* was being read, censored and licensed by Herbert only weeks before

the performance of *Cymbeline*, hints at possible metadramatic interconnections between the plays and masques performed that season.

29 These additions were included in a new quarto published shortly after the royal performance which, as with *King Lear* Q1, is given prominent mention on the title page.

30 Work on the ceiling itself, however, does not seem to have taken place until some time between 1634 and the 1640s (Strong 1980: 13).

Conclusions

1 This uncertainty may change. Sarah Lindenbaum's ongoing project, catalogued in the blog *Frances Wolfreston Hor Bouks*, has expanded the known corpus of Wolfreston's library from around 130 to 230 titles.

WORKS CITED

Primary Sources

Allott, Robert (1600), *Englands Parnassus*, London.

Bale, John (1544), *A Brefe Chronycle*. London.

Bale, John, ed. (1548), *A Godly Medytacion*, by Marguerite of Navarre, trans. Elizabeth Tudor (later Elizabeth I), London.

Blundeville, Thomas (1599), *The Art of Logic*. London.

Bolton, Edmund, *Hypercritica* (c. 1618; pub. 1722): in *Annalium Continuatio*, Nicolas Triveti et al., Oxford.

'Bridge House Weekly Payments Book 1(2): Account for 1420–1' (1995), in Vanessa Harding and Laura Wright, eds, *London Bridge: Selected Accounts and Rentals, 1381–1538*, London: London Record Society, 65–113.

Buc, George (1605), *Daphnis*, London.

Buc, George (1982), *The History of King Richard III* [London, 1619], ed. Arthur Noel Kincaid, Gloucester: Sutton.

Buchanan, George (2009), *Rerum Scoticarum Historia* [Edinburgh, 1582], trans. Dana F. Sutton, Birmingham: U of Birmingham.

By the Queene (1593a), *The Queenes Most Excellent Maiestie Being Credibly Enformed That the Infection of the Plague Is at This Present Greatly Increased and Dispersed*, London.

By the Queene (1593b), *The Queenes Most Excellent Maiestie, Vnderstanding that the Infection of the Plague in the Cities of London and Westminster Doth Yet Continue*, London.

Cambini, Andrea (1562), *Two Very Notable Commentaries*, trans. John Shute, London.

Camden, William (1610), *Britannia* [London, 1586], trans. Philemon Holland, London.

Caesar, Julius (1996), *Seven Commentaries on the Gallic War*, trans. Carolyn Hammond, Oxford: Oxford UP.

Caradoc of Llancarvan (1584), *The Historie of Cambria*, trans. Humphrey Lhoyd, London.

Carew, Thomas (1634), *Coelum Britanicum*, London.

Caxton, William (1480), *Cronicles of Englond*, Westminster.

Chapman, George (1598), *Achilles Shield*, London.

Chapman, George (1606), *Sir Gyles Goosecappe*, London.

Clapham, John (1602), *The Historie of England*, London.

Clapham, John (1606), *The Historie of Great Britainne*, London.

Coryate, Thomas (1611), *The Odcombian Banquet*, London.

Crooke, Helkiah (1615), *Mikrokosmographia*, London.

Daniel, Samuel (1612), *The First Part of the Historie of England*, London.

Davenant, William (1636), *The Witts*, London.

de Granada, Luis (1598), *Spirituall and Heauenlie Exercises*, trans. Francis Meres, London.

Dekker, Thomas (1604), *The Magnificent Entertainment*, London.

de Nicolay, Nicholas (1585), *The Nauigations, Peregrinations and Voyages, Made into Turkie*, London.

Drayton, Michael (1593), *Englands Heroical Epistles*, London.

Drayton, Michael (1612), *Poly–Olbion*, London.

D'Urfrey, Thomas (1682), *The Injured Princess*, London.

Elder, John (1555), *The Copie of a Letter Sent in to Scotlande*, London.

Eliot, John (1593), *Ortho–Epia Gallica*, London.

Fabyan, Robert (1516), *The Newe Cronycle*, London.

Fenne, Thomas (1590), *Fennes Fruites*. London.

Fletcher, John (1656), *The Faithful Shepherdess*, London.

Florio, John (1611), *Queen Anna's New World of Words*, London.

Fuimus Troes (1633), London.

Foxe, John (1570), *The First Volume of the Ecclesiasticall History*, London.

Fraunce, Abraham (1588), *The Lawiers Logike*, London.

G., I. (1615), *A Refutation of the Apologie for Actors*, London.

Geoffrey of Monmouth (2007), *The History of the Kings of Britain* [*c.* 1130], trans. Neil Wright, ed. Michael D. Reeve, Woodbridge: Boydell.

Goffe, Thomas (1632), *The Courageous Turke*, London.

Grafton, Richard (1569), *Chronicle at Large*, London.

Greene, Robert (1594), *The Honorable Historie of Frier Bacon, and Frier Bongay*, London.

Greene, Robert, and Thomas Lodge (1594), *Looking Glass for London and England*, London.

Hardyng, John (1543), *The Chronicle of Ihon Hardyng*, London.

Hariot, Thomas (1588), *A Briefe and True Report of the New Found Land of Virginia*, London.

Harrington, John (*c.* 1609), 'Catalogue of Plays' [Add. MS 27632, f.43r], *Shakespeare Documented*: https://shakespearedocumented. folger.edu/exhibition/document/sir-john-haringtons-catalogue-play s-ownership-shakespeare-quartos [accessed 15 February 2015].

Harvey, Richard (1593), *Philadelphus*, London.

Harsnett, Samuel (1603), *A Declaration of Egregious Popish Impostures*, London.

Herbert, Henry (1996), *The Control and Censorship of Caroline Drama: The Records of Sir Henry Herbert, Master of the Revels 1623–73*, ed. N. W. Bawcutt, Oxford: Clarendon.

Henslowe, Philip (2002), *Henslowe's Diary*, ed. R. A. Foakes, Cambridge: Cambridge UP.

Heywood, Thomas (1611), *The Golden Age*, London.

Heywood, Thomas (1612), *Apology for Actors*, London.

Heywood, Thomas (1613), *The Silver Age*, London.

Heywood, Thomas (1632), *The Second Part of the Iron Age*, London.

Higgins, John (1574), *The First Parte of the Mirour for Magistrates*, London.

The Holie Bible (1568), London.

Holinshed, Raphael (1577), *Chronicles*, London.

Holinshed, Raphael (1588), *The First and Second Volumes of Chronicles*, London.

Hughes, Thomas (1587), *Certaine Deu[is]es and Shewes Presented to Her Maiestie* [The Misfortunes of Arthur], London.

The Ioyfull Receyuing of the Queenes Most Excellent Maiestie (1578), London.

James VI & I, *Royal MS 18 B XV*, British Library collections online: https://www.bl.uk/collection-items/autograph-manuscript-of-k ing-james-vi-and-is-basilikon-doron-or-the-kings-gift [accessed 18 September 2016].

James VI & I (1599), *Basilikon Doron*, Edinburgh.

James VI & I (1973), *Stuart Royal Proclamations*, ed. James F. Larkin and Paul L. Hughes, 2 vols, Oxford: Clarendon.

James VI & I (1994), *Political Writings*, ed. Johann P. Sommerville, Cambridge: Cambridge UP.

James VI & I (1996), *True Law of Free Monarchies and Basilikon Doron* [London, 1603], eds Daniel Fischlin and Mark Fortier, Toronto: Centre for Reformation and Renaissance Studies.

Jewell, William (1612), *The Golden Cabinet of True Treasure*, London.

Jonson, Ben (1600), *Every Man Out of His Humour*, London.

Jonson, Ben (1604), *His Part of King Iames His Royall and Magnificent Entertainment*, London, 1604.

Kellwaye, Simon (1593), *A Defensatiue Against the Plague*, London.

Kelton, Arthur (1547), *A Chronycle with a Genealogie*, London.

A Knacke to Knowe a Knaue (1594), London.

Knolles, Richard, *The Generall Historie of the Turkes*, London, 1603.

Lanquet, Thomas (1560), *Coopers Chronicle*, London.

Locrine (1595), London.

Lodge, Thomas (1579), *Protogenes*, London.

Lodge, Thomas (1593), 'Complaint of Elstred', in *Phillis*, London.

Lodge, Thomas (1594), *The Wounds of Civil War*, London.

Lodge, Thomas (1596), *Wits Miserie*, London.

Lyte, Henry (1588), *Light of Britayne*, London.

Machyn, Henry (1848), *The Diary of Henry Machyn Citizen and Merchant-Taylor of London (1550–1563)*, ed. J. G. Nichols, London: Camden Society.

Marlowe, Christopher (1590), *Tamburlaine*, London.

Meres, Francis (1598), *Palladis Tamia*, London.

Milton, John (1637), *A Masque Presented at Ludlow Castle*, London.

Munday, Anthony (1605), *The Triumphes of Re-vnited Britania*, London.

Munday, Anthony (1612), *A Brief Chronicle*, London.

Nashe, Thomas (1592), *Pierce Penniless*, London.

Nashe, Thomas (1596), *Have with You to Saffron Waldon*, London.

No-Body and Some-Body (1606), London.

Niccols, Richard, ed. (1610), 'To the Reader', in *A Mirour for Magistrates*, by John Higgins et al. London.

Norton, Thomas, and Thomas Sackville (1565), *Gorboduc*, London.

Norton, Thomas, and Thomas Sackville (1570), *Ferrex and Porrex*, London.

Norton, Thomas, and Thomas Sackville (1590), 'Gorboduc', in John Perrin, ed., *The Serpent of Division*, London.

Peele, George (1584), *The Araygnement of Paris*, London.

Peele, George (1585), *The Deuice of the Pageant Borne Before Woolstone Dixi Lord Maior of the Citie of London*, London.

Peele, George (1593), *King Edward the First*, London.

Peele, George (1594), *The Battel of Alcazar*, London.

Puttenham, George (1589), *The Arte of English Poesie*, London.

Records of Early English Drama: York (1979), eds Alexandra F. Johnston and Margaret Rogerson, 2 vols, Manchester: Manchester UP.

Records of Early English Drama: Newcastle-Upon-Tyne (1982), ed. J. J. Anderson, Manchester: Manchester UP.

Records of Early English Drama: Norwich (1984), ed. David Galloway, London: U of Toronto P.

Records of Early English Drama: Herefordshire and Worcestershire (1990), ed. David N. Klausner, London: U of Toronto P.

Records of Early English Drama: Somerset (1996), ed. James Stokes, London: British Library and U of Toronto P.

Records of Early English Drama: Bristol (1997), ed. Mark C. Pilkinton, London: U of Toronto P.

Records of Early English Drama; Oxford (2004), eds John R. Elliott, Alan H. Nelson, Alexandra F. Johnston, and Diana Wyatt, 2 vols, London: British Library.

Records of Early English Drama: Civic London (2015), ed. Anne Lancashire, 3 vols, Cambridge: D. S. Brewer.

Ross, John (2010), *Britannica* [1607], ed. Richard F Hardin, Birmingham: U of Birmingham: http://www.philological.bham.ac.uk/ross/ [accessed 11 November 2015].

Shakespeare, William (1608), *The True Chronicle Historie of the Life and Death of King Lear and His Three Daughters*, London.

Shakespeare, William (1623), *Mr. William Shakespeare's Comedies, Histories and Tragedies*, London.

Shakespeare, William (1994), *Titus Andronicus* [London, 1594], ed. Jonathan Bate, London: Bloomsbury.

Shakespeare, William (1995), *Antony and Cleopatra* [London, 1623], ed. John Wilders, London: Bloomsbury.

Shakespeare, William (1997), *King Lear* [London, 1608; 1623], ed. R. A. Foakes, London: Bloomsbury.

Shakespeare, William (2017), *Cymbeline* [London, 1623], ed. Valerie Wayne, London: Bloomsbury.

Shirley, James (1633), *The Triumph of Peace*, London.

Sidney, Philip (1593), *The Countess of Pembrokes Arcadia*, London.

Slatyer, William (1622), *Palae-Albion*, London.

Slatyer, William (1630), *Genethliacon*, London.

Speed, John (1611), *The History of Great Britain*, London.

Spenser, Edmund (1590), *The Faerie Queene*, London.

Spenser, Edmund (1591), 'Ruines of Time', in *Complaints*, London.

Spenser, Edmund (1596), *The Faerie Queene*, London.

Stow, John (1565), *A Summarie of Englyshe Chronicles*, London.

Stow, John (1580), *The Chronicles of England*, London.

Stow, John (1598), *A Suruay of London*, London.

Stow, John (1615), *The Annales, or a Generall Chronicle of England*, London.

Tasso, Torquato (1594), *Godfrey of Bulloigne*, trans. R. C., London.

Taylor, John (1630), *A Memorial of All the English Monarchs*, London.

Thompson, Aaron, trans. (1718), *The British History*, by Geoffrey of Monmouth, London.

Townshend, Aurelian (1632), *Albions Trivmph*, London.

The Troublesome Raigne of Iohn King of England (1591), London.

The True Chronicle Historie of the Whole Life and Death of Thomas Lord Cromwell (1602), London.

The True Chronicle History of King Leir, and His Three Daughters (1605), London.

A Trve Chronologi of All the Kings of England from Brvte the First King vnto Our Most Sacred King Charles (*c.* 1635), London.

Vergil, Poydore (2005), *Anglia Historia* [Basel, 1534], trans. Dana F. Sutton, Birmingham: U of Birmingham: http://www.philological.bham.ac.uk/polverg/ [accessed 6 October 2014].

Verstegan, Richard (1605), *A Restitution of Decayed Intelligence*, Antwerp.

Virgil, *The XII Bookes of Æneidos*, trans. Thomas Phaër, London, 1584.

Warner, William (1602), *Albions England*, London.

Weever, John (1631), *Ancient Funerall Monuments*, London.

Wilson, Thomas (1612), *A Christian Dictionarie*, London.

Secondary Sources

Abbott, D. M. (2004), 'Buchanan, George (1506–1582)', in *Oxford Dictionary of National Biography*, Oxford: Oxford UP: https://doi.org/10.1093/ref:odnb/3837 [accessed 1 February 2017].

Adolph, Anthony (2017), *Brutus of Troy: And the Quest for the Ancestry of the British*, Barnsley: Pen and Sword.

Angus, Bill (2020), 'The Night, the Crossroads and the Stake: Shakespeare and the Outcast Dead', in Lisa Hopkins and Bill Angus, eds, *Reading the Road, from Shakespeare's Crossways to Bunyan's Highways*, Edinburgh: Edinburgh UP, 151–70.

Archdeacon, Anthony (2012), 'The Publication of *No-Body and Some-Body*: Humanism, History and Economics in the Early Jacobean Public Theatre', *EMLS* 16:1: n. pag.

Archer, Ian W. (2014), 'John Stow, Citizen and Historian', in Ian Gadd and Alexandra Gillespie, eds, *John Stow (1525–1605) and the Making of the English Past*, London: The British Library, 13–26.

Ashe, Laura (2012), 'Holinshed and Mythical History', in Ian W. Archer and Paulina Kewes, eds, *The Oxford Handbook of Holinshed's Chronicles*, Oxford: Oxford UP, 155–71.

Astington, John H. (2009), 'Introduction', *Shakespeare Studies* 37: 19–24.

Atherton, Ian, and Julie Sanders (2006), 'Introduction', in Ian Atherton and Julie Sanders, eds, *The 1630s: Interdisciplinary Essays on Culture and Politics in the Caroline Era*, Manchester: Manchester UP, 1–27.

Attreed, Lorraine (1994), 'The Politics of Welcome: Ceremonies and Constitutional Development in Later Medieval English Towns', in Barbara A. Hanawalt and Kathryn L. Reyerson, eds, *City and Spectacle in Medieval Europe*, Minneapolis: U of Minnesota P, 208–34.

Axton, Marie (1970), 'Robert Dudley and the Inner Temple Revels', *The Historical Journal* 13:3: 365–78.

Axton, Marie (1977), *The Queen's Two Bodies: Drama and the Elizabethan Succession*, London: Royal Historical Society.

Barrett, J. K. (2016), *Untold Futures: Time and Literary Culture in Renaissance England*, Cornell UP.

Barroll, Leeds (2001), *Anna of Denmark, Queen of England: A Cultural Biography*, Philadelphia: U of Pennsylvania P.

Barron, W. R. J. (2002), 'The Idiom and the Audience of Laȝamon's *Brut*', in Rosamund Allen, Lucy Perry and Jane Roberts, eds, *Laȝamon: Contexts, Language and Interpretation*, Exeter: Short Run Press, 164–5.

Barthes, Roland (1993), *Mythologies* [Paris: Editions du Seuil, 1957], trans. Annette Lavers, London: Vintage.

Bate, Jonathan (2007), 'Introduction to *Cymbeline*', in Jonathan Bate and Eric Rasmussen, eds, *William Shakespeare: Complete Works*, Basingstoke: Macmillan, 2240–4.

Berek, Peter (1982), 'Tamburlaine's Weak Sons', *Renaissance Literature* 13: 55–82.

Bergeron, David (1980), '*Cymbeline*: Shakespeare's Last Roman Play', *Shakespeare Quarterly* 31:1, 31–41.

Birken, William (2004), 'Crooke, Helkiah (1576–1648), Physician and Anatomist', in *Oxford Dictionary of National Biography*, Oxford: Oxford UP: https://doi.org/10.1093/ref:odnb/6775 [accessed 1 March 2017].

Blayney, Peter (1982), *The Texts of King Lear and Their Origins*, Cambridge: Cambridge UP.

Blayney, Peter (1996), 'Introduction', in Charlton Hinman, ed., *The First Folio of Shakespeare: The Norton Facsimile*, 2nd edn, London: Norton.

Bowling, Joseph (2017), '"Part Shame, Part Spirit Renewed": Affect, National Origins, and Report in Shakespeare's Cymbeline', *Renaissance Drama* 45:1: 81–106.

Briggs, Julia (1990), 'Middleton's Forgotten Tragedy: *Hengist, King of Kent*', *Review of English Studies* 41: 479–95.

Brink, J. R. (2008), 'What Does Shakespeare Leave Out of King Lear?' in Jeffrey Kahan, ed., *King Lear: New Critical Essays*, New York: Routledge, 208–30.

Brinkley, Roberta Florence (1932), *Arthurian Legend in the Seventeenth Century*, London: Oxford UP.

Brown, Keith M. (1994), 'The Vanishing Emperor: British Kingship and Its Decline 1603–1707', in Roger A. Mason, ed., *Scots and Britons: Scottish Political Thought and the Union of 1603*, Cambridge: Cambridge UP, 58–87.

Brown, Keith M. (2008), 'Monarchy and Government, 1603–1637', in Jenny Wormald, ed., *The Short Oxford History of the British Isles: The Seventeenth Century*, Oxford: Oxford UP, 13–48.

Bruda, Paul (1992), 'The *Mirror for Magistrates* and the Politics of Readership', *Studies in English Literature* 32:1: 1–13.

Bryan, Elizabeth J. (2006), 'Dialoguing Hands in MS Hatton 50: Reformation Readers of the Middle English Prose Brut', in

William Marx and Raluca Radulescu, eds, *Readers and Writers of the Prose Brut*, Lampeter: Trivium, 131–87.

Bullough, Geoffrey (1969), 'Pre-Conquest Historical Themes in Elizabethan Drama', in Derek Albert Pearsall and Ronald Allan Waldon, eds, *Medieval Literature and Civilization: Studies in Memory of G. N. Garmonsway*, London: Athlone, 289–321.

Burke, Peter (1969), *The Renaissance Sense of the Past*, London: Edward Arnold.

Butler, Chris, ed. (2007), *Fuimus Troes*, Sheffield Hallam University: https://extra.shu.ac.uk/emls/iemls/renplays/fuimustroes.htm [accessed 1 August 2015].

Butler, Martin (1984), *Theatre and Crisis: 1632–1642*, Cambridge: Cambridge UP.

Bzdyl, Donald G., trans. (1989), *Brut: A History of the Britons*, by Laȝamon, Binghamton, 1989.

Caciola, Nancy (1996), 'Wraiths, Revenants and Ritual in Medieval Culture', *Past & Present* 152: 3–45.

Caldwell, Robert A. (1956), 'Wace's *Roman De Brut* and the Variant Version of Geoffrey of Monmouth's *Historia Regum Britanniae*', *Speculum* 31:4: 675–82.

Capp, Bernard (1979), *Astrology and the Popular Press: English Almanacs 1500–1800*, London: Faber and Faber.

Capp, Bernard (1993), *The World of John Taylor the Water Poet, 1578–1653*, Oxford: Clarendon.

Carney, Sophie (2013), 'The Queen's House at Greenwich: The Material Cultures of the Courts of Queen Anna of Denmark and Queen Henrietta Maria, 1603–1642', PhD thesis, U of Roehampton.

Carpenter, John (2006), 'Placing Thomas Deloney', *Journal of Narrative Theory* 36:2: 125–62.

Carr, Joan (1978), '*Cymbeline* and the Validity of Myth', *Studies in Philology* 75:3: 316–30.

Cauthen, I. B. Jr. (1962), 'Gorboduc, Ferrex and Porrex: The First Two Quartos', *Studies in Bibliography* 15: 231–3.

Chapman, Alison (2007), 'Marking Time: Astrology, Almanacs, and English Protestantism', *Renaissance Quarterly* 60: 4: 1257–90.

Clegg, Cyndia Susan (2008), 'King Lear and Early Seventeenth-Century Print Culture', in Jeffrey Kahan, ed., *King Lear: New Critical Essays*, New York: Routledge, 155–83.

Cohen, Jeffrey (1999), *Of Giants: Sex, Monsters, and the Middle Ages*, London: U of Minnesota P.

Connolly, Annaliese (2007), 'Peele's David and Bethsabe: Reconsidering Biblical Drama of the Long 1590s', *Early Modern Literary Studies* 16: 1–20.

Cooper, Helen (2004), *The English Romance in Time: Transforming Motifs from Geoffrey of Monmouth to the Death of Shakespeare*, Oxford: Oxford UP.

Crick, Julia C. (1991), *The Historia Regum Britannie of Geoffrey of Monmouth: Dissemination and Reception in the Later Middle Ages*, Cambridge: Brewer.

Crumley, Clinton J. (2001), 'Questioning History in *Cymbeline*', *Studies in English Literature, 1500–1900* 41:2: 297–315.

Cull, Marisa S. (2010), 'Contextualising 1610: *Cymbeline, The Valiant Welshman,* and the Princes of Wales', in Willy Maley and Philip Schwyzer, eds, *Shakespeare and Wales: From the Marches to the Assembly*, Farnham: Ashgate, 127–42.

Curran, John (1997), 'Royalty Unlearned, Honor Untaught: British Savages and Historiographical Change in *Cymbeline*', *Comparative Drama* 31:2: 277–303.

Curran, John (1999), 'Geoffrey of Monmouth in Renaissance Drama: Imagining Non–History', *Modern Philology* 97:1: 1–20.

Curran, John (2002), *Roman Invasions: The British History Protestant Anti-Romanism and the Historical Imagination in England, 1530–1660*, London: Associated UP.

Davies, Rees (1996), *The Matter of Britain and the Matter of England: An Inaugural Lecture Delivered Before the University of Oxford on 29 February 1996*, Oxford: Oxford UP.

DEEP: Database of Early English Playbooks (2007), eds Alan B. Farmer and Zachary Lesser, http://deep.sas.upenn.edu/ [accessed 19 October 2014].

de Grazia, Margreta (2013), '*King Lear* in BC Albion', in Ruth Morse, Helen Cooper and Peter Holland, eds, *Medieval Shakespeare: Pasts and Presents*, Cambridge: Cambridge UP, 138–56.

de Grazia, Margreta, and Peter Stallybrass (1993), 'The Materiality of the Shakespearean Text', *Shakespeare Quarterly* 44:3: 255–83.

de Guevara, Mariluz Beltran (2013), 'Is Not Parchment Made of Sheepskins? Ay, My Lord, and of Calfskins Too…', *British Library Collection Care Blog*: https://blogs.bl.uk/collectioncare/

2013/09/parchment-conservation-lyte-geneaology.html [accessed 18 November 2015].

Devereux, E. J. (1990), 'Empty Tuns and Unfruitful Grafts: Richard Grafton's Historical Publications', *Sixteenth Century Journal* 21:1: 33–56.

Dimmock, Matthew (2005), *New Turkes: Dramatising Islam and the Ottomans in Early Modern England*, Aldershot: Ashgate.

Doran, Susan (1995), 'Juno Versus Diana: The Treatment of Elizabeth I's Marriage in Plays and Entertainments, 1561–1581', *Historical Journal* 38:2: 257–74.

Draper, John W. (1937), 'The Occasion of *King Lear*', *Studies in Philology* 34: 176–85.

Drukker, Tamar (2003), 'Thirty-Three Murderous Sisters: A Pre-Trojan Foundation Myth in the Middle English Prose *Brut* Chronicle', *Review of English Studies* 54:216: 449–63.

Drukker, Tamar (2006), 'I Read Therefore I Write: Readers' Marginalia in Some Brut Manuscripts', in William Marx and Raluca Radulescu, eds, *Readers and Writers of the Prose Brut*, Lampeter: Trivium Publications, 97–130.

Dutton, Richard (1986), 'King Lear, The Triumphs of Reunited Britannia and "The Matter of Britain"', *Literature and History* 12:2: 139–51.

Duxfield, Andrew (2016), *Christopher Marlowe and the Failure to Unify*, London: Routledge.

Elliott, John R. (1997), 'Early Staging in Oxford', in John D. Cox and David Scott Kastan, eds, *A New History of Early English Drama*. New York: Columbia UP, 68–76.

Escobedo, Andrew (2004), *Nationalism and Historical Loss in Renaissance England: Foxe, Dee, Spenser*, Milton, London: Cornell UP.

Escobedo, Andrew (2008), 'From Britannia to England: *Cymbeline* and the Beginning of Nations', *Shakespeare Quarterly* 59: 60–87.

Farley-Hills, David (1990), *Shakespeare and the Rival Playwrights, 1600–1606*, London: Routledge.

Farmer, Alan and Zachary Lesser (2005), 'The Popularity of Playbooks Revisited', *Shakespeare Quarterly* 56:1: 1–32.

Feerick, Jean (2003), '"A Nation . . . Now Degenerate": Shakespeare's *Cymbeline*, Nova Britannia, and the Role of Diet and Climate in Reproducing Races', *Early American Studies* 1:2: 30–71.

Felperin, Howard (1972), *Shakespearean Romance*, Princeton: Princeton UP.

Ferguson, Arthur B. (1993), *Utter Antiquity: Perceptions of Prehistory in Renaissance England*, London: Duke UP.

Fleming, Peter (2013), *Time, Space, and Power in Later Medieval Bristol*, working paper, University of the West of England.

Floyd-Wilson, Mary (2002), 'Delving to the Root: *Cymbeline*, Scotland, and the English Race', in David J. Baker and Willy Maley, eds, *British Identities and English Renaissance Literature*, Cambridge: Cambridge UP, 101–18.

Foakes, R. A., ed. (1997), *King Lear* [by William Shakespeare, London, 1608], Walton-on-Thames: Nelson.

Forse, James (2014), 'To Die or Not to Die, That Is the Question: Borrowing and Adapting the King Lear Legend in the Anonymous *The True Chronicle History of King Leir* and Shakespeare's *King Lear*', *Ben Jonson Journal* 21:1: 53–72.

Fox, Adam (2000), *Oral and Literate Culture in England: 1500–1700*, Oxford: Oxford UP.

Freeman, Arthur, and Janet Ing Freeman (2004), *John Payne Collier: Scholarship and Forgery in the Nineteenth Century*, 2 vols, New Haven: Yale UP.

Furness, H. H., ed. (1913), *Cymbeline: A New Variorum Edition* [by William Shakespeare, London, 1623], Philadelphia: Lippincott.

Geller, Lila (1980), 'Cymbeline and the Imagery of Covenant Theology', *Studies in English Literature, 1500–1900* 20:2: 241–55.

Gerritsen, Johan (1964), 'Venus Preserved: Some Notes on Frances Wolfreston', *English Studies* 45: 271–4.

Gibbons, Brian (1993), *Shakespeare and Multiplicity*, Cambridge: Cambridge UP.

Gillespie, Alexandra (2004), 'Introduction', in Ian Gadd and Alexandra Gillespie, eds, *John Stow (1525–1605) and the Making of the English Past*, London: The British Library.

Gillespie, Alexandra, and Oliver D. Harris (2012), 'Holinshed and the Native Chronicle Tradition', in Ian W. Archer and Paulina Kewes, eds, *The Oxford Handbook of Holinshed's Chronicles*, Oxford: Oxford UP, 135–51.

Goldberg, Jonathan (1983), *James I and the Politics of Literature: Jonson, Shakespeare, Donne, and Their Contemporaries*, London: John Hopkins UP.

Gooch, Jane Lytton, ed. (1981), *The Lamentable Tragedie of Locrine* [London, 1595], New York: Garland.

Grafton, Anthony (1975), 'Joseph Scaliger and Historical Chronology: The Rise and Fall of a Discipline', *History and Theory* 14:2: 156–85.

Grafton, Anthony (1993), *Joseph Scaliger: A Study in the History of Classical Scholarship*, 2 vols, Oxford: Clarendon.

Grafton, Anthony (2003), 'The Renaissance & the Reformation of Chronology', *Daedalus* 132:2: 74–85.

Grafton, Anthony, and Lisa Jardine (1990), 'Studied for Action: How Gabriel Harvey Read His Livy', *Past & Present* 129: 30–78.

Griffin, Andrew (2019), *Untimely Deaths in Renaissance Drama*, Toronto: Toronto UP.

Griffin, Benjamin (2001), *Playing the Past: Approaches to English Historical Drama, 1385–1600*, Woodbridge: Brewer.

Griffith, Eva (2013), *A Jacobean Company and Its Playhouse: The Queen's Servants at the Red Bull Theatre (c. 1605–1619)*, Cambridge: Cambridge UP.

Groves, Beatrice (2011), '"They Repented at the Preaching of Ionas and Beholde, a Greater Thaen Ionas Is Here": *A Looking Glass for London and England*, Hosea and the Destruction of Jerusalem', in Adrian Street, ed., *Early Modern Drama and the Bible: Contexts and Readings, 1570–1625*, Basingstoke: Palgrave Macmillan, 139–55.

Gurr, Andrew (2007), 'The Work of Elizabethan Plotters, and *2 The Seven Deadly Sins*', *Early Theatre* 10:1: 67–87.

Gurr, Andrew (2009), 'Professional Playing in London and Superior Cambridge Responses', *Shakespeare Studies* 37: 43–53.

Hackel, Heidi Brayman (1999), 'The "Great Variety" of Readers', in David Scott Kastan, ed., *A Companion to Shakespeare*, London: Blackwell, 139–57.

Hadfield, Andrew (1994), *Literature, Politics and National Identity: Reformation to Renaissance*, Cambridge: Cambridge UP.

Hadfield, Andrew (2004), *Shakespeare, Spenser, and the Matter of Britain*, Basingstoke: Palgrave Macmillan.

Hadfield, Andrew (2005), 'Thomas Lodge and English Republicanism', *Nordic Journal of English Studies* 4:2: 89–104.

Hadfield, Andrew (2016), 'Richard Niccols and Tudor Nostalgia', in Harriet Archer and Andrew Hadfield, eds, *A Mirror for*

Magistrates in Context: Literature, History, and Politics in Early Modern England, Cambridge: Cambridge UP, 164–80.

Halio, Jay L., ed. (2005), *The Tragedy of King Lear* [by William Shakespeare, 1608], Cambridge: Cambridge UP.

Hall, Alice (2008), 'Plague in London: A Case Study of the Biological and Social Pressures Exerted by 300 Years of *Yersinia Pestis*', MA dissertation, Oregon State University.

Halpern, Richard (1991), *The Poetics of Primitive Accumulation: English Renaissance Culture and the Genealogy of Capital*, London: Cornell UP.

Hardin, Richard F. (1992), 'Geoffrey Among the Lawyers: *Britannica* (1607) by John Ross of the Inner Temple', *Sixteenth Century Journal* 23:2: 235–49.

Harding, Vanessa, and Laura Wright (1995), 'Introduction', Vanessa Harding and Laura Wright, eds, *London Bridge: Selected Accounts and Rentals, 1381–1538*, London: London Record Society, vii–xxix.

Hardman, Phillipa (2003), 'Evidence of Readership in Fifteenth-Century Household Miscellanies', *Poetica* 60: 15–30.

Harris, Jonathan Gil (2008), 'Ludgate Time: Simon Eyre's Oath and the Temporal Economies of *The Shoemaker's Holiday*', *Huntington Library Quarterly* 71:1: 11–32.

Harris, Jonathan Gil (2009), *Untimely Matter in the Time of Shakespeare*, U of Pennsylvania P.

Helgerson, Richard (1992), *Forms of Nationhood: The Elizabethan Writing of England*, Chicago: U of Chicago P.

Hill, Tracey (2004), *Anthony Munday and Civic Culture: Theatre, History and Power in Early Modern London, 1580–1633*, Manchester: Manchester UP.

Hill, Tracey (2008), '"Representing the Awefull Authoritie of Soveraigne Majestie": Monarchs and Mayors in Anthony Munday's *The Triumphs of Reunited Britania*', in Glenn Burgess, Rowland Wymer and Jason Lawrence, eds, *The Accession of James I: Historical and Cultural Consequences*, Basingstoke: Palgrave, 15–33.

Hill, Tracey (2010), *Pageantry and Power: A Cultural History of the Early Modern Lord Mayor's Show, 1585–1639*, Manchester: Manchester UP.

Hirst, Derek (1986), *Authority and Conflict: England 1603–1658*, London: Edward Arnold.

Hopkins, Lisa (2002), 'We Were the Trojans: British National
    Identities in 1633', *Renaissance Studies* 16:1: 36–51.
Hopkins, Lisa (2010), 'Cymbeline, the *Translatio Imperii*, and the
    Matter of Britain', in Willy Maley and Philip Schwyzer, eds,
    Shakespeare and Wales: From the Marches to the Assembly,
    Farnham: Ashgate, 143–56.
Hopkins, Lisa (2017), *From the Romans to the Normans on the
    English Renaissance Stage*, Kalamazoo: Medieval Institute.
Howlett, D. R. (1995), 'The Literary Context of Geoffrey of
    Monmouth: An Essay on the Fabrication of Sources', *Arthuriana*
    5:3: 25–69.
Hunt, Maurice (2002), 'Dismemberment, Corporal Reconstitution,
    and the Body Politic in *Cymbeline*', *Studies in Philology* 99:4:
    404–31.
Ingledew, Francis (1994), 'The Book of Troy and the Genealogical
    Construction of History: The Case of Geoffrey of Monmouth's
    Historia regum Britanniae', *Speculum* 69:3: 665–704.
Innes, Paul (2007), '*Cymbeline* and Empire', *Critical Survey* 19:2:
    1–18.
Iser, Wolfgang (1978), *The Act of Reading: A Theory of Aesthetic
    Response* [*Der Akt des Lesens*, Munich: Wilhelm Fink, 1976],
    London: John Hopkins UP.
James, Heather (1997), *Shakespeare's Troy: Drama, Politics, and the
    Translation of Empire*, Cambridge: Cambridge UP.
James, Henry, and Greg Walker (1995), 'The Politics of *Gorboduc*',
    English Historical Review 110:435: 109–21.
Johnston, Alexandra (2009), 'The Politics of Civic Drama and
    Ceremony in Late Medieval and Early Modern Britain', in John
    Fitzpatrick, ed., *The Idea of the City: Early Modern, Modern,
    and Post-Modern Locations and Communities*, Newcastle-Upon-
    Tyne: Cambridge Scholars, 21–38.
Jones, Emrys (1961), 'Stuart *Cymbeline*', *Essays in Criticism* 11:
    84–99.
Jones, Timothy (1994), 'Geoffrey of Monmouth, "Fouke le Fitz
    Waryn," and National Mythology', *Studies in Philology* 91:3:
    233–49.
Kastan, David Scott (1982), *Shakespeare and the Shapes of Time*,
    London: Macmillan.
Kastan, David Scott, and Aaron T. Pratt (2012), 'Printers, Publishers,
    and the *Chronicles* as Artefact', in Ian W. Archer and Paulina

Kewes, eds, *The Oxford Handbook of Holinshed's Chronicles*, Oxford: Oxford UP, 21–42.

Kathman, David (2004), 'Reconsidering "The Seven Deadly Sins"', *Early Theatre* 7:1: 13–44.

Keeler, Laura (1946), 'The *Historia Regum Britanniae* and Four Mediaeval Chroniclers', *Speculum* 21:1: 24–37.

Kendrick, T. D. (1950), *British Antiquity*, London: Methuen.

Kenward, Claire (2017), 'Sights to Make an Alexander? Reading Homer on the Early Modern Stage', *Classical Receptions Journal* 9:1: 79–102.

Kerrigan, John (2008), *Archipelagic English Literature, History, and Politics 1603–170*, Oxford: Oxford UP.

Kewes, Paulina (2003), 'The Elizabethan History Play: A True Genre?', in Richard Dutton and Jean E. Howard, eds, *A Companion to Shakespeare's Works, Volume II: The Histories*, London: Blackwell, 170–93.

Kewes, Paulina (2006), 'History and Its Uses', in Paulina Kewes, ed., *The Uses of History in Early Modern England*, San Marino: Huntingdon Library, 1–30.

Kewes, Paulina (2016), '"Ierusalem thou dydst promyse to buylde vp": Kingship, Counsel, and Early Elizabethan Drama', in Jacqueline Rose, ed., *The Politics of Counsel in England and Scotland, 1286–1707*, Oxford: Oxford UP, 171–92.

King, Ros (2005), *Cymbeline: Constructions of Britain*, Aldershot: Ashgate.

Kipling, Gordon (1997), 'Wonderful Spectacle: Theatre and Civic Culture', in John D. Cox and David Scott Kastan, eds, *A New History of Early English Drama*, New York: Columbia UP, 153–71.

Knowles, James, ed. (2012), 'The Entertainment at Althorpe, [by Ben Jonson, London, 1603]', in David Bevington, Martin Butler and Ian Donaldson, eds, *The Cambridge Edition of the Works of Ben Jonson*, 7 vols, Cambridge: Cambridge UP.

Knowles, R. (2002), 'How Shakespeare Knew *King Leir*', *Shakespeare Survey* 55: 12–35.

Knutson, Roslyn L. (2010), 'What's so Special About 1594?' *Shakespeare Quarterly* 61:4: 449–67.

Kretzschmar, William A. (1992), 'Caxton's Sense of History', *Journal of English and Germanic Philology* 91:4: 510–28.

Lamont, Margaret (2010), 'Becoming English: Rowenne's Wassail, Language, and National Identity in the Medieval Prose *Brut*', *Studies in Philology* 107:3: 283–309.

Landry, D. E. (1982), 'Dreams as History: The Strange Unity of *Cymbeline*', *Shakespeare Quarterly* 33:1: 68–79.

Langley, Eric (2009), *Narcissism and Suicide in Shakespeare and His Contemporaries*, Oxford: Oxford UP.

Leckie, R. William, Jr. (1981), *The Passage of Dominion: Geoffrey of Monmouth and the Periodization of Insular History in the Twelfth Century*, Toronto: U of Toronto P.

Lecky, Kat (2014), 'Naturalization in the *Mirror* and *A Mask*', *Studies in English Literature 1500-1900* 54:1: 125–42.

Lee, Sidney, ed. (1909), *King Leir* [by William Shakespeare, London, 1605], Chatto & Windus.

Lesser, Zachary (2004), *Renaissance Drama and the Politics of Publication: Readings in the English Book Trade*, Cambridge: Cambridge UP.

Levy, F. J. (1967), *Tudor Historical Thought*, San Marino: Huntingdon Library.

Lewalski, Barbara K. (1998), 'Milton's *Comus* and the Politics of Masquing', in David Bevington and Peter Holbrook, eds, *The Politics of the Stuart Masque*, Cambridge: Cambridge UP, 296–320.

Lidster, Amy (2017), 'Producing the History Play: The Agency of Repertory Companies, Stationers, and Patronage Networks in Early Modern England', PhD thesis, King's College, London.

Lost Plays Database (2009), eds Roslyn L. Knutson, David McInnis, and Matthew Steggle, Washington: Folger Shakespeare Library: https://lostplays.folger.edu [accessed 18 January 2020].

Lyons, Tara L. (2016), 'Shakespeare in Print Before 1623', in Emma Smith, ed., *The Cambridge Companion to Shakespeare's First Folio*, Cambridge: Cambridge UP, 1–17.

MacColl, Alan (2006), 'The Meaning of "Britain" in Medieval and Early Modern England', *Journal of British Studies* 45:2: 248–69.

Macdonald, Michael, and Terence R. Murphy (1990), *Sleepless Souls: Suicide in Early Modern England*, Oxford: Clarendon.

MacDougall, Hugh A. (1982), *Racial Myth in English History*, Montreal: UP of New England.

Maley, Willy (1999), 'Postcolonial Shakespeare: British Identity Formation and *Cymbeline*', in Jennifer Richards and James Knowles, eds, *Shakespeare's Late Plays: New Readings*, Edinburgh: Edinburgh UP, 145–57.

Manley, Lawrence (1995), 'Of Sites and Rites', in David L. Smith, Richard Strier and David Bevington, eds, *The Theatrical City: Culture, Theatre, and Politics in London 1576–1649*, Cambridge: Cambridge UP, 35–54.

Manley, Lawrence (2011), *Literature and Culture in Early Modern England*, Cambridge: Cambridge UP.

Manley, Lawrence (2014), 'Lost Plays and the Repertory of Lord Strange's Men', in David McInnis and Matthew Steggle, eds, *Lost Plays in Shakespeare's England*, London: Palgrave Macmillan, 163–86.

Manley, Lawrence, and Sally-Beth MacLean (2014), *Lord Strange's Men and Their Plays*, New Haven: Yale UP.

Mann, David (2013), 'Heywood's *Silver Age*: A Flight Too Far?' *Medieval & Renaissance Drama in England* 26: 184–203.

Marcus, Leah S. (1988), *Puzzling Shakespeare: Local Reading and Its Discontents*, London: U of California P.

Marcus, Leah S. (1996), *Unediting the Renaissance: Shakespeare, Marlowe, and Milton*, London: Routledge.

Marsh, Christopher (2019), 'Best-Selling Ballads and the Female Voices of Thomas Deloney', *Huntington Library Quarterly* 82:1: 127–54.

Marshall, Cynthia (1991), *Last Things and Last Plays: Shakespearean Eschatology*, Carbondale: Southern Illinois UP.

Marshall, Tristan (2000), *Theatre and Empire: Great Britain and the London Stages Under James VI and I*, Manchester: Manchester UP.

Marvin, Julia (2005), 'Havelok in the Prose *Brut* Tradition', *Studies in Philology* 102:3: 280–306.

Marvin, Julia, trans. (2006), *The Oldest Anglo-Norman Prose Brut Chronicle*, Woodbridge: Boydell.

Marvin, Julia (2017), *The Construction of Vernacular History in the Anglo-Norman Prose Brut Chronicle: The Manuscript Culture of Late Medieval England*, York: York Medieval.

Marx, William, and Raluca Radulescu. 'Introduction', in William Marx and Raluca Radulescu, eds, *Readers and Writers of the Prose Brut*, Lampeter: Trivium Publications, xiii–xvi.

Mason, Roger A. (1987), 'Scotching the Brut: Politics, History and National Myth in Sixteenth-Century Britain', in Roger A. Mason, ed., *Scotland and England: 1286–1815*, Edinburgh: John Donald, 60–84.

McDonald, Russ (2006), *Shakespeare's Late Style*, Cambridge: Cambridge UP.

McEachern, Claire (1996), *The Poetics of English Nationhood: 1590–1612*, Cambridge: Cambridge UP.

McInnis, David and Matthew Steggle, eds (2014), *Lost Plays in Shakespeare's England*, London: Palgrave Macmillan.

McKerrow, R. B., ed. (1910), *A Dictionary of Printers and Booksellers in England, Scotland, and Ireland, and of Foreign Printers of English Books, 1557–1640*, London: Bibliographical Society.

McManus, Clare (2002), *Women on the Renaissance Stage: Anna of Denmark and Female Masquing in the Stuart Court 1590–1619*, Manchester: Manchester UP.

McManus, Clare (2008), 'What Ish My Nation?: The Culture of the Seventeenth-Century British Isles', in Jenny Wormald, ed., *The Short Oxford History of the British Isles: The Seventeenth Century*, Oxford: Oxford UP, 182–222.

McMillin, Scott, and Sally-Beth MacLean (1998), *The Queen's Men and Their Plays*, Cambridge: Cambridge UP.

McMullan, Gordon (2007), 'The Colonisation of Britain on the Early Modern Stage', in Gordon McMullan and David Matthews, eds, *Reading the Medieval in Early Modern England*, Cambridge: Cambridge UP, 119–42.

Meagher, John C. (1968), 'The First Progress of Henry VII', *Renaissance Drama* 1: 45–73.

Michelsson, Elisabeth (1999), *Appropriating King Arthur: The Arthurian Legend in English Drama and Entertainments 1485–1625*, Uppsala: Coronet Books.

Michie, Donald M., ed. (1991), *A Critical Edition of The True Chronicle History of King Leir and His Three Daughters, Gonorill, Ragan and Cordella* [London, 1605], New York: Garland.

Mikalachki, Jodi (1995), 'The Masculine Romance of Roman Britain: *Cymbeline* and Early Modern English Nationalism', *Shakespeare Quarterly* 46: 3: 301–22.

Miller-Tomlinson, Tracey (2017), 'Queer History in *Cymbeline*', *Shakespeare* 12:3: 225–40.

Mills, Jerry Leath (1978), 'Prudence, History, and the Prince in *The Faerie Queene*, Book II', *Huntington Library Quarterly* 41:2: 83–101.

Moffet, Robin (1962), 'Cymbeline and the Nativity', *Shakespeare Quarterly* 13:2: 207–18.

Morash, Christopher (2001), *A History of Irish Theatre, 1601–2000*, Cambridge: Cambridge UP.

Morgan, Paul (1989), 'Frances Wolfreston and "Hor Bouks": A Seventeenth-Century Woman Book-Collector', *The Library* 6–11:3: 197–219.

Morse, Ruth (2013), 'Shakespeare and the Remains of Britain', in Ruth Morse, Helen Cooper and Peter Holland, eds, *Medieval Shakespeare: Pasts and Presents*, Cambridge: Cambridge UP, 119–37.

Mortimer, Ian (2002), 'Tudor Chronicler or Sixteenth-Century Diarist? Henry Machyn and the Nature of His Manuscript', *Sixteenth Century Journal* 33:4: 981–98.

Murphy, Erin (2011), 'Sabrina and the Making of English History in *Poly-Olbion* and *A Maske Presented at Ludlow Castle*', *Studies in English Literature 1500–1900* 51:1: 87–110.

Olson, Rebecca (2010), 'Before the Arras: Textile Description and Innogen's Translation in *Cymbeline*', *Modern Philology* 108:1: 45–64.

O'Malley, C. D. (1968), 'Helkiah Crooke, M.D, F.R.C.P., 1576–1648', *Bulletin of the History of Medicine* 42: 1–18.

Orgel, Stephen (1967), *The Jonsonian Masque*, Cambridge: Harvard UP.

Orgel, Stephen (1979), 'Shakespeare and the Kinds of Drama', *Critical Inquiry* 6:1: 107–23.

Pace, Edwin (2012), 'Geoffrey's 'Very Old Book' and Penda of Mercia', *Arthuriana* 22:2: 53–74.

Parker, Patricia (1989), 'Romance and Empire: Anachronistic *Cymbeline*', in George M. Logan and Gordon Teskey, eds, *Unfolded Tales: Essays on Renaissance Romance*, Cornell UP, 189–207.

Parry, Graham (1981), *The Golden Age Restor'd: The Culture of the Stuart Court, 1603–42*, Manchester: Manchester UP.

Parry, Graham (2000), 'Ancient Britons and Early Stuarts', in Robin Headlam Wells, Glenn Burgess and Rowland Wymer, eds,

Neo-Historicism: Studies in Renaissance Literature, History and Politics, Woodbridge: D.S. Brewer, 153–78.

Parsons, A. E. (1929), 'The Trojan Legend in England: Some Instance of Its Application to the Politics of the Times', *Modern Language Review* 24:4: 394–408.

Patterson, Annabel (1989), *Shakespeare and the Popular Voice*, Oxford: Blackwell.

Patterson, Annabel (1994), *Reading Holinshed's Chronicles*, London: U of Chicago P.

Patterson, W. B. (2011), *James VI and the Reunion of Christendom*, London: Century.

Peck, Linda Levy (1991), 'Introduction', in Lind Levy Peck, ed., *The Mental World of the Jacobean Court*, Cambridge: Cambridge UP, 1–17.

Penny, Andrew (1997), 'John Foxe, The Acts and Monuments and the Development of Prophetic Interpretation', in David Loades, ed., *John Foxe and the English Reformation*, Aldershot: Scolar Press, 252–77.

Peterson, Kaara L. (2006), 'Historica Passio: Early Modern Medicine, King Lear, and Editorial Practice', *Shakespeare Quarterly* 57:1: 1–22.

Pettegree, Andrew (2004), 'Day, John (1521/2–1584)', in *Oxford Dictionary of National Biography*, Oxford: Oxford UP: https://doi.org/10.1093/ref:odnb/7367 [accessed 1 September 2015].

Piggott, Stuart (1988), *Ancient Britons and the Antiquarian Imagination*, London: Thames & Hudson.

Pitcher, John (1993), 'Names in *Cymbeline*', *Essays in Criticism* 43:1: 1–16.

Pocock, J. G. A. (1975), 'British History: A Plea for a New Subject', *The Journal of Modern History* 47:4: 601–21.

Prescott, Anne Lake (1991), 'Marginal Discourse: Drayton's Muse and Selden's "Story"', *Studies in Philology* 88:3: 307–28.

Radulescu, Raluca (2006), 'Gentry Readers of the *Brut* and Genealogical Material', in William Marx and Raluca Radulescu, eds, *Readers and Writers of the Prose Brut*, Lampeter: Trivium, 189–202.

Rasmussen, Eric (2016), 'Publishing the First Folio', in Emma Smith, ed., *The Cambridge Companion to Shakespeare's First Folio*, Cambridge: Cambridge UP, 18–29.

Richardson, Jennifer, and Richard Wistreich (2019), 'Introduction: Voicing Text 1500–1700', *Huntington Library Quarterly* 82:1: 3–16.

Robertson, K. (1998), 'Geoffrey of Monmouth and the Translation of Insular Historiography', *Arthuriana* 8:4: 42–57.

Robinson-Self, Philip (2018), *Early Modern Britain's Relationship to Its Past: the Historiographical Fortunes of the Legends of Brute, Albina, and Scota*. Kalamazoo: Western Michigan University.

Rothstein, Marian (1990), 'Etymology, Genealogy, and the Immutability of Origins', *Renaissance Quarterly* 43:2: 332–47.

Russell, Conrad (2011), *King James VI and I and His English Parliaments: The Trevelyan Lectures Delivered at the University of Cambridge 1995*, eds Richard Cust and Andrew Thrush, Oxford: Oxford UP.

Sager, Jenny (2013), *The Aesthetics of Spectacle in Early Modern Drama and Modern Cinema Robert Greene's Theatre of Attractions*, New York: Palgrave Macmillan.

Samson, Alexander (1999), 'The Marriage of Philip of Habsburg and Mary Tudor and Anti-Spanish Sentiment in England: Political Economies and Culture, 1553–1557', PhD thesis, Queen Mary University of London.

Sanderson, Richard K. (1992), 'Suicide as Message and Metadrama in English Renaissance Tragedy', *Comparative Drama* 3: 199–217.

Schlueter, June (2016), 'Across the Narrow Sea: The 1620 Leipzig Volume of English Plays', in Joseph Candido, ed., *The Text, the Play, and the Globe*, Madison: Farleigh-Dickinson UP, 231–50.

Schwyzer, Philip (1997), 'Purity and Danger on the West Bank of the Severn: The Cultural Geography of *A Masque Presented at Ludlow Castle*, 1634', *Representations* 60: 222–48.

Schwyzer, Philip (2004), *Literature, Nationalism, and Memory in Early Modern England and Wales*, Cambridge: Cambridge UP.

Schwyzer, Philip (2008), 'The Jacobean Union Controversy and *King Lear*', in Glenn Burgess, Rowland Wymer and Jason Lawrence, eds, *The Accession of James I: Historical and Cultural Consequences*, Basingstoke: Palgrave, 34–47.

Shapiro, James (2015), *1606: The Year of Lear*, London: Faber & Faber.

Sharpe, Kevin (1987), *Criticism and Compliment: The Politics of Literature in the England of Charles I*, Cambridge: Cambridge UP.

Sharpe, Will (2013), 'Authorship and Attribution', in Jonathan Bate
    and Eric Rasmussen, eds, *William Shakespeare and Others:
    Collaborative Plays*, Basingstoke: Palgrave Macmillan.
Smith, Emma (2016a), *The Making of Shakespeare's First Folio*,
    Oxford: Bodleian Library.
Smith, Emma (2016b), 'Reading the First Folio', in Emma Smith,
    ed., *The Cambridge Companion to Shakespeare's First Folio*,
    Cambridge: Cambridge UP, 155–69.
Smith, Emma (2016c), *Shakespeare's First Folio: Four Centuries of
    an Iconic Book*, Oxford: Oxford UP, 2016.
Smith-Laing, Tim (2012), 'Note on References to the *Chronicles*', in
    Ian W. Archer and Paulina Kewes, eds, *The Oxford Handbook of
    Holinshed's Chronicles*, Oxford: Oxford UP, xix–xxi.
Steggle, Matthew (2000), 'Spenser's Ludgate: A Topical Reference in
    The Faerie Queene II.x', *Notes and Queries* 47:1: 34–7.
Steggle, Matthew (2015), *Digital Humanities and the Lost
    Drama of Early Modern England: Ten Case Studies*, Farnham:
    Ashgate.
Stephens, Walter (1989), *Giants in Those Days: Folklore, Ancient
    History, and Nationalism*, Lincoln: U of Nebraska P.
Stock, Brian (1983), *The Implications of Literacy: Written Language
    and Models of Interpretation in the Eleventh and Twelfth
    Centuries*, Princeton: Princeton UP.
Strong, Roy (1980), *Britannia Triumphans: Inigo Jones, Reubens,
    and Whitehall Palace*, London: Thames and Hudson.
Syme, Holger Schott (2012), 'Thomas Creede, William Barley,
    and the Venture of Printing Plays', in Marta Straznicky, ed.,
    Shakespeare's Stationers: Studies in Cultural Bibliography,
    Philadelphia: U of Pennsylvania P, 28–46.
Tatlock, J. S. P. (1950), *The Legendary History of Britain: Geoffrey
    of Monmouth's 'Historia Regum Britanniae' and Its Early
    Vernacular Versions*, Berkeley: U of California P.
Taylor, Gary (2006), 'Making Meaning Marketing Shakespeare
    1623', in Peter Holland and Stephen Orgel, eds, *From
    Performance to Print in Shakespeare's England*, Palgrave
    Macmillan, 55–72.
Teramura, Misha (2014), 'Brute Parts: From Troy to Britain at the
    Rose, 1595–1600', in David McInnis and Matthew Steggle,
    eds, *Lost Plays in Shakespeare's England*, London: Palgrave
    Macmillan, 127–47.

WORKS CITED

Tolhurst, Fiona (1998), 'Geoffrey of Monmouth's *Historia Regum Britannie* and the Critics', *Arthuriana* 8:4: 3–11.

Tonry, Kathleen (2012), 'Reading History in Caxton's *Polychronicon*', *Journal of English and Germanic Philology* 111:2: 169–98.

Tyler, Elizabeth M. (2013), 'Trojans in Anglo-Saxon England: Precedent Without Descent', *Review of English Studies* 64:263: 1–20.

van Es, Bart (2002), *Spenser's Forms of History*, Oxford: Oxford UP.

Vanhoutte, Jacqueline (2000), 'University Community, Authority, and the Motherland in Sackville and Norton's *Gorboduc*', *Studies in English Literature, 1500–1900* 40:2: 227–39.

Veyne, Paul (1988), *Did the Greeks Believe in Their Myths?: An Essay in the Constitutive Imagination* [*Les Gregs ont-ils cru a leurs mythes?*, Editions de Seuil, 1983], trans. Paula Wissing, London: U of Chicago P.

Vines, Amy Noelle (2006), '"Thys Ys Her Owne Boke": Women Reading the Middle English Prose *Brut* Chronicle', in William Marx and Raluca Radulescu, eds, *Readers and Writers of the Prose Brut*, Lampeter: Trivium, 71–96.

Vitkus, Daniel J., ed. (2000), *Three Turk Plays from Early Modern England*, New York: Columbia UP.

Walsh, Brian (2009), *Shakespeare, the Queen's Men and the Elizabethan Performance of History*, Cambridge: Cambridge UP.

Watt, Tessa (1991), *Cheap Print and Popular Piety, 1550–1640*, Cambridge: Cambridge UP.

Wayne, Valerie (2015), 'The First Folio's Arrangement and Its Finale', *Shakespeare Quarterly* 66:4: 389–408.

Wayne, Valerie, ed. (2017), *Cymbeline* [by William Shakespeare, London, 1623], London: Thompson.

Weijer, Neil (2016), 'History Reimagined: Filling the Gaps in England's Ancient Past', in Earle Havens, ed., *Fakes, Lies, and Forgeries*, Sheridan Libraries: Johns Hopkins University, 43–66.

Weir, Alison (1996), *Britain's Royal Families: The Complete Genealogy*, 2nd edn, London: Bodley Head.

Wells, Stanley, ed. (2000), *King Lear* [by William Shakespeare], Oxford: Oxford UP.

Whitted, Brent (2009), 'Street Politics: Charles I and the Inns of Court's *Triumph of Peace*', *The Seventeenth Century* 24: 1–25.

Wickham, Glynne (1980), 'Riddle and Emblem: A Study in the Dramatic Structure of *Cymbeline*', in John Carey, ed., *English Renaissance Studies: Presented to Dame Helen Gardner on Her 70th Birthday*, Oxford: Clarendon Press, 94–113.

Wiggins, Alison (2010), 'Frances Wolfreston's *Chaucer*', in Anne Lawrence-Mathers and Philippa Hardman, eds, *Women and Writing c. 1340–c. 1650: The Domestication of Print Culture*, Woodbridge: Boydell, 77–89.

Wiggins, Martin (2012–), *British Drama (1533–1642): A Catalogue*, 9 vols, Oxford: Oxford UP.

Williamson, Arthur (2008), 'Radical Britain: David Hume of Godscoft and the Challenge to the Jacobean British Vision', in Glenn Burgess, Rowland Wymer and Jason Lawrence, eds, *The Accession of James I: Historical and Cultural Consequences*, Basingstoke: Palgrave, 48–68.

Winston, Jessica (2005), 'Expanding the Political Nation: *Gorboduc* at the Inns of Court and Succession Revisited', *Early Theatre* 8:1: 11–34.

Winston, Jessica (2006), 'Seneca in Early Elizabethan England', *Renaissance Quarterly* 59:1: 29–58.

Woolf, D. R. (1986), 'Speech, Text, and Time: The Sense of Hearing and the Sense of the Past in Renaissance England', *Albion: A Quarterly Journal Concerned with British Studies* 18:2: 159–93.

Woolf, D. R. (1987), 'Erudition and the Idea of History in Renaissance England', *Renaissance Quarterly* 40: 11–48.

Woolf, D. R. (1988), 'Genre into Artefact: The Decline of the English Chronicle in the Sixteenth Century', *Sixteenth Century Journal* 19:3: 321–54.

Woolf, D. R. (1997), 'A Feminine Past? Gender, Genre, and Historical Knowledge in England, 1500–1800', *American Historical Review* 3:1: 645–79.

Woolf, D. R. (1999), 'Shapes of History', in David Scott Kastan, ed., *A Companion to Shakespeare*, London: Blackwell, 186–205.

Woolf, D. R. (2003), *The Social Circulation of the Past*, Oxford: Oxford UP.

Woolf, D. R. (2005), 'From Hystories to the Historical: Five Transitions in Thinking about the Past, 1500–1700', *Huntington Library Quarterly* 68:1–2: 33–70.

Worden, Blair (2005), 'Historians and Poets', *Huntington Library Quarterly* 68:1–2: 71–93.

Wormald, Jenny (1991), 'James VI and I, *Basilikon Doron* and *The Trew Law of Free Monarchies*: The Scottish Context and the English Translation', in Linda Levy Peck, ed., *The Mental World of the Jacobean Court*, Cambridge: Cambridge UP, 36–54.

Wormald, Jenny (1994), 'The Union of 1603', in Roger A. Mason, ed., *Scots and Britons: Scottish Political Thought and the Union of 1603*, Cambridge: Cambridge UP, 17–40.

Wymer, Rowland (1999), 'The Tempest and the Origins of Britain', *Critical Survey* 11:1: 3–14.

Yates, Frances A. (1975), *Shakespeare's Last Plays: A New Approach*, London: Routledge.

INDEX

CPSIA information can be obtained
at www.ICGtesting.com
Printed in the USA
LVHW081746191022
731081LV00008B/736

9 781350 232822